THE MAINE ISLANDS

THE MAINE

in Story

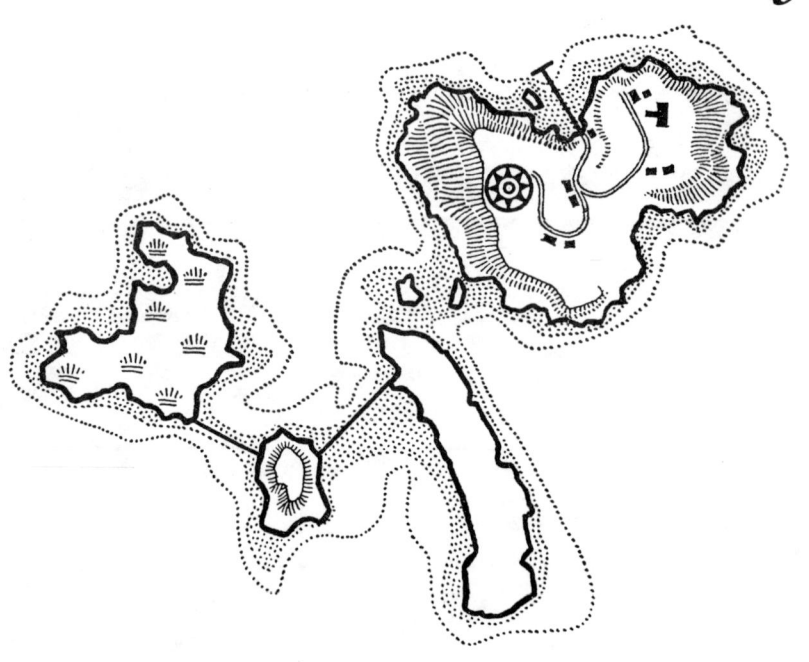

ISLANDS
and Legend

by DOROTHY SIMPSON

From material compiled by
THE MAINE WRITERS RESEARCH CLUB

Copyright © Dorothy Simpson, 1987

Reprinted June, 1987 by Blackberry
ISBN 0-942396-51-0
Blackberry Books
Chimney Farm
RRI-Box 228
Nobleboro, Maine 04555

Originally published in 1960
by J.B. Lippincott Company

"Cover Photo by Beth Leonard"

*Printed in the United States of America
By National Reproductions Corporation*

To Charles E. Campbell
A Friend to Many Writers

CONTENTS

    LANDFALL   13

I THE WESTERN COAST: *Appledore to Cape Elizabeth*
    The Isles of Shoals   19
    Boon Island   25
    The Islands of Saco Bay   28
    Richmond Island   33

II CASCO BAY
    The Islands of Portland Harbor   45
        Cushing, Peaks
    Long Island   53
    Chebeague   59
    Jewell Island   63
    Mackworth Island   68
    Cousins Island   73
    Harpswell's Islands   78
        Sebascodegan, Orr's, Bailey, Pond, Haskell, Malaga, Ragged, The Smaller Harpswell Islands, The Dead Ship of Harpswell

III THE MIDDLE COAST: *Cape Small to Port Clyde*
    Swan Island   109
    The Boothbay Islands   115
        Southport, Squirrel, Mouse, Ram, Fisherman's, Damariscove
    The Islands of Muscongus Bay   129
        Loud's, Hog
    Monhegan   137

IV	PENOBSCOT BAY	
	Matinicus	145
	Matinicus Rock	
	Criehaven	152
	Monroe's Island and Sheep Island	156
	The Fox Islands	159
	Vinalhaven, North Haven, Hurricane	
	Islesboro	169
	Verona	174
	Deer Isle	176
	Isle au Haut	178
V	EASTWARD FROM PENOBSCOT: *Blue Hill Bay to Passamaquoddy Bay*	
	Swan's Island	183
	Bartlett's Island	189
	Mount Desert Island	193
	The Cranberry Isles	199
	The Maine Sea Coast Missionary Society	206
	Beals Island and Great Wass Island	210
	St. Croix	214

DEPARTURE	219
Acknowledgments	223
A Selective Bibliography	226
Appendix: THE TIDEWATER ISLANDS OF MAINE	228
Index	244

MAPS

drawn by Guy Fleming

THE MAINE COAST	pages 10-11
THE ISLES OF SHOALS	facing page 19
THE ISLANDS OF SACO BAY	page 29
CASCO BAY	facing page 45
THE MIDDLE COAST	facing page 109
PENOBSCOT BAY	facing page 145
THE MOUNT DESERT REGION	facing page 183

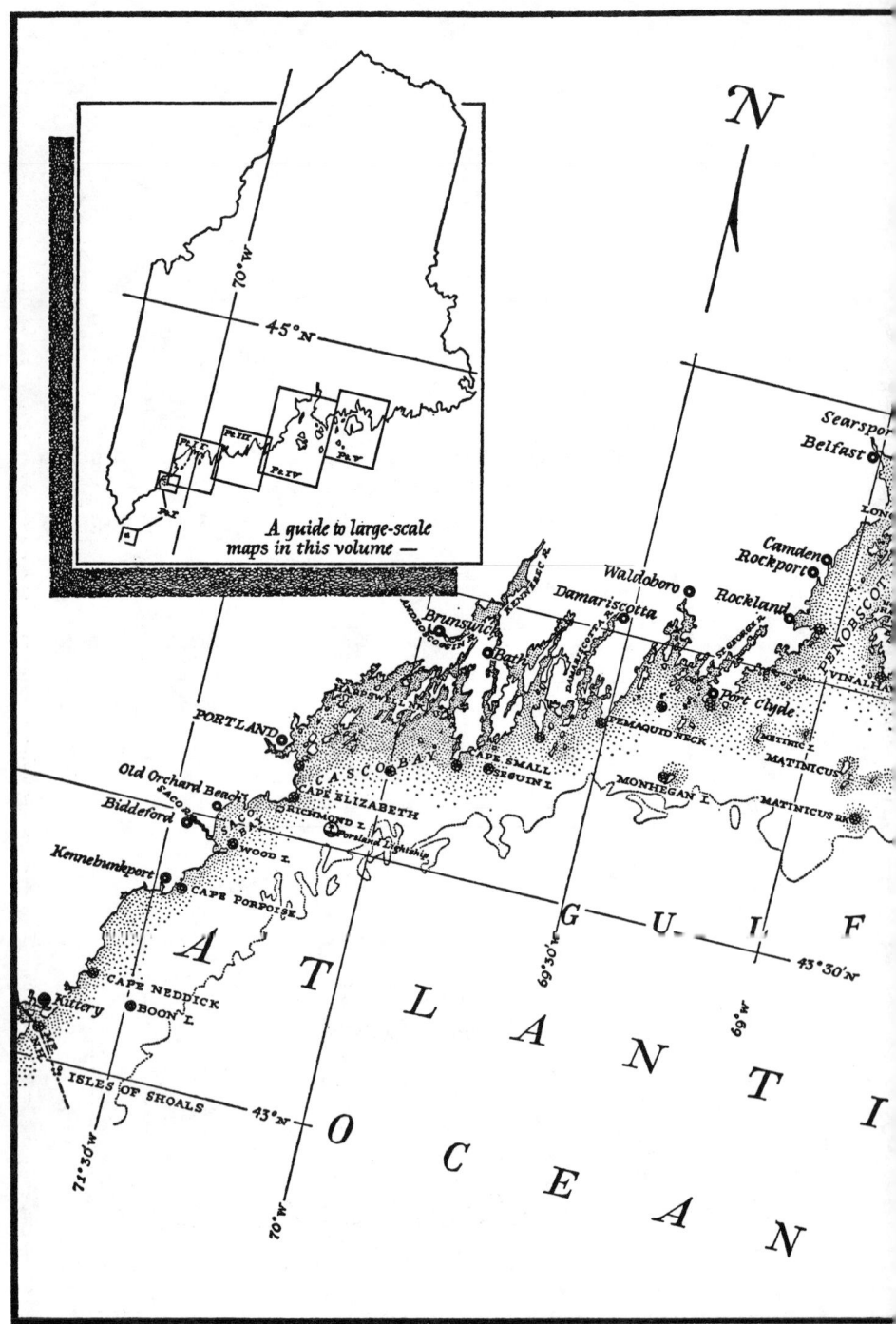

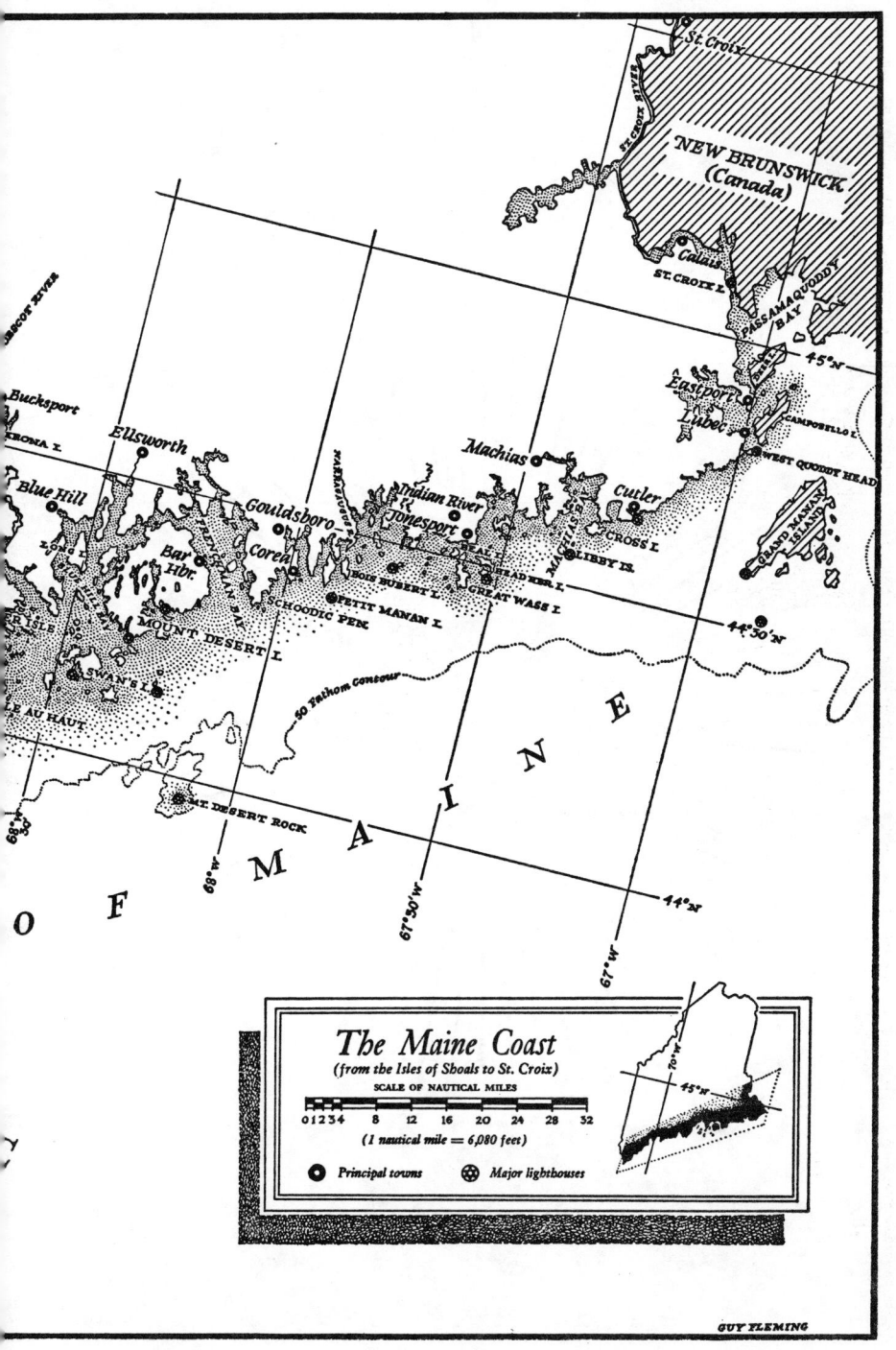

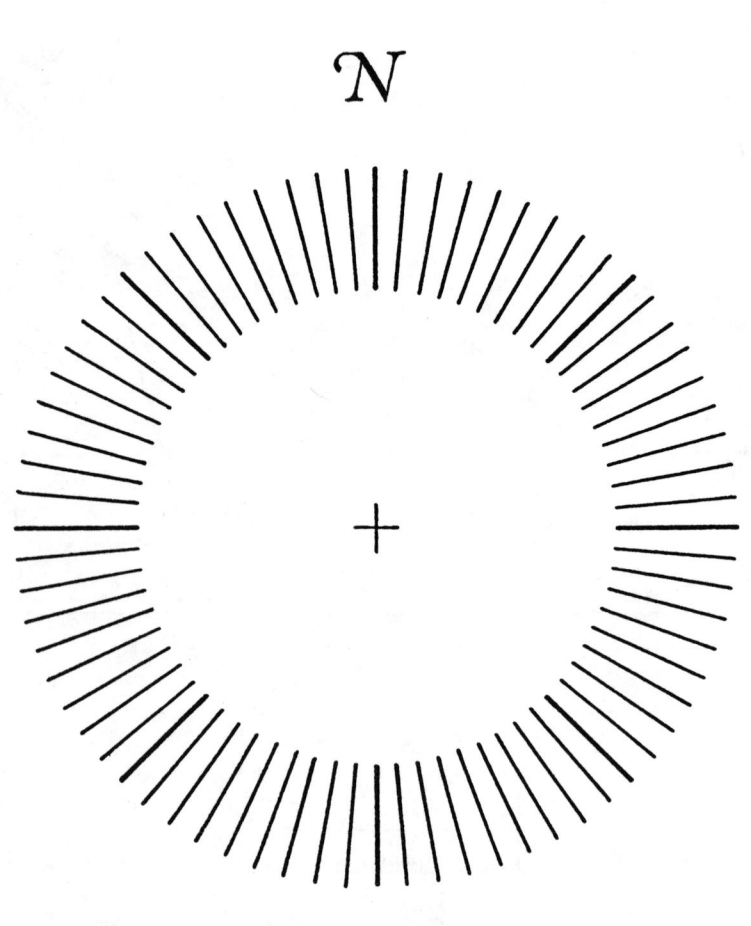

LANDFALL

ONE EITHER LOVES ISLANDS or loathes them; there are no nuances in between. Thus to leave even one island out of this collection seems the worst kind of disloyalty on the part of the island-lovers of the Maine Writers Research Club, who gathered the material. But since there are some two thousand islands along the coast of Maine—counting all the little ones, which are just as important to the true islander as the big ones—the club members found it a sad necessity to leave out rather more than a few. To anyone whose favorite island has been slighted, apologies—the club's, and mine—are offered with compassionate understanding.

Each island, even the smallest, has its own sovereign importance as an individual. This goes for them all along the entire coast. If no one lives on an island now, it was profoundly significant to someone *once*; to the person who named it, to the person who found shelter on it when he was wrecked, to the person who tried to live on it and was driven off by one fate or another. You can be sure that if no human being lives on it, it is a sanctuary to other creatures who are important in their own right, migrating birds and nesting ones, breeding seals, and animals who can swim to it for refuge from the mainland, if it is close enough.

People are always leaving islands because they think they have had enough of them, and other people are always going back to the islands which they once knew, or else they are discovering new islands. A man buys a piece of island and thus becomes heir to the whole in his mind and heart, and suffers a mortal wound when someone who really hasn't the make-up for an islander buys another piece of the island and tries to live on it exactly as he would on the mainland. If a man is lucky enough to possess a whole island—even if it's the merest speck of rock and turf, and a few spruce trees and raspberry bushes—but can spend only a few summer weeks on it, spiritually he is an islander all year round. This is particularly true of children who have island summers. They become islanders for life at an early age.

As for those who are born on islands where their fathers were born, and where their great-great-grandfathers were the first settlers after the Revolution, some accept their heritage with pride and thank God they are not as other men; and some fight against it and go away, but even when they are successfully established somewhere else they are always homesick for something which they will not look in the face.

Take an eagle's-eye view of the coast of Maine today, at the long fingers of rock thrusting out into the great bays, the gemmy spatter of islands from the Isles of Shoals to Grand Manan, and try to see it as it was long before the coming of the Red Paint people, the Abenaki, the Norsemen, Champlain, Pring, Verrazano, Gomez, and the rest.

The islands are really the tops of drowned mountains. The cooling earth in aeons past pushed up folds of molten rock in heights and furrows, as shaking a rug or carpet will send little waves speeding across the surface of the cloth. In Casco Bay, for example, you can actually visualize the folding process as you look out at the islands, folded regularly from northeast to southwest. Then the violence of glaciers tore the Maine coastline to shreds and let in the sea around the rocky hilltops, which became islands. When you are on them you may trace with your fingers on their sheets of prehistoric ledge the glacial scrapes from north to south, left to show how the sea of ice once moved, massive and irrevocable, down over the land. The beaches of Maine islands are strewn with rocks of every known vintage, rocks brought from hundreds of miles away and dropped into the places where they will remain until erosion or another ice age moves them on.

This happened millions of years before the Red Paint people made their now hard-to-find cemeteries. When the French, English, Spanish, and Dutch explorers sailed among these islands they had been as they are for a long time. But many of those which the eagle's eye sees today as barren were densely wooded. And as the European ships sailed through the bright, beautiful, silent summer world of their time, these islands which enchanted them were not deserted. They were a part of the Indians' universe, they were used and loved, so much that even today we pick up flint tools and weapons on our beaches, and walk over old shell heaps on our way to swim.

Beginning in the 1600's a new civilization rose on the islands that took Champlain's eye, and Smith's, Pring's, and Levett's. They were natural fortifications, and besides, what man doesn't enjoy owning his own little continent? And so all along the coast there grew up an active, productive island life. It was difficult living at times, especially in the early winters before the settlers had learned how best to survive, but the fish were plentiful, and at first there were good relations with the Indians who brought furs to trade. There were happy times; Englishmen celebrated Christmas in the traditional way, and set up maypoles at Damariscove and Monhegan as wicked Thomas Morton did at Merrymount.

Most of the islands that are empty today, or are just being discovered by people searching for an escape from the crowd, were a part of this thriving little world. But then as the Indians' resentment grew, and the French fought against the loss of a good part of their Acadie, a whole way of life was wiped out in blood and smoke. How many people today know that way of life ever existed? For most of us the settling of the islands began after the Revolutionary War, and on many populated islands the continuity has been unbroken ever since. Yet it is possible to find those ancient cellar holes, as it is possible to find traces of the Indian occupancy, and in old records the names are clear to read.

What did these seventeenth-century Englishmen find on their islands? Not Utopia, certainly, but something else which they had come far to seek, and which they cherished when they found it. It was probably the same thing that dwellers on islands have always found.

That something has not changed. It simply takes different forms. The man who has always lived on an island and has his work there, who can make a living, may often threaten to leave and go where life is softer and easier, but he does not go until he is carried off, because in his deepest, most secret self he cannot imagine living anywhere else; he is too much a creature of the tides that rise and fall about his small planet. Alternatively, though, he would settle for having everyone *else* move off the island and leave him alone on it.

The man who finds his island later in life, and goes to it whenever he can, escapes the rush and confusion of his mainland existence only to find *himself* on his island—or rather, the early, innocent, primal self that lived at ease with nature, and greeted each rising sun as a fresh miracle.

DOROTHY SIMPSON

[I]

The Western Coast

APPLEDORE TO CAPE ELIZABETH

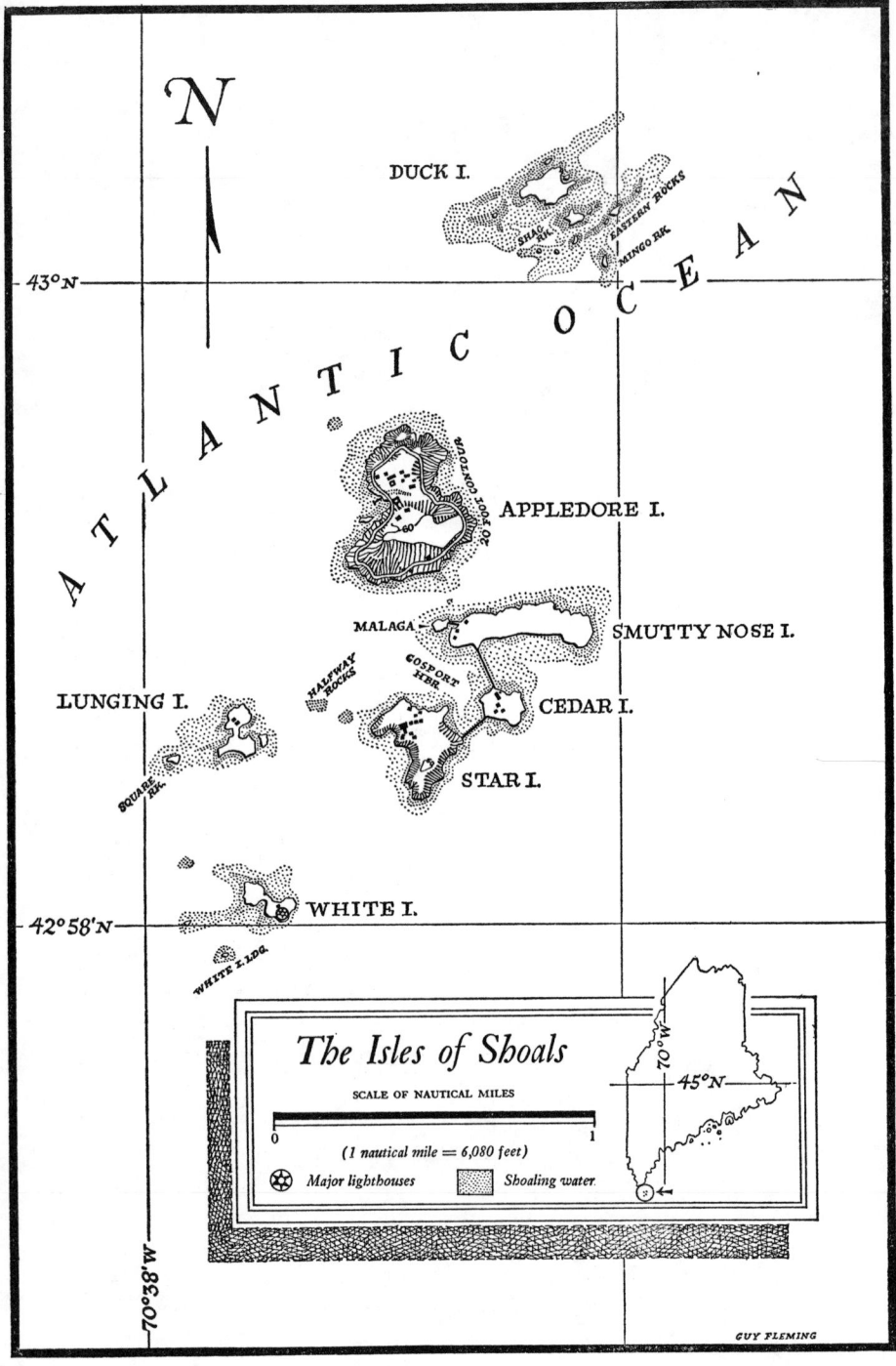

THE ISLES OF SHOALS

THE ISLANDS OF MAINE begin properly with Appledore, Smutty Nose, Malaga, Cedar, and Duck, the five northerly isles of that rocky cluster off Portsmouth, New Hampshire, called the Isles of Shoals. Before some imaginative fisherman or navigator poetically christened them thus, either because of the shoal waters and ledges about them or the "shoals" or schools of fish that gave the first settlers a rich living, they were known as Smith's Isles, and appeared on early maps greatly exaggerated in size. Whether or not Captain John Smith discovered them, he is credited with it by some sources.

To those of us who from grade school have been accustomed to think of John Smith as an ageless, monolithic sort of character, neatly tucked away at Jamestown with Pocahontas, it comes as rather a surprise to find that "Captain Jack" was a ubiquitous figure who traveled up and down the Atlantic coast with astonishing frequency and ease, considering the difficulties of transportation in those days. Smith was only twenty-six when Jamestown was founded, and had been a hard-fighting soldier of fortune since he was sixteen; to him the exploration of the New World was only one more bright challenge in a life that was full of flung gauntlets. One can imagine the trepidation with which other explorers landed on strange islands, fully expecting Captain Jack, that indefatigable island-hopper, to emerge from the nearest woods with his hand outstretched in welcome. Apparently he simply was not able to resist even the smallest lump of rock and turf if it was completely surrounded by water.

Appledore, a half-mile long and almost as wide, was once called Hog. Why? Was it shaped like a hog? There are so many Hog Islands along the Maine coast that the name shows a distressing lack of imagination on someone's part. At last some homesick Englishman renamed this one Appledore, for his home village in England.

Appledore is separated by a narrow channel from the island next largest in size, Smutty Nose, so named for its rocky black point projecting into the sea, contrasting sharply with the pale gneiss of which the islands are chiefly formed. Smutty Nose was thus called in 1684, when the Court for the Western Islands sat there, and the name appears also in the written record of one of the many wrecks that turned the Shoals into a graveyard: "Ship Sagunto stranded on Smotinose Isle, Jany. 14th, 1813."

Smutty Nose is connected by breakwaters with Malaga, which is little more than a small rock, with Cedar, and with Star, which belongs to New Hampshire. Duck Island, fifth in Maine's group, is a bird rock to the northeast.

The first fishermen in the Isles of Shoals, settling on Appledore, then Hog, in the early 1600's, lived well from the sea. Celia Thaxter in *Among the Isles of Shoals* says that for more than a century before the Revolution there were from three to six hundred islanders at the Shoals, with a well-run town government and a catch of from three to four thousand quintals of fish, sold to Spain and taken to Portsmouth for the West Indies market.

It is said, of a somewhat later time, that the Shoals were so far ahead of the mainland in literacy that pupils came from the coast for "literary instruction." This opens up new vistas for the imagination. What poets, scholars, and learned clergy dwelt on these sea-ringed Pleiades? What an ideal civilization this might have been, as rich as anything in the Grecian past.

That the very first settlers were determined to keep the islands monastically pure is proved by some of the provisions in their charter, which we know about only through handed-down stories. One rule forbade goats and swine on the islands—sensible, because these animals running wild would disturb the drying fish and muddy the springs. But another rule said that no woman should ever live on the islands.

In 1647 a hot-headed young iconoclast perpetrated a triple violation of the code by bringing over from the mainland not only a

The Western Coast · 21

goat and a pig, but a wife. The savage battle raged all the way up to the General Court of Massachusetts, where the final judgment ordered young Reynolds to get rid of his livestock. As for his wife, the Court ruled, "if no further complaint came against her she might enjoy the company of her husband."

So then other wives came, and something probably quite perfect in its own way passed out of existence. But the school with its excellent educational opportunities probably came after the wives and the first babies, as did the church.

After the settlement on Appledore, there was another on Star Island, which became a village called Gosport in 1715. It had a church built from the timbers of a Spanish wreck. Here a clergyman, John Tuck, for forty years preached to the Shoalers, christened them, married them, and buried them. And here came the tall Spanish ships to trade with the Yankees for loads of fish. As late as 1730 and even later the vessels sailed from Bilbao with their dark and earringed crews, and there must have been many a Shoaler who locked up his daughter against their exotic Iberian charms, or else was left with a black-eyed grandchild come winter.

Growing up in those days at the Shoals was a boy who was to become famous as a soldier. This was William Pepperell, born in 1696 on Appledore. His father, also William, was a Cornishman who had settled on the island in 1676. (It may have been he who changed the name of the island from Hog to Appledore.) The younger William was put at the head of an expedition against the fortress of Louisbourg, on Cape Breton, in March, 1745, in retaliation for French attacks against New England fishermen. Maine sent over a thousand men to join this audacious Yankee exploit.

How the New Englanders won is not clear; the fort was strongly armed, the French were well-trained, and the colonists were not. They died by the hundreds in the icy swamps under the walls of the fort, those who were not killed by their own exploding cannon. It was probably sheer bull-headedness that carried the battle for them at last, along with the purely voluntary help of a British naval squadron that happened to be in the vicinity. William Pepperell was made a baronet by George II—the first native American to be so honored—for his part in the campaign, and he became a hero to the colonists. He did not retire upon his laurels, but was busy with Maine and Massachusetts doings for the rest of his life. He died in 1759.

With the Revolution the Shoalers scattered to the coast towns. Probably many of them fought with distinction; those who were loyalists survived or not, depending on the temper of the natives. But it was the certain end of another epoch in the Shoals' existence, just as one had ended when young Reynolds fetched him home a wife.

After the Revolution there was no religion on the Shoals but that of New England rum. The islanders soon had a reputation for being drunken, quarrelsome, and depraved. It was suspected that many of the wrecks that took place were caused deliberately. Still, there were a few hard-working citizens, men of integrity, and teachers and ministers who came there to save what was worth salvaging in the way of human material.

It was at this dark time, which was between the end of the Revolution and about 1820, that the Haley family lived on Smutty Nose. Captain Samuel Haley seems to have been a person of some substance and honor. The Spanish ship *Sagunto* was wrecked on the island in January, 1813, and fourteen sailors died in the snow as they crawled from their breaking ship toward the light in the Haley house, while the Haleys were all unaware. They found the bodies the next day, to their horror, but all they could do was give them a decent burial on the island. It is said that the ghosts of the Spanish sailors have haunted the shores for years, trying to stop passing vessels and beg passage back to Spain.

There were always tales of pirates' using the Shoals for headquarters; one was the notorious Edward Lowe, who terrorized the New England coast in the years 1722-23, and who seems to have been a psychopathic killer. Even his crew hated him and at last set him adrift. One of the ghosts is a lovely golden-haired maiden said to guard the treasure of Teach, or Blackbeard; she is successful in her vigil, because no one has ever found it. However, Captain Haley did turn up four bars of solid silver under a rock, and used his wealth to build one of the breakwaters at his island.

The Shoals began to change for the better after 1820, though no one knows why, unless the constant labors of those who had never given up the Shoalers as lost souls had begun to pay off. The burned-down church was rebuilt, town meetings were resumed; conditions were so improved that, when Thomas Laighton of Portsmouth became disillusioned with New Hampshire politics and wanted to get away from it all, he asked for the job of keeper of the White Island Light at the Shoals, and moved his wife and babies out there.

This move is important to Maine because in 1847 Laighton built one of the first summer hotels in New England, on Maine's island of Appledore. (He built another later, on Star.) To Laighton's Hotel came Nathaniel Hawthorne, who wrote enthusiastically of it; and Whittier, Thomas Bailey Aldrich, James Russell Lowell, Frances Hodgson Burnett, and many others through the years. Meanwhile, Laighton's daughter Celia was growing up, recording in her sensitive mind all the sights, sounds, and scents of these islands. When she married Levi Thaxter and went to Massachusetts to live, she wrote down all the impressions that had become a part of her. It is her poetry—including the famous "sandpiper" one—and such evocative, vivid, and unsentimental recollections as those in *Among the Isles of Shoals* that for many years have given these islands life even for those who have never seen them. Celia Thaxter is buried with her family near the ruins of the hotel on Appledore, and now there is a museum there in memory of her.

But if the Laightons brought the Shoals to life in one way, so that the name "Appledore" even today causes a wave of pleasant impressions, the name "Smutty Nose" suggests something quite different. On the night of March 5, 1873—and this was between two of those delightful Appledore summers, it is the dark side of the coin—Louis Wagner rowed ten miles out from Portsmouth in a stolen dory, murdered with an ax Karen Christensen and her sister-in-law Anetha Christensen, and rowed back.

Knowing the women were alone on the island, because the men were in Portsmouth after bait for their trawls, Wagner had gone out to see if they had money hidden in the house. Edmund Pearson in *Murder on Smutty Nose* gives the story in its setting of vast, icy, moonlit silence: we see the three women in the house, the madman's entrance; we hear the screams that no one else heard, and we see the blood on the snow. The surviving girl, Maren, ran frantically, in her bare feet and nightgown, the dog running with her; the two of them crouched in a crevice in the rocks until daylight, the girl hugging the dog against her breast. At daylight she was able to attract the attention of someone on Appledore. The men came, and saw what they would never forget as long as they lived.

Louis Wagner was one of the two last men to be put to death in Maine, and it may be that their execution was the deciding factor in a long battle over the moral issues involved in capital punishment. Wagner's death was put off, again and again, for two years, so that he must have died many times before the final event in the old lime kiln in the prison yard at Thomaston. The other murderer, one John True Gordon, was dying from a suicide attempt when they hanged him. For the officials who performed them, and for those who watched, the executions were pretty harrowing. There was a good deal of public disapproval—except, no doubt, on the part of those who found the dead women on Smutty Nose—and so the death penalty was abolished in Maine.

Today the Isles of Shoals live a quiet but useful existence. Ghosts are still supposed to walk, phantom ships have been observed: Philip Babb, who was once a butcher on Appledore, wanders around in his butcher's coat, carrying his sharp knife; modern draggermen swear they have seen supernatural fires lighting the skies around the Shoals. But apart from this activity, there is the more mundane kind at the Coast Guard station and at the White Island light. The University of New Hampshire holds summer courses in its marine laboratories at the Shoals. There is a writers' conference on Star Island each year, and a summer-long series of religious conferences sponsored by the Isles of Shoals Unitarian Association, which owns Star Island and the hotel there, and some land and buildings on Appledore. The Association has plans to restore the ancient village of Gosport, and already several stone cottages have been built.

Perhaps in time the memory of the Shoals' bad years and of the murder on Smutty Nose will be wiped out entirely by the healthy and creative life the new "Shoalers" have designed for Celia Thaxter's and Samuel Haley's and John Tuck's islands.

BOON ISLAND

BOON ISLAND, apparently more lighthouse than island, lies a little way off the Yorks. A small, low island, it was easily *not* seen by early shipping, and probably accounted for many a death at sea, but the first recorded wreck in the history of the coast is that of the *Increase* in 1682. The *Increase* was an early variety of coaster, doing a good trading business between Plymouth and Pemaquid. This was in the promising days before the Indian wars drove everyone to the westward, when each island had its fishermen, each mainland settlement had farmers and trappers with goods to sell.

The *Increase* was wrecked on this low-lying reefy islet one summer day, and four survivors—three white men and an Indian—dragged themselves ashore. They were better off than the survivors of the *Nottingham Galley*, which was wrecked there in December some thirty years later, for the *Increase*'s crew was able to get fish and gulls' eggs, and didn't suffer from the cold. Still, no ship passed, nothing moved on the green shore opposite, and at the end of a month the men were desperate.

Then one day they saw a column of smoke rising from Mount Agamenticus, on the mainland, and so they hurried to build a fire of their own. It was seen by a group of Indians, who had sent up the great smoke on Mount Agamenticus in memory of a beloved and respected Indian named Aspinquid. He had been converted to Christianity by John Eliot of Massachusetts, and had lived such a good life that he was a sort of saint to Indians all over Maine. They met each year on Agamenticus to perform memorial rites in his name.

The rescued men of the *Increase* considered their salvation to be a great boon conferred on them by God, and so they named the island Boon Island.

Most of us non-seagoing islanders had never heard of Boon Island until Kenneth Roberts wrote a book about it. After that the words "Boon Island Light" seemed to have a familiar ring about them; for there is a lighthouse there now, and the twenty-five-day nightmare of the crew of the *Nottingham Galley* has never been repeated in the history of the coast. To read the account by the ship's captain, John Dean, and his brother is to open a door into a world of wet cold that rots the flesh and dissolves the bones, of soul-destroying desolation made all the more horrible because the mainland was so close. "Four leagues to the eastward of Piscataqua," the narrative says.

Wrecked on the rock on the eleventh of December, 1710, Captain Dean did what he could to keep his men alive and sane, though two died almost at once and two more died in an attempt to reach the mainland on a raft they had constructed from the wreck. The others lived on rockweed and two or three mussels apiece each day; mussels were difficult to get and eventually the men's empty stomachs refused them. Once they minced a green hide and ate it, and they shared a gull. Meanwhile fingers and toes froze and rotted, and revolting ulcers appeared.

Those who were able worked under the captain's command, first to make a suitable shelter of timbers and canvas, then to construct some means of transportation. They lost their hammer and ax. They were harried by strong winds and high seas, from first one direction and then another. They became frighteningly weak. It is certain that their lives were saved by the flesh of the dead carpenter, carefully portioned out by the captain. He found, however, that with a slow gain in strength from this food some of the men became wild and brutish, and would have fought for more. It took all Dean's power of command to keep order.

On the second of January, 1711, the survivors were discovered by a shallop from the mainland. She couldn't come ashore because of the rough seas, but sent in a man in a small "cannoe," who was somewhat "affrighted" by the dreadful appearance of the derelicts. But he saw for himself the condition of the men, who were too weak to leave the shelter, and he helped them build a fire and then left, not without being almost drowned himself in the wild water. The shallop was lost on its way back to the mainland, but the crew was saved. As soon as they got ashore they sent word to Portsmouth about the Boon Island wreck, and after two stormy days—which in their way were worse for the survivors than all the others, perhaps for the very reason that delivery was so close—men came from Portsmouth with a shallop and a large canoe, and in two hours had carried the weak men on their backs from the rock to their craft.

Other vessels had come out too, as soon as the seas flattened. The captain and his brother Jasper Dean in their narrative have nothing but praise and thanks for the generous kindness of the New Englanders: the tender care which the crew received, the feeding and the nursing, the clothing provided.

The unpleasant aftermath, to be expected because there is always someone to start whispered gossip, was not concerned with the fact that the crew survived by eating the carpenter. Instead, it was put about that the captain and his brother, who owned seven-eighths of the ship, had deliberately conspired to wreck the vessel on Boon Island for the insurance. That the ridiculous accusation does not need a rebuttal is the answer put forth in the brief and dignified statement signed by Jasper Dean, John Dean, and by young Miles Whitworth, who owned the remaining eighth of the ship and was also a Boon Island castaway, the "Young Gentleman" of the narrative. Sensibly the statement points out that if the owners had intended to wreck the ship they would have chosen a different place to do it, with an eye out for their own survival; *not* the sodden, freezing, nightmare territory of Boon Island in a bad December.

Today Boon Island is a light station, inhabited by the keeper and his family. It seems strange that the traces of an ordeal such as that of the *Nottingham Galley*'s survivors can be completely wiped away, that one can stand on Boon Island today, hearing the pleasant wash of summer surf and the cries of the gulls, and not remember that there once men prayed, wept, and in a fury of terror cursed Providence and each other. It is all someone else's bad dream; and yet it happened.

THE ISLANDS OF SACO BAY

STRATTON, BLUFF, WOOD, Negro, Stage, Ram, and Eagle—and how many other even more minute islands—form a gilt chain lying along summer seas; even those that are barren possess their own particular beauty and keep all year round their warm topaz color that from a little distance looks as soft as tawny plush. The faintest slope or most shallow dip shows in sunshine as an enchanting contour, and one of the loveliest sights in Maine is a red winter sunset turning barren islands to rosy-gold across an icy blue sea. Many birds find sanctuary on these during the migration periods, and a treeless island does not seem bare when the song sparrows come or when Canada Geese circle down to rest in a secluded cove. Wild flowers star the tangling grasses from May till frost, and berries usually grow thick and rich from wild-strawberry time to cranberry picking.

As one explores the Saco Bay islands, most of which are uninhabited now (in strictly human terms), one is accompanied by a great sense of their past. It begins with the tremendous upheaval of nature that created them; then follows a period of incredibly rich wild life and vegetation of which we can have only the faintest idea, and inhabitation by a race that antedated the Indians as we know them. The Indians considered the mainland and the islands as their own, and they were right. If ever innocents lived in a Garden of Eden, it was they: the pure and savage freedom they possessed has never been surpassed anywhere. The islands were necessary to them; they paddled out in their canoes to hold summer encampments and great councils, to hunt seabirds, to spear fish, to gather shellfish, berries and nuts.

The first white men who came were, from the Indians' point of

The Western Coast · 29

view, villains, but from their own all of them were brave, and most were honorable.

What sort of man was John Stratton, for whom Stratton Island is named, no one knows. He came from Shotley, in Suffolk, and was probably a gentleman of some importance; he had a grant of 2,000

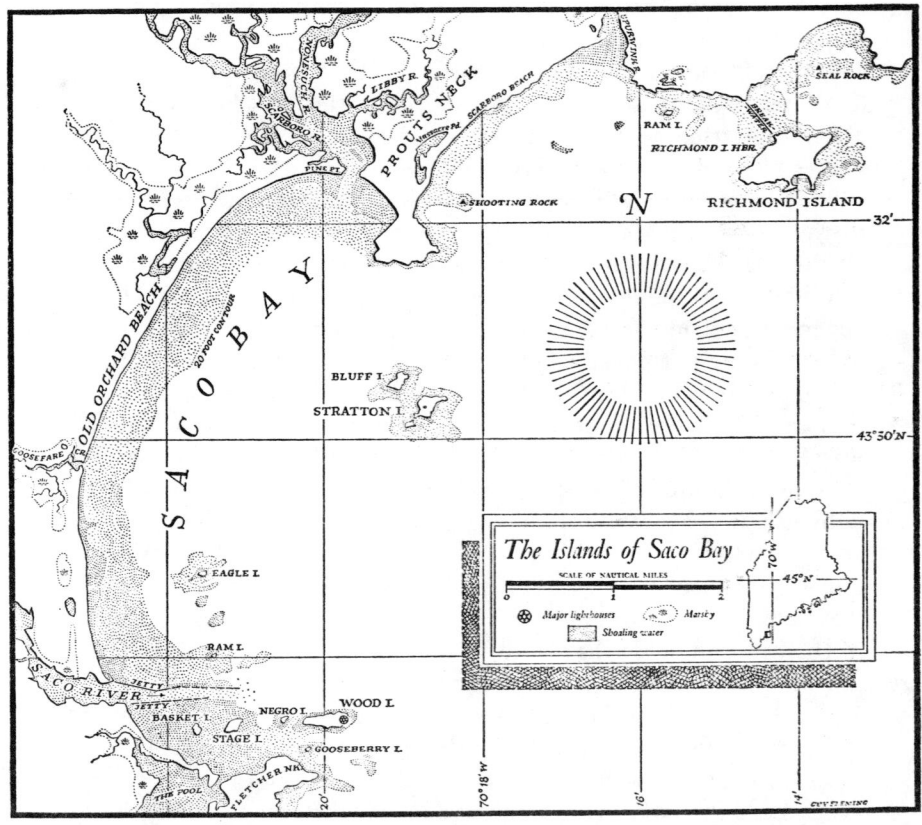

acres on the mainland near Cape Porpoise, as well as the island. We know that he was living in Salem in 1637, when he was defendant in a suit over a brass kettle. Stratton was apparently dispossessed of his lands by Sir Ferdinando Gorges, of the Plymouth Council, of whom we shall hear more; no reasons are given, and though he later sued for repossession, apparently he lost. That is all that is recorded of Stratton the man.

Stratton, the island, lies four and a half miles off Pine Point; it is the larger of two islands due west of Prout's Neck, Scarboro. (The other, smaller island, barren, is called Bluff. Both lie within the Saco town limits.) John Stratton stayed on Stratton long enough only to leave his name; he was little more than the wind blowing over the island, yet he must have sailed across from the mainland and walked on the shores and through the woods, gone hunting here—perhaps for muskrats at the big pond that still lies among the cattails; perhaps he stood and looked out to sea in the very place where we stand now, and thought of England.

John Stratton may be seen as a symbol of all the men who came to the islands of Maine—the sly or the honorable, the adventurer or the planter, the agnostic or the theologian, the Puritan or the Cavalier. The moving spirit behind their endeavors—though he never set foot in the New World himself—was the West Country nobleman Sir Ferdinando Gorges, who in 1616 began his career of backing colonial enterprises. Gorges, after a gallant military career, was awarded the command of the fort at Plymouth, where he watched the ships setting out for America and the West Indies. As he came to know more of the land across the sea, of its people, its wild life, its geography, he decided to take a hand in its development. Though many of his efforts failed—in fact Gorges considered himself a failure—he was really the founder of Maine; as A. L. Rowse has pointed out in *The Elizabethans and America*, "It is only in the careerist sense that he did not succeed, for in fact his efforts did bear fruit, even if others enjoyed the rewards."

Gorges and Stratton are typical of these seventeenth-century men, who lived in a world that was growing so fast, reaching out in all directions—both mentally and physically—with such greedy excitement that we, living in an age in which there is nowhere left to go but the moon, almost envy them. In the time of Ferdinando Gorges and John Stratton, Galileo was getting into trouble in Italy for daring to say the earth moved; in England Harvey was working out his theory of the circulation of the blood, and Ben Jonson was still alive. George Fox, who was to found the Society of Friends, was a little boy, Descartes and Corneille were active in France, and

The Western Coast · 31

in Belgium Franz Hals was painting his laughing cavaliers, so that we know how John Stratton and his contemporaries dressed for fine occasions.

In Stratton Island's later history, after John Stratton was dispossessed, it was a farm and pastured a large dairy herd. The cattle were taken back and forth to the mainland in large scows. Young cattle were taken to Bluff Island for grazing, sometimes in comfort by boat and sometimes made to swim from Stratton at low tide.

During World War II the island was kept empty because of its possibly strategic location. Now both Stratton and Bluff, as well as Richmond Island off Cape Elizabeth, have been designated as wild-life sanctuaries by the heirs of the late Phineas Sprague of Boston and Scarboro. Stratton possesses a unique rock formation, and tons of its round, many-colored beach rocks have been carried off over the years to decorate fireplaces.

Four and a half miles across the water from Prout's Neck, Wood Island forms a natural breakwater for Biddeford Pool. It is a small island, thirty-odd acres in all, about eight hundred yards long, and very narrow, though it was probably once much wider.

It too is barren, though Folsom's *History of Saco* says of Wood Island in 1830: "The vine is not found there now, nor the walnut, but a great growth still covers the island. Beech, oak, maplebass, ash, fir or spruce, moose wood, pine and hornbeams and birch cover its surface, which covers about thirty-six acres." This lovely forest must have gone the way of the wild grape and the nut trees that so enchanted the early explorers. Fires and wasteful cutting without subsequent reforestation have turned many an island from a magnificent botanical garden into a hump of rock and turf that could represent the top of a volcano that died out a few million years ago.

Wood is important today because of its sixty-two-foot lighthouse; the revolving red light is visible for thirteen miles and is a familiar and friendly signal to trawlers, lobstermen coming home after dark, and yachtsmen cruising through the summer nights.

Negro Island lies west of Wood and is connected by a bar with a scrap of solid ground called Rocky Bar, which is as good a description of it as any. Stage Island, now entirely barren, lies eight hundred yards west of Negro, and is convoyed by Ram and

Eagle, which are small, bare, and rocky. Stage is set apart from the others by the gray stone geodetic monument, forty feet high, which stands at its northwest corner. Built in 1825, it is known as the Stage Island Monument, and is the official guide leading vessels into Biddeford Pool. A bar of pebbles leads from Stage Island to the mainland.

Stage Island was once called Gibbins Island, for a James Gibbins who came to Saco in 1642. It was probably much bigger then than it is now—an estimated four hundred yards in length. As Gibbins Island it played a small but exceedingly lively part in the Revolution. It belonged then to a Colonel Cutts, a shipbuilder. One day the British frigate *Bulwark* anchored offshore, and landed a hundred and fifty men on the island, who set fire to four ships, two of them still on the stocks. Colonel Cutts confronted the British commander, Captain Milne, and offered ransom money to save his beauties, the *Hermione*, the *Catherine*, the *Equator*, and a nameless sloop. But Milne was brutally obdurate, and so the Colonel saw his splendid vessels wilfully destroyed before his eyes. It must have been rather like watching his children murdered, and, though details are lacking, we can imagine the sickening sound of flames crackling through the hulls as the fine work of the carpenters and joiners was eaten away before their eyes, the smoke rising to heaven as if from some monstrous sacrifice.

After that, the seamen raided Colonel Cutts's stores. In the meantime people had gathered fearfully on the nearest mainland shore, seeing the frigate lying off the island, and the smoke and flame of tremendous fires. They were terrified of a raid on the mainland which could destroy their holdings and stock, burn their homes, and turn them into paupers in the space of an hour.

However, one Jesse Tarbox of Fletcher's Neck had the presence of mind to call the militia. They came marching down "at a late hour," we are told, and again drama is conveyed in a few bare words. They must have been reluctant warriors, and who can blame them? What a relief when they reached the shore and heard floating over the water the music of the band playing on the *Bulwark* as the frigate sailed away!

Because of the Stage Island raid, a special town meeting was held in Saco. One resolution reads; "To direct the Selectmen to have constantly in readiness one thousand rations and the means of conveying same to wherever the militia shall march, an alarm given and a sufficient quantity of provisions shall be sent after them." The thought of having plenty to eat during their next engagement with the enemy couldn't have been very cheering to the militia; it is rather like the condemned man's being assured of a hearty breakfast before he is hanged. This is not to malign the men who were ready to shoulder a musket to protect the holdings they had almost literally clawed out of the wilderness; but the thought of facing such a tough, nail-hard, well-armed crew of British seamen as burned the Stage Island vessels would have made anybody hesitate.

The *Bulwark* never came back to harass the rest of the community, and after a while it was said that Captain Milne had only meant to settle a private grudge with Colonel Cutts, a speculation that gives an intimate touch to the war. In any event, because of the burning of four new ships, and quite possibly because of a private fight between an American shipbuilder and a British naval officer, Stage Island won its immortality in island history.

RICHMOND ISLAND

SEEN FROM A PASSING YACHT on a fine day when it is rich and green with summer, or from the mainland when choppy autumn seas hide the bar or snow blows in a tenuous veil over its rocks and fields until they can barely be seen from half a mile away, Richmond is simply another one of the hundreds of islands along the Maine coast. There is nothing about it now to tell of its hundreds of years of history, some of it blood-soaked, some of it rich with warmth, humor, and creative industry.

Lying south of Cape Elizabeth, between the cape and the mouth of the Spurwink River, Richmond covers about two hundred acres, is about one mile long, and three-quarters of a mile wide at its broadest point. The names of its capes and inlets—Watch Point, Adams Head, Western Head, Broad Cove, Clam Cove, and Mussel Cove—are fairly ordinary, as such names go, until we read the island's history and wonder who of those early islanders named them. Who watched for Indians from Watch Point? Was it Walter Bagnall, who was murdered by Indians after all? And did John Winter's maids gather mussels in Mussel Cove and discuss furtively Mrs. Winter's harsh tongue, and dare each other to write to Mr. Trelawny in Devon to complain? And did young Mrs. Gibson walk unhappily on Western Head, wishing that she and her clergyman husband could live where other women wouldn't resent her? They are all gone now, but we can reconstruct their stories from scattered references to Richmond in the records, and from the Trelawny papers, which give a detailed account of life on the island from 1630 to 1645.

The island's lush growth of grapes made the early Dutch navigators call the place "*Wingards Eylant*." The Italian explorers knew it as "Winte" or "Wingut" Island. Samuel de Champlain, enthusiastic about the great natural beauty of the place, called it "the Isle of Bacchus." In 1607 it was visited by the Sagadahoc colonists, who apparently discovered it by accident when they missed the mouth of the Sagahadoc on their voyage from St. George. They called it the "Seagirt Refuge."

To a patent-holder or an adventurer looking for a place he could claim by one means or another, the island was most desirable because of its location; it had a safe anchorage, and a wealth of trees and shrubs that signified rich soil for pasturage and crops. As more settlers came to this part of the coast, the island became even more important as the center of a growing coastwise trading business.

Some historians believe that Richmond received its name from the Duke of Richmond, one of the forty members of the Plymouth Council, who won the island in a lottery on May 29, 1623. But most authorities hold that the island was named for George Richmond, whose headquarters were there in the 1620's. No details of his life on the island have been found, but through lists of transferred property one gathers that he was the head of a colonial enterprise which employed fishermen and shipbuilders.

George Richmond came from Bandonbridge, a town in Ireland about twenty miles west of Cork. After an Irish uprising there, Queen Elizabeth had granted Bandonbridge to companies of English planters, who at once came into conflict with the Irish, the threat of Spanish ships, and the hostility of the newly-founded Anglican church, since many of these colonists were Puritans. It is easy to see why the Bandonists sought a new place of refuge. When the *Mayflower* sailed in 1620 George Richmond was already settled on or in the vicinity of Richmond Island, with men in his employ, a vessel which they built here, and extensive goods, which shows that the search for space and religious freedom had been going on long before the Plymouth Colony was founded.

Records show that Walter Bagnall and John Peverly were living on the island from 1628 to 1631. Bagnall had come from England with a young explorer, Captain Christopher Levett, and stayed behind when Levett returned home. Another fact gives Bagnall definite personality and color, and makes him out to be a bit of a rogue: he was an associate of Thomas Morton, who horrified the Puritans of Massachusetts with his maypole on Merrymount and its attendant rites in worship of Hymen. Bagnall sounds like an adventurer, but by the time he had acquired a fortune through shrewd dealings with the Indians he must have longed for respectability as an accredited landowner, for he was anxious to establish his legal claim to Richmond Island. Peverly went back to England and managed to attain a grant in his and Bagnall's names, but before he returned with it Bagnall was murdered on the island by Indians in 1631.

He may have deserved it, or it may have been a brutal and unprovoked attack; in any event, his death was avenged the next year when Captain Neale, returning with an expedition from the pursuit of the pirate Dixey Bull off Pemaquid, landed on the island. He found there an Indian chief, Black William of Saugus, and executed him at once, though there was no evidence that he was involved in Bagnall's murder.

Now we come to Robert Trelawny, a man of Devon who never set foot on these shores and yet made his mark on our history. The Plymouth Council in 1631 gave to Robert Trelawny a grant of land including Richmond Island and all of Cape Elizabeth. Trelawny and his partner, Moses Goodyear, were given the grant because they had "spent large sums in the discovery of those parts and to encourage them to settle a plantation there." On July 21, 1632, Richard Vines, agent for Sir Ferdinando Gorges of the Council, gave possession of the territory covered by the grant to John Winter as the agent for Robert Trelawny. Thomas Cammock, a relative of the Earl of Warwick, also a member of the council, had expected to take over for Trelawny, but an accident delayed his arrival in America and Winter assumed all responsibilities.

Winter was familiar with the coast of Maine, having been in the area for several years. After taking possession, he went back to England, returning in 1633 with men and materials, and proceeded to establish a complete trading center on Richmond Island.

Through Winter's extensive correspondence Trelawny was kept informed of the trials and problems which beset the settlement three thousand miles from its owner. All did not go too well during Winter's first year. On January 18, 1634, he wrote a homesick letter to Trelawny, stating, "I have an interest to come home next winter; so with all our company that is here with me."

Yet they persevered through their homesickness, and stayed on. In June, 1634, Winter wrote:

> I have build a house at Richmond Island that is forty feet in length and eighteen feet broad within the sides, besides the chimney and the chimney is large with an oven in each end of him and he is so large we can place our chittle [kettle] within the clavel piece. We can brew and bake and boyle our chittles all at once in him with the help of another house built under the side of our house where we have sett our eight ceves, and mill and martar [corn was first crushed with a mortar and then sifted]. I have two chambers in him and all our men lies in on them and every man has his close borded cabbin. I have room to make more close borded cabbins, if I have need of them and in the other chamber, I have room enough to put the ship's sails into and all our dry goods which are in casks and I have a storehouse in him which will hold eighteen to twenty tons of casks underneath. Underneath I have a citchin [kitchen] for our men to eat and drink in and a steward room that will hold two tons in casks, which we put our bread and beans into, everyone of these rooms has locks and keys.

In 1635 Winter made another trip home, and returned in 1636 with a minister for the area, Richard Gibson, and part of the Winter family—his wife and one daughter, Sara.

When trading became active, Winter was able to keep his men occupied all the year. The adjoining mainland and several of the other islands began to attract settlers, many of whom were fishermen and carpenters. In the fifteen years in which Winter carried on his trading, ships were built on the island and cruised from Virginia to Penobscot Bay, as well as making periodic trips to Europe. One of the vessels built carried 600 tons, and one 300 tons. Their cargoes consisted of oil, furs, and, oddly enough, "fish peas," now known as roe or caviar. The *Richmond*, commanded by Captain Marius Hawkins, carried oak staves; these were in great demand for use in making casks for wine storage.

Stephen Sargent drew plans for a ship, launched at the island in July, 1641, about which her builder wrote home, "She swimmed as upright as might be when she was launched and was very stiff in her side." This two-decker had a fifty-foot keel, a nine-foot hold, and was four and a half feet between decks. She sailed for Bilbao, under command of her builder, with a cargo of salt fish, fish oil, and fish peas.

The average fishing boat displaced 200 tons and carried a crew of fifty men. Before a voyage, each man contributed twenty shillings for provisions. They fished on shares—one-third for expenses (nets, lines, and such), one-third for the crew, and one-third for the owners. The cost of each voyage was about 800 pounds. Three trips a year was the average, and during the cold winter months the men spent their time preparing cargoes for shipment, repairing gear, and, when it was possible for Mr. Winter to find work for them, they built and improved the buildings on the island.

Later, when smaller boats were used, a crew of four was carried for fishing near home. One of these men was the cook, and also took charge of landing the fish on shore and curing them. Mackerel and herring were salted down on rocks, dried carefully, and used as bait. Other fish were cured more painstakingly on frames—called "flakes"—and piled in a dark place. They were then covered with salt hay from the marshes and left there until it was time to ship them.

Yet, though Winter made Trelawny's patent show a profit, and appears to have been entirely honest in his dealings with his employer, the correspondence of those days reveals that he was a difficult man. He cut Thomas Cammock's hay with no idea of paying for it. He ordered George Cleeves, or Cleeve, to relinquish his home and constantly harassed him, even after Cleeves and his partner, Richard Tucker, had made a new settlement in what is now Portland. He claimed extensive holdings as agent for the Trelawny estates.

In justice to Winter, it must be admitted that trespassers gave him a hard time, ignoring his orders, settling down wherever they pleased and staying indefinitely, demanding food and shelter. And probably he had his share of those who refused to pull their own weight, who caused quarrels, who trifled with the maids. But there is no hiding the fact that he was tactless, grasping, and unpopular.

In Winter's letters there are lists of materials which he ordered from England for his family. From these we know that the ladies were well-dressed. At a launching "Madam Winter" and Sara were gay in scarlet petticoats, lace-trimmed coats and waistcoats. John Winter wore a "sad"-colored coat with long-lapeled waistcoat of scarlet, silver buckles on his knees, woven Irish stockings, and a steeple-crowned hat.

We know from her husband's letters that Mrs. Winter had troubles from the moment of her arrival on Richmond. There are accounts of a slander suit brought because George Cleeves was heard to speak disrespectfully of her. We can only hope that she found enough social life among the ladies of the nearby mainland to compensate for her trials with bound-out girls, the crews from the vessels, and her efforts to marry off her daughter Sara.

There were difficulties and heartaches among the maids. The work was terribly hard for some of the girls who had come to seek their fortunes, and the prospect of Indians and wild beasts was far more frightening in reality than it had seemed at home in England. And if they were not overworked or afraid, they were bored when the boats were out and all the young men gone. One of Winter's letters says:

> You write me of some yll reports is given of my Wyfe for beating the maid; yf a faire way will not do yt, beatings must, sometimes,

uppon such idlle girrells as she is. Yf you thinke yt fitt for my wyfe to do all the worke & the maid sitt still, she must forebeare her hands to strike, for then the works will ly undonn. She hath bin now 2 yeares ½ in the house, & I do not thinks she hath risen 20 times before my Wyfe hath bin up to Call her, & many tymes light the fire before she Comes out of her bed. She hath twize gon a mechinge [missing] in the woodes, which we haue bin faine to send all our Company to seeke. We cann hardly keep her within doores after we are gonn to bed, except we Carry the key of the doore to bed with us. She never Could melke Cow nor goat since she Came hither. Our men do not desire to haue her boyle the kittell for them she is so sluttish. She Cannot be trusted to serue a few piggs, but my wyfe most Commonly must be with her. She hath written home, I heare, that she was faine to ly uppon goates skins. She might take some goates skins to ly in her bedd, but not given to her lodginge. For a yeare 'quarter or more she lay with my daughter uppon a good feather bed before my daughter beinge lacke 3 or 4 daies to Sacco, the maid goes into bed with her Cloth & stockins & would not take the paines to plucke of her Cloths; her bedd after was a doust bed & she had 2 Coverletts to ly on her, but sheets she had none after that time she was found to be so sluttish. Her beating that she hath had never hurt her body nor limes. she is so fat & soggy she Cann hardly do any worke. This I write all the Company will justify. If this maid at her lasy tymes, when she hath bin found in her ill accyons, do not deserue 2 or 3 blowes, I pray Judge You who hath most reason to Complaine, my wyfe or the maid.

Life was good on Richmond Island. There were plenty of cows and goats, and pigs too. (Horses were not brought over until later.) "You also write me that you ar informed that my wyfe will giue the men no mylke," Winter wrote Trelawny. "Yt may be that she will not giue every on mylke as often as they Com for yt, but I know that all the Company haue mylke 4, 5 & 6 meales in a weeke, boyled with flower, which som of them haue Complained haue had mylke to often."

One sad event is recorded by Winter:

In 1639 the maid Tomson had a hard fortune. Yt was her Chance to be drowned Cominge over the barr after our Cowes, & very little water on the barr, not aboue ½ foote, & we Cannot Judge how yt should be, accept that her hatt did blow from her head, & she to saue her hatt stept on the side of the barr. A great many of our Company saw when she was drowned, & run with all speed to save her, but she was dead before they Could Com to her. I thinke yf she had lived she would have proved a good servant in the house; she would do more worke than 3 such maides as Prysylla [the subject of the long complaint above] is.

Several men who had come out with Winter, leaving their wives in England, were charged with money advanced to the women by Trelawny. Benjamin Stevens, Steven Lapthorn, and Roger Slatterlay all had their troubles. "You may please to forbear to give his wyfe any more money." Charles Hatch made the same request to Trelawny, as "he had not heard from her what she had done with previous money."

The keeping of English holidays and the customary celebrations are noted in several deeds and transfers. Richard Vines issued a deed for rental, the charge to be "Fifteen shillings yearly, to be paid at the feast of Saynt Michaell, the ark angell, two days work of one man at harvest, and one fatt gowse on the twenty fifth of December." The Christmas Eve service, doubtless conducted by young Richard Gibson, ushered in the twelve days of frolicking and feasting.

Richard Gibson, the scholar and theologian who had come over in 1636 with Mr. and Mrs. Winter and Sara, ministered to the households of the surrounding area (including Black Point and Saco) for three years and eight months. As a university man, he must have experienced some lonely moments. No greater contrast to Magdalen College at Oxford could have been found than on the coast of Maine. But we find frequent gifts of wine from Trelawny to Gibson and a bequest of twelve pounds for him in his will. The young minister must have been active and popular on Richmond. We read how some of the men who left Winter and went fishing for themselves built "the parsonage house, chapel with all the other appurtenances, at their own proper costs and charges, and made choice of Mr. Richard Gibson to be the first parson of said parsonage."

This would have been gratifying to Gibson, especially as he had lost favor with John Winter because he did not marry Sara. The Winters had hoped, and expected, ever since they had all come out on the boat together from England, that Gibson would one day marry their daughter. Poor Sara must have counted on it, and assumed a comfortably proprietary air toward him, while her mother was overwhelmingly maternal, both of them preening a little when mothers and daughters in the mainland settlements gazed hungrily at him as he preached, or tutored their small sons and brothers.

When he said he was going to marry Mary Lewis of Saco, there was a scene. More than that, there was a rush of slanderous gossip about his fiancée. It was unfortunate that the Gibsons had to live on Richmond Island after their marriage, with Mrs. Winter and Sara as close neighbors and not bothering to swallow their injured pride. But when Richard Gibson wrote to Trelawny that he was leaving the island after Michaelmas, he said it was Winter's discourtesy that was driving him.

The Gibsons had been asked to settle at Passcattaway (Portsmouth) where they were made very welcome, but soon there was trouble with the Puritans at Boston, who, now that they were securely established, had decided to stamp out the pernicious Anglican influence to the north of them. The Gibsons eventually left Portsmouth for England, as an alternative to being jailed in America for such crimes as infant baptism.

Gibson's successor on Richmond was Robert Jordan, who had come to America with his relative, Thomas Purchase of Brunswick. He must have known Gibson; surely he knew of the way the Winters had behaved when Richard didn't marry Sara. He married Sara himself, and in the light of his subsequent behavior it looks as if he expected to be marrying Richmond Island as well. Jordan served in Gibson's place as a clergyman for a short time, but he too was hectored by the General Court in Massachusetts for his Church of England goings-on. Finally he left the ministry and became a man of business.

Political disturbances arose at home, and the Trelawny estates were taken over by the Crown in 1640; Trelawny died in prison. After the owner's death, with his heirs disinherited insofar as the plantation was concerned, Winter obtained legal possession of the patent. He left the island to his grandson, John Jordan, son of Robert and Sara. But Robert didn't intend to let Richmond slip so easily out of his reach. He petitioned the court for a distribution of Winter's estate and won six hundred pounds, and an order allowing him to seize the entire grant. Thereby he acquired a title by which all the properties have been cleared ever since. When young John Jordan married Elizabeth Styleman of Boston, his father deeded part of Richmond Island to him.

    At the end of the bloody period of the Indian wars which cleared the islands of inhabitants and destroyed the buildings, the heirs of former owners began to appear. Settlers straggled back, recalling the fertile fields, the fish and game. Again they were pioneers, for homes must be built and land recleared. The Jordan heirs came back to claim their inheritance, Richmond Island, and held it until 1777, when Clement Jordan sold half the island to Jedediah Preble. Clement was the last Jordan to own the complete island, and in the next year he sold the other half to Preble. Thus was broken the last direct link with Robert Trelawny, the good Devon man.

    Now owned by the Phineas Sprague heirs, who have made it a wild-life sanctuary, Richmond lies aloof but not lonely. It has birds and beasts for companions, and its ghosts.

[II]

Casco Bay

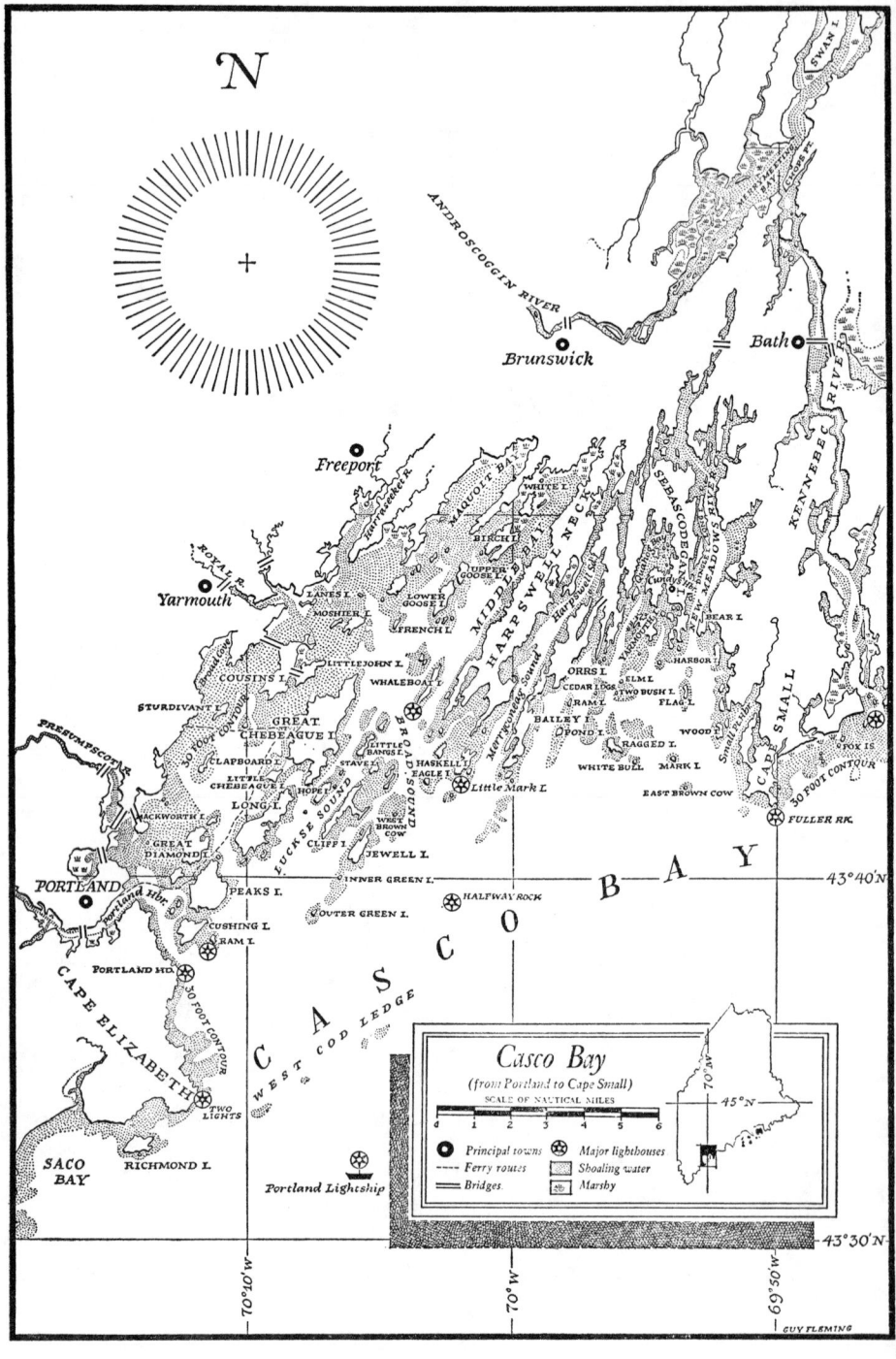

THE ISLANDS OF
PORTLAND HARBOR

CHRISTOPHER LEVETT, who sailed from England in 1623 at the head of an expedition to the New World, was one of the first white men to stand on some of the islands in what he called "Cascoe" Bay. This Levett, beloved of Samoset and the sagamores, is a man to whom our modern hearts instinctively warm. Tracing his journeys along the coast of Maine, we feel we know him well.

What he looked like we do not know, so we are at liberty to make our own picture of this English seafarer, captain in His Majesty's Navy, explorer and colonizer in the New World. Perhaps he was lean and fair and blue-eyed. He was almost certainly young when he landed at the Isles of Shoals in the autumn of 1623, bearing from Sir Ferdinando Gorges a grant of 6,000 acres at a location to be chosen by himself. We know that he had a sober and responsible head, for he had been appointed to the New England Council, whose power extended from the 40th to the 48th parallel, from the Atlantic to the Pacific, and was almost absolute, even to control of shipping on the high seas.

From the Isles of Shoals Levett sailed up to one David Thompson's small colony at the mouth of the Piscataqua, and thence on a journey of exploration with his fifty men. It must have been winter then, or close to it, but their training in the British Navy would have made Levett and his men tough enough for almost anything; these were not like the later settlers who came to the wilderness fresh from their mild English winters and cultivated land.

Still, it was hard enough for Levett and his men, that winter when they explored the York River, the Kennebunk, and the Saco. Then they set out from what is now Biddeford Pool and went along the coast to what is now Portland harbor, and here Levett discovered a perfect harbor formed by four islands; today they are Cushing, Peaks, Diamond, and House. He called the region Quack, which was as near as the Indians could get to York, his native shire.

He explored the territory as far as the Sagadahoc, and rowed up the Fore River, which he named Levett's River. (Let us hope it was spring by that time.) While he was exploring the Presumpscot, which, he said, had a "bigger fall than the fall of London Bridge," he met the Indians of the place. They received him hospitably; he must have been the sort of person to give the best possible impression of the white man, so that they did not see him as the harbinger of the destruction of their way of life.

So here is a young Englishman living in the home of the chief, Skitterygusset, learning the language, eating the food, as much at ease as if he were walking the quarterdeck of his ship. Other chiefs traveled long distances to see him, bringing furs to barter, and they must have been satisfied with their trading. The great Samoset gave him a beaver skin as a gift, and this was a sign of great respect and admiration; it was also the gesture made by one strong man to another whom he considered his equal. In the dark and bloody history of the whites and Indians, Levett's meeting with the red men reads like an idyll.

Cushing Island

Old Whitehead is one of the most magnificent features of Cushing Island; perhaps this great granite cliff, rising one hundred and fifty feet above Portland harbor, perpetually whitewashed by gulls and shags, was what made Christopher Levett choose this island of all those he had seen for the one where he would live.

He didn't simply move onto the island, however, but first asked permission of the Indian chief Cagawescoe. Levett's constantly friendly relations with the Indians protected him even more effectively than did the stone dwelling he erected on Cushing. The house was fortified against the unneighborly Tarratines, who made the islands and shores of "Cascoe" Bay their summer headquarters. Apparently the sagamores of the region were glad to have a little bolstering against this invasion of summer people.

Levett returned to England shortly after this, leaving ten men to guard his fortifications, and promising to come back. He never did, unfortunately, and the ten men eventually scattered. Some may have married into Indian families, or branched out on expeditions of their own, or they may have been captured by the Tarratines after all. Now only the traces of an ancient cellar hole show where Levett's house was.

Levett sold his Casco Bay interests to some Plymouth (England) merchants. A Mr. Wright of that company passed on the title of Cushing Island to George Cleeves who, as we have seen, later had trouble with John Winter of Richmond Island and eventually founded the city of Portland. Cleeves bequeathed the island to his daughter Elizabeth, who married Michael Mitton, one of the Peaks Island settlers. When their daughter Sarah married a James Andrews, the island was her dowry.

James Andrews kept the island from 1667 to 1698. In this time it was known successively by three names: Andrews, Portland, and Fort Island, for the first official fort on the island. When the Indian wars broke out in the 1670's, and the New England settlers were mowed down like corn in a hailstorm, refugees from the mainland fled to the garrison on Andrews Island. They built a new redoubt which must have protected them, but for a while they were without food or ammunition, and existed on berries and fish. A George Felt is remembered because he took a few men and risked a trip to nearby Peaks Island to get some sheep left there by settlers who had escaped massacre and sailed to Boston. The savages let them land on Peaks and then murdered them.

There is a whole drama in that unornamented sentence; one sees the men, weakened with malnutrition but strengthened in turn by desperation and the fact that the women and children in the fort were depending on them, rowing across to the other island. The sea would have to be quite calm, and it was probably dark; perhaps it was a summer night, so mild and still and starlit that it makes the aftermath even more frightful. Thinking that the Indians had no reason to come back to the island after making it into a shambles, they landed on a sheltered beach. And then the Indians fell on them with knives and tomahawks. If it was a quiet night, the listeners at the fort may have heard the shouts and the screams across the calm water; or the slaughter may have been swift and silent. Then, as the night went on and daylight came but no boat returned from Peaks, those waiting would have known the truth at last.

Well, fish and berries are better than nothing, and we visualize a detail sent to fish for cunners off the rocks, or even, at high tide, out into a cove—one with no headlands behind which an Indian canoe could hide—while a watch was stationed at strategic spots all about. Some of the settlers did survive, for James Andrews lived to give up his island in 1698. His fort must have been a good one, for traces of it existed up to the Civil War; in 1754, when Governor William Shirley signed a treaty with the Indians, there were 800 soldiers on the island.

John Rouse of Marshfield, Massachusetts, who bought the island in 1698, or at least took title to it, transferred it to a John Brown of the same town. Neither of them ever lived on the island. Brown sold to John Robinson of Newbury, Massachusetts, Robinson to Nathaniel Jones, and in 1735 Jones sold to Captain Joshua Bangs. During Bangs's possession and for the next hundred years, the island was called Bangs Island, and only the fort recalled the nightmare of the Indian wars that had gone on for so long.

Now another Massachusetts man migrated northward; Ezekiel Cushing, a minister's son, bought the island for $2300. He made his fortune in the West Indian trade and lived accordingly; at the home he built, called "The Homestead in the Willows," he entertained extravagantly and often, and his cellar had a fame all its own. He was commander of a regiment of the County, the highest military rank in the District of Maine at that time, and was selectman of the town of Falmouth. After three years he sold the island back to Joshua Bangs and left, eventually buying Long Island, where he lived the same pleasant existence until he died.

After Captain Bangs's death, his son-in-law Brigadier Jedediah Preble, who once owned Richmond Island, had possession. In the years between 1760 and 1812—doubtless rich and exciting years, if we could know all that went on there in that period—the island was broken up into parcels, for in 1812 a Simon Skillings, who sounds like a character out of Dickens, moved into "The Homestead in the Willows" and began to buy up the island piecemeal. By 1823 he owned six-sevenths of the land, while the other one-seventh was held—stubbornly, we presume—by the heirs of Jedediah Preble. Perhaps Skillings did not try to buy their seventh, but on the other hand, if he did try, there must have been some bitter battles over the years.

In 1858 both the Skillings and Preble heirs gave up and sold out to Lemuel Cushing, a fourth cousin of Ezekiel. This Cushing did not plan to live on the moat-encircled fastness, as his relative had. He built, instead, a large brick hotel on a height overlooking Casco Bay. It cost $10,000, which in 1858 could pay for quite an establishment. He named it "The Ottawa," after his home in the Ottawa Valley near Montreal. Wealthy Canadians came south in the summer to rusticate in the Maine air, watch the sails on Casco Bay, and eat lobster at night that had been caught that morning. The hotel burned in 1886, but Cushing sold stock and rebuilt his inn at a cost of $75,000. Prices were going up. And because of the overhead and the short tourist season, he eventually sold his establishment for $16,000.

This second hotel also burned, in 1917, and was never rebuilt. Only a part of a chimney and a huge fireplace remain where once the guests danced and strolled and played croquet through the leisurely summers of an age that ended in 1917 all over the world just as irrevocably as the Cushing hotel burned to the ground.

At about the time of the Spanish-American War the Government bought a large tract on the island at Spring Point, overlooking Old Whitehead, and established a fort there with a garrison of heavy artillery. Numerous brick buildings were erected to quarter officers and enlisted men. With a fine loyalty to the island's past and a chivalrous salute to the man who built the first fortification there, someone named the fort for' Christopher Levett. If his ghost ever walked there, it must have stood aghast to see the great twelve-inch and sixteen-inch guns whose concussion could be felt for incredibly long distances.

The fort was in use during World Wars I and II, and then was abandoned. The 125 acres of land and the buildings were sold in 1957 to a private investor. A 500-foot underground tunnel, built at the turn of the century, is the feature that fascinates most small boys.

Though there is no hotel, many Portland families maintain summer homes on the island today.

Peaks Island

The island in Portland harbor later to be called Peaks took Christopher Levett's fancy especially. It had good fishing and much fowl, he said. But this could be said of any island in those early days before white men had set foot in the deep forests full of game, or set oars to the seas swarming with huge cod.

Just as Levett singled out this one particular island, so did the Bracketts and the Palmers choose it in the mid-1600's, and later the Sterlings, Trefethens, and Mittons; the Munjoys and Trotts. The island of 720 acres was the largest of the four Levett first saw in 1623, and lay on a line between Long Island to the northeast and what is now South Portland to the southwest. A lovely island, as they all are; but this one must indeed have represented a new world to the first settlers. It was not an easy life they had, but it was free, and no life, even in the towns, was easy in those days. To get to the mainland settlements the islanders had to cross water, but that was probably much safer than passing through woods where there was always a chance of being attacked by a wildcat or a hostile Indian.

So with its freedom to work and to produce, its space for breathing, its bounty from the sea, the life on Peaks Island must have been good and satisfying in many ways, until it was destroyed in the blood and smoke of the Indian wars. The Bracketts and the Palmers were almost completely wiped out in an attack in October, 1689, by the Canadas, the Norridgewocks, and the Penobscots. Only the action of Major Benjamin Church and his men, who had been stationed on the island to guard Falmouth, kept the battle from being a complete massacre. But the settlement was destroyed the next year.

As the terror burned itself out, the brave settlers began to come back to rebuild what must have seemed in retrospect a Utopian existence. Newcomers filled the place of those who had died, or who chose not to come back and run the risk of seeing their hard-built homes burned and their families and livestock killed.

Once more in a Maine October, during the Revolution, war touched the island but in a less horrible and intimate fashion. A British ship anchored between House and Hog Islands, and from the houses of Thomas Brackett and of Benjamin Trott the red coats of British soldiers showed clearly in the blazing autumn sunlight. Later the soldiers landed and paraded the Peaks roads with their band, and Peaks children must have tumbled out to the enchantment of fifes and drums, even though their elders tried to keep them in the house. The soldiers went away again, and that was the war on Peaks Island.

For a time the island was called Palmer's, probably for John Palmer, one of the survivors of the attack in October, 1689. It was also called Munjoy's, Mitton's, and Michael's Island. This last has an oddly Miltonian ring, but it wasn't named for the Archangel Michael but rather for Michael Mitton, one of the major land-owners, who married the Elizabeth Cleeves who inherited Cushing.

Then another islander, Samuel Peaks, distinguished himself sufficiently to have the island finally and permanently named after him. He married George Munjoy's widow—perhaps that is the way he distinguished himself.

Though there seems to have been a fairly good-sized settlement on the island at the time of the Indian raids, there were only three houses there in Revolutionary days, when the redcoats came ashore and paraded the island. Captain John Waite was the third householder, along with Thomas Brackett and Benjamin Trott. Captain Waite owned 160 acres, and the Trotts and the Bracketts owned the other 560 acres, Thomas Brackett and his brother having come into their land when they married Michael Mitton's daughters. Later Benjamin Trott bought their share and became the principal landowner.

During the quiet years after the Revolution, Peaks was simply a fishing village in which the islanders lived a self-sufficient life, building their boats, tending their nets and curing their fish, growing gardens and children. The names ring Scottish, Irish, English, Dutch; besides the old ones, there are Woodbury, Parsons, Jones, Skillings, Scott. These people built a new stratum of America over the rocks and turf where the first Americans had their clambakes and council fires.

The island wasn't quite self-sufficient, at that. Many a boat has gone over to Portland to bring back a doctor to help into the world an island child, who would hear pounding surf within the first hour of his life and perhaps within the last hour of it.

The wife of a man who was born on the island in a February blizzard tells how some of the women retained the "second sight" of their Gaelic ancestors. Her husband's grandmother prepared her man's coffin one winter night before anyone but herself knew that he had been drowned. And she knew it only through that most secret, mysterious, inner knowledge that has no words, only certainty. It is a gift that one used to meet with often on the islands and was as much a part of their special atmosphere as the smell of rockweed and the crying of gulls. It was nothing that could be defined, and yet it was there, making of its possessor an island also.

It is said that "The Wreck of the Hesperus" was inspired by the wreck of the schooner *Helen Eliza* which ran ashore on Peaks Island in 1869, with only one survivor. The ship was broken to pieces on the rocks. The survivor's story is a tragedy that seems almost too classic to be true. He had already been through a hurricane in the West Indies, where also he had been the sole survivor. So after the Peaks Island wreck he decided it was clearly indicated that he should give up the sea before it made a third attempt to drown him and succeeded. He went farming in New Hampshire, a good distance from the coast, only to skid off a slippery log over a stream, and drown.

In the 1890's Peaks had an amusement area known as Greenwood Park, and later a repertory theater, run by a Portland man named Bart MacCullum. One could take the three-mile steamer trip out to Peaks, and see the play, for twenty-five cents in all. Who is to say those weren't the good old days?

Peaks has a large summer colony now, and it also has year-round residents who commute to Portland by boat, to school and business. Technically a part of the big city of Portland, it is still geographically and spiritually an island. That fifteen-minute boat ride is the decompression period for the summer resident, the student, the commuter, and the shopper. Once they land on the home wharf, the old and lasting values reassert themselves, and the city might as well be a hundred miles away as three.

LONG ISLAND

LOOKING AT A CHART of the coast of Maine, more particularly at the jeweled archipelago beginning at the vast confluence of the Androscoggin, the Kennebec, and the Sheepscot, and spangling the sea with all sizes of islands down to the bold promontory of Cape Elizabeth, one gains a vivid and disturbing sense of flow, or motion, as if the islands were a great armada forever sailing toward the southwest with the surf of ages breaking about their rocky bows. Not a modern armada of wolfish gray ships; old half-forgotten names come to mind, belonging to the vessels that once sailed among these islands or were built on their fields and launched down their steep beaches: pinks, snows, shallops, pinnaces, and later that pure Yankee descendant of the Viking long ship, the dory.

Long Island is one of the fleet, lying between Peaks and Chebeague. Though at some early time Dutch explorers had named the island "*Lange Eylande*," the first recorded ownership was that of Captain John Mason and Sir Ferdinando Gorges. The island passed through many hands. In one deed it was said to contain "six hundred and fifty acres be it more or less bounded westerly by house wife's Sound So called the other end toward the Northeast reaching down to Luxtons Sound So called—Dated Sixth day of Janry Anno Domi. One thousand Seven hundred and Six/7."

Luxtons Sound was doubtless named for George Luxton, who lived on the island in 1640. Now it's Luckse Sound—an odd change, as it's so much harder to say. Housewife's Sound is now probably Husseys Sound. But who was the housewife for whom it was first so called and what did she do to glorify her calling rather than her own name? Perhaps several women contributed; perhaps they were picking wild berries, or the grapes which used to grow with an almost Dionysian prodigality on the islands, and saw Indian canoes approaching and gave the warning. Or perhaps they simply had their vegetable gardens overlooking the sound, or pastured the cows there in summer, and did nothing especially heroic (besides cooking, washing, sewing, having babies, losing them, loading muskets for the men in Indian raids, and enjoying all the other amenities of gracious living on an island in the 1600's).

The Indians, of course, enjoyed the island first as they did all the others, and Long Island with its many springs was particularly beloved. They came from their winter villages as soon as the ice was out of the rivers; perhaps we should add the canoe to the list of craft that haunt the archipelago, for in the spring the canoes came down all the rivers out into the great bay of Aucocisco (as the Indians called it) to the islands of fruits, forests, and flowers, with game on those close to the mainland, with clams to dig, and fish to spear from the rocks. The Indians worked hard because they had to leave before autumn storms began, but it must have been a happy time for all that.

They camped on the inland side of the island, but the children played on the seaward side, in the cove they called Little Harbor. Later, a Frenchman, Louis Elerette of Bordeaux, named it *Havre de Grâce*. The cove is still a good anchorage, never freezing over, and protected by a natural breakwater of ledges, The Stepping Stones, to the eastward, and by Obed's Rock and The Nubble to the south. But it is a good deal smaller than it was in the Indians' day, with the years' accumulation of shell, rocks, and sand.

The Singing Beach curves out to The Nubble. There are varying descriptions of the beach's song. For some it is the "crunch, crunch of marching feet," and for others, providing the wind is right, it sounds "strange musical notes of great beauty." There is a fairly wide margin of choice in between. If this phenomenon existed when the Indians came to the island, it must have been a convenient sound-effect for their shaman or medicine man when he wanted to make a point without any argument from his flock.

Long Island was owned from 1667 to 1683 by Richard Russell, and then by his son James. The island was deserted after the Indian wars, and the Russells tried hard to resettle it, but the terror of savages was still too vivid. James sold the island to a John Smith (not Captain) in 1706 and Smith had no better luck in inducing pioneers to come. Sometime after 1735 the property at last came into the hands of Colonel Ezekiel Cushing, he who built "The Homestead in The Willows" on Cushing Island. He settled his brother Ignatius and his family on Long Island, built them a home, and helped them lay out a farm at the west end. This was the first permanent home on Long Island.

Now other people came, and Long Island became an ideal farming and fishing community. Colonel Cushing settled there in the grand fashion, living the life of a country squire. A charming picture has been handed down of the Colonel's Negro servant, old Cato, driving around the island in the chaise behind the white mare, accompanied by four-year-old Dinah, doing family errands from farm to farm; perhaps collecting at one house a beautifully-done ironing, all the ruffles goffered to perfection, and at another delivering calves'-foot jelly from the Big House to a woman just recovering from childbirth.

Colonel Cushing served his guests with "clam boil," the predecessor of clam chowder. Everyone sipped the broth from clam shells and felt himself growing healthier by the moment. In those days people used to recite:

"Clams is physic the year all through;
Come eat my clams, bid the doctors adieu."

When the Colonel died he left the island to his children. In addition, his daughters Hannah and Phebe received twelve-acre Marsh Island, on the south side of Long Island. His son Thomas got the little island called Overset.

Today the descendants of the families that followed the Cushings still live on Long Island. They have provided many seafaring men, who went to sea as small boys and kept to the water for the rest of their lives. Long Island men were great ones to take command, and they were responsible for some of the most successful fishing vessels along the coast.

The Long Islanders witnessed or took part in many a shipwreck. One with a happy ending occurred in January, 1891. The schooner

Ada Barker was driven ashore on a nearby ledge called Junk of Pork. It must have been quite some time before the Long Islanders were able to reach the crew; there may have been a long spell of wild seas and winds. Anyway, when they reached the Junk of Pork they found the men had salvaged cabin doors and canvas from the wreck and built themselves a snug shelter. They had hams, beef, and a barrel partly full of flour from which they had been making fritters and gingerbread dough. They even had frying pans, and had made their fire with wood from the wreck.

In 1835 a Francis Cushing and one McKenny, ship chandlers of Portland, delivered the mail to the island by sail. Freight and passengers were carried the same way. It was a long-remembered day on Long Island when, in 1870, Captain Ricker brought out the steamboat *Henrietta* from Portland. They might even have had a band playing on the Landing, and speeches. If not, they should have! The *Henrietta* was followed by the *Express*, skippered by Alfred Oliver. In 1872 Captain Redman's *Sea Flower* began to make the trip; she could carry 150 people. In June, 1883, the *Emita*, registered to carry 500 passengers, made her maiden trip among the islands of Casco Bay.

In the early days of carrying passengers and freight, the captain and a deckhand did everything, sharing the profits. Some little boats —sixty-five feet or so—still go out to the islands along the coast where only small communities of fishermen live and there are no crowds of tourists and summer people. But the air of adventure these small, seaworthy, and sometimes rakish craft gave a trip to the islands in the past is sadly lacking today except in a few places where boats like the *Mary A.*, out of Rockland to Matinicus and Criehaven, still make their runs.

In the 1880's Long Island passed into a jolly, band-concert-in-the-park, picnic-by-the-sea period, with mandolins, white flannels, straw sailors, and, doubtless, parasols. It was great fun to sail out to Long Island for a clambake. The tables set under the trees for the Maine Commercial Travellers' picnic in 1886 would have stretched for a mile if they had been placed end to end. The clambake burned over ten cords of wood. The quantity and variety of pies must have been something to dream about. At least one picnicker was bold enough to admit he had tried to get a sample of each, because he subsequently announced anonymously in the local paper: "A young man wishes to apologize for having been so greedy as to consume nine pieces of pie at the Travellers' picnic last week."

There were moonlight sails accompanied by music, and dancing after the passengers reached the island and went up over the landings—Doughty's, Ponce, Cushing, and Cleaves. A tame bear was the star of one of the picnics, and the island men took turns wrestling with him, but nobody was able to get him down. The trainer was feeling pretty smug about it until a young islander named Charles McVane asked for a chance, and threw the bear so quickly that nobody saw what happened, or ever knew afterward. If the trainer was astonished, the bear was dumfounded. He refused to get up until he was tempted by a fresh fish, and Charles was thereafter known as the Strong Man of Long Island.

In 1887 old Stephen Pettengill and his wife claimed to be the oldest residents on the island. They were eighty-seven and eighty-five respectively, children of the century, Stephen reaching his adulthood in the year 1820, when Maine became a state in her own right and no longer a resentful stepdaughter of Massachusetts. Stephen said that when he built his house on Long Island in 1832 there were but four houses on the island, yet in 1887 only one of those early houses remained, besides his own. In a way this sums up the history of all islands: cabins built, destroyed, the ruins grown over, becoming field and forest, and in turn being cleared and built upon. A hollow in the grass where cranberries grow was once a cellar hole. Apple trees wild in a spruce wood were once someone's tame treasure. The alders have stolen the early pastures and many a spring has been choked off and lost; we don't know over whose bones we walk. Oddly enough, what is turned up oftenest are relics of the early, innocent time of the Indians, before the white men came.

There have been other changes. In 1824 a Miss Page taught the first school classes in a barn. Today, after a series of one-room schools, Long Island has a new school built in 1945. The early settlers, trying to pass down their own small store of learning to their children, welcoming the arrival of a scholarly clergyman or even reaching the point of affluence where they might hire a schoolmaster, would not believe their eyes today.

In the late 1800's the David Wallaces gave land for a Methodist

Episcopal church, which was built by the work and contributions of the women. This leads us back to the woman or women for whom Housewife's Sound was named. Women have evidently been a vital force all through Long Island's history. In 1901 the parsonage was built, and in 1913 the parishioners built an addition on the church and installed a furnace. In 1927 the beautifully-named St. Mary-Star-of-the-Sea Chapel was dedicated, a summer church for the Catholic members of the population.

During World War II the Navy established a base on Long Island; another drastic change to astonish any wandering souls who still had the temerity to linger about their cellar holes. An Honor Guard of sailors from this base unveiled the Long Island Honor Roll one September day in 1954. One hundred and sixty men from Long Island went to war, and six gold stars recall those who did not return.

Long Island, three miles long and covering almost a thousand acres, today has three hundred houses. At one time the island had three hotels, the Dirigo House, the Cushing House, and the Granite Spring Hotel, but those glorious days of rocking on the porch are gone forever, and the summer population of nearly 1200 is distributed among the houses. When the last of the summer people depart after Labor Day what a mighty quiet must prevail! The ears of the 200-odd permanent residents must fairly ring with emptiness. With their telephones, their electricity, their off-island work, their children going to high school in Portland, they are at times far more mainlanders than islanders; yet there is a difference. There are some who cannot forget what their ancestors knew in this place, the remoteness, the silence, the imperviousness of the surrounding sea; the sure sense of being an islander and therefore in some way different from other men.

CHEBEAGUE

LIKE A MINIATURE ROMAN WALL wandering over the face of Scotland, the stone wall that marked the three-mile width of Great Chebeague in the days when the island belonged to two men can still be traced from the outer shore, in and out of woods where it is sometimes briefly lost, and thence to the inner bay and the faint hollow that is the cellar hole of the first house on the island.

There are supposed to be 365 islands in Casco Bay, one for every day of the year, but by actual count there are only 222. One could perhaps sneak in some ledges, but to be absolutely an island it must have enough room for a man to stand on. One must draw the line somewhere. There is no doubt about Chebeague, however, which is one of the largest. It is five miles long from stem to stern; like most of the other islands that lie like ships at anchor in Casco Bay, it heads into the prevailing southwesterly winds and tails to the northeast. In winter it takes an hour and a half by boat to cover the seven or so miles out to it from Portland.

According to one source, the island's name is Indian for "Cold Spring Water" another holds it to mean "Island of Many Springs." The island has been inhabited from so far back that there is no history of those who first came to it; some of the curious artifacts that have been turned up are inexplicable in terms of the Indians who used it in the period just before, and contemporaneous with, the first white explorers. By comparison with these strange objects, the tools and weapons of the later Indians seem almost modern.

Chebeague has its ancient graves also, raising further questions about those whose feet trod this turf and these rocks so many hundred years ago. Were these who were laid away on Chebeague some who died there during summer encampments or in battle?

Or were their bodies brought in ceremony across the waters, and laid away with the prescribed rites of mourning in these places sanctified as burial grounds? And were the places taboo afterwards, and did later Indian children dare each other to walk near them? Did young men try to prove their courage to the girls—unknown to the elders, of course—by visiting the old burial grounds at midnight during the fragrant summer darkness?

One civilization tops another here, as seven cities lie one above another on the site of Troy. English and French fishermen once came trapping and fishing on Chebeague, though not simultaneously, unless these common men—no, *un*common men, who wandered the Atlantic as casually as gulls in vessels that didn't look as functionally tough as a gull's wing—established a policy of live and let live that was impossible between their home governments. Later there were permanent settlements, as permanent as anything could be when death came so swiftly in one form or another, and the old cellar holes and cemeteries dimly remain along the shore near Johnson's and Chandler's Coves, and in other places too.

Now all the island shipping uses Chandler's Cove as home harbor. It is usually free of ice. One year it achieved a kind of fame when President Franklin D. Roosevelt anchored his yacht there. What a fascinating game for the mind to play, imagining all the residents from the days of pre-history onward, clustering around the shore to watch the goings-on. There might be among them a band of more or less familiar souls, for a company that was part of the 1745 expedition against Louisbourg camped on the island one night. And we can only hope that if the young man in the treasure story who was tied up in knots put in an appearance, he would be untied.

This story may be apocryphal, but it is true to the same extent as many others: practically every one of the Casco islands is supposed to have been visited by the pirates Teach or Kidd. Judging by all the legends they must have buried, between them, enough treasure to pay off the national debt and make it possible to suspend income taxes for five years.

One day long ago a leathery and ferocious old party with one eye is said to have landed on Chebeague, and during a rum spree in the ordinary confided that in his fairly innocent youth he had once sailed with pirates, and that his captain had buried a magnificent treasure, gold and silver and precious gems, on this very island. As the story got around, the community was pretty excited, but there was something about that one frightful eye that discouraged friendly advances. So old Gimlet Eye stumped around by himself, until one ambitious young man saw a chance to make a quick fortune.

He wasn't able to trail the old man, but finally he approached him with an offer of assistance in return for a share of the take. He was ordered out of the way with a fine lot of tarry curses. This did not scare him. Try never was beat, as they used to say in those days, and in no time at all the bold young man discovered the retired pirate digging vigorously amidst a sizable excavation.

Another thing they used to say in those days was that discretion is the better part of valor; so the hero returned home for help. When Gimlet Eye was surprised at his dig, he let go with a really poetic and imaginative stream of profanity in several languages, and awed everyone into a respectful and admiring silence. But when he had to stop for breath, the young man jumped brazenly over the rope barrier into the pit to look things over. Then Gimlet Eye cursed him.

"I call on Almighty God," he roared, "and all you looking on, to witness that in less than a year this young nitwit will be tied in knots even as this rope is now."

This was considered uproariously funny. The next morning Gimlet Eye had disappeared, and the sand and rocks had been tumbled back into the hole. But one of the village playboys said that on his way home from the pub the night before he had seen three men lugging a heavy chest down over the beach to a boat, which then pulled away into the foggy dark. Of course he might have had a touch of the poet, and dreamed this up as a suitable ending to the affair, but one can't help hoping old Gimlet Eye really did find his treasure.

There was a sequel, however. A year hadn't passed when the rash hero of the escapade fell overboard from his fishing boat, and came down with chills and fever. Soon his arms and legs were doubled up in cramps, and they were so when he died. In a sense he was tied up in knots. The final macabre touch to the story was that his bones had to be broken before he could be laid in his casket.

In those days and for many years afterward Chebeague was one of those self-sufficient little worlds of salt-water farms. Men lived off both the sea and the land. Then it was possible to see the water from almost any point on the island, for the virgin forests had been cleared away to make room for pastures and raising crops. As the day of the horse passed, and fewer people kept cows where every family had used to have at least one, the woods stole back their own; poplars shimmer and white birches gleam where once fields of oats rippled like a green sea. The old farms have disappeared.

Times have changed in other respects. Once there were more than a thousand people in the town, and more than one industry. "Stone slooping," the building and manning of vessels to carry granite from the quarries up the coast, once made the island rich. Clams were so plentiful there was a canning business on the island. Now stone slooping is a part of the past when we were a nation of creators rather than consumers. Green crabs and lack of conservation practices have done away with clams. The great schools of herring bypass Chebeague for deeper and colder waters farther north, as the cod have done.

Chebeague today is a part of Cumberland, but it has an independent air of living its own life all year round, and the two hundred or so islanders go fishing as they always have. What if there are golf links, a hotel, boardinghouses, cottages, boats for rent, and fishing parties? They are merely so much froth swirling on the surface of the deep-running waters of daily existence.

Still the islanders tell proudly of the great old oak tree on Indian Point, cherished by Wentworth Ricker in 1791 and still standing after the hurricane of 1938, a monument to its own persistence and the loving care of many men. Chebeague is one of the islands that has kept up an unbroken continuity with its past. The community is vigorous in its living, in its religious and social and educational life. Many summer people have now become permanent islanders, finding there some answer to a long-felt need. There is something about having a moat around one, whether it is a half-mile wide, or seven, or ten!

JEWELL ISLAND

Jewell Island is indeed one of the prettiest jewels in the Casco collection, but it was prosaically named for George Jewell, a seafaring man who once owned it. It is also the outermost island of the western group, lying halfway along an imaginary line drawn from the tip of Harpswell Neck to Cape Elizabeth.

Jewell Island came into prominence in the year 1676, when the settlers on Merryconeag Neck (Harpswell Neck) and the vicinity were alarmed by news brought them from Boston and Salem of the Indian raids in Massachusetts; King Philip's War had begun. Captain Joseph Donnell, who sailed the coast bringing salt and provisions to the fishermen and taking away their fish, now brought orders from the Massachusetts General Court to the settlers. They were to leave their homes and go to the outlying islands where, supposedly, the Indians couldn't reach them.

The news was frightening, because these settlers had always been on good terms with the Indians; distressing, because they were just beginning to get their roots into the soil, to feel they were at home on their land. Still, there was good rich cornland on the Green Islands that tailed a mile or so off Jewell's southwest tip. They would move out to Jewell because Captain Donnell's father owned the island, and the son had given the settlers permission to build a garrison there.

In less than a week the move had been made, and the garrison was being built. Everyone helped, every child old enough to look after himself had some chore: running errands, whittling out tree nails, bringing clay from the shore to caulk between the logs. The corn had to be planted, clams dug, the stock looked after. But everyone felt happy and confident in his new security. It was firmly believed that no Indians would dare paddle so far out to sea.

Here is where the Potts family rises to the surface of the stream of history, and it would be interesting to calculate the exact number of persons alive today because a Potts child happened to be in a certain spot on a certain day, and knew how to load and fire his father's musket.

Richard and Margaret Potts with their children lived on Potts Point, at the end of Merryconeag Neck. Young Thomas Potts was about nine at the time of the remove to Jewell. Like the other children in the party, he probably spent a pleasant summer out there, in spite of the stories, brought by Captain Donnell and other mariners, of the Indian raids that were spreading like a rapid and lethal epidemic up the coast. Soon after the Merryconeag settlers moved to Jewell, thirty-five people were killed or captured in Back Cove at Falmouth, and the survivors got out to Long Island. The few who escaped a raid on Casco Neck sailed out to Jewell, and relaxed. Of course the Indians wouldn't dare come out here in their frail canoes.

The corn grew richly on the Green Islands, fertilized by years of gull droppings. The sea was as full of fish as it ever was. It was a good summer. The second day of September was as lovely as only a September day on the coast of Maine, more particularly on a Maine *island*, can be. We know it was perfect weather, because the women took the washing down to the brook, prepared to make a day of it, while the smaller children played in and out of the water like little otters. The men took off in the long boats to cut the corn on the Green Islands, and every boy or girl who could wield a knife was taken along.

That is, all but Thomas Potts, who was left behind to man the garrison. He must have felt very important and at the same time very happy, because no one expected anything bad to happen. Otherwise a nine-year-old would not have been left as a lookout. The Indian raids ashore were real enough—he'd heard the survivors' ghastly stories—but on a sparkling late-summer day so far out to sea there seemed no chance of violence.

When he saw the eight sea canoes, they were less than a quarter of a mile away, between Cliff and Jewell. There were four Indians in each canoe. The boy rushed through the woods to the garrison and, with remarkable steadiness and nerve for a terrified child, loaded his father's musket—a complicated process—and fired the alarm. One source says that he hurried back to the shore and fired directly at the Indians; however it happened, he truly manned the garrison that day. The warning shot sent the women and small children rushing for the garrison house.

The Indians had meanwhile reached the shore, and the men on the Green Islands were rowing home with all their strength—all but one of them, John Damarell, who went in his sloop toward Richmond for help. The others headed for Long Cove on Jewell, instead of trying to land in the very face of the Indians' muskets, and by the time the Indians got around the rugged shore, the settlers had landed and were ready for them, while the women came storming down from the garrison house. The Indians took to their canoes and paddled rapidly back to Cliff Island.

It is not certain whether or not any of the settlers were killed, but they did have men wounded. This first brush with the reality of the Indian wars must have been doubly horrifying because they had felt so safe until now. John Damarell sailed up from Richmond Island that afternoon with several sloops, and the settlers loaded the women and children aboard these, and followed back to Richmond in their own boats.

At Richmond they were safe, but not for long; during that long autumn the Indians destroyed every dwelling between the Piscataqua and the Kennebec. There was not one building left standing in the Province of Maine, islands or mainland. But the Potts family and the other refugees of Jewell Island had gone to Pennsylvania by that time, where the Indians were more friendly and where there was more land to clear and plant in corn, to make up for that which was never gathered on the Green Islands that September day. They never came back to Potts Point on Merryconeag Neck. Later, when young Thomas inherited the property there, he sold it to one Benjamin Marston.

Like all the other islands along the coast, Jewell is supposed to contain buried treasure; perhaps this is the most famous cache of all, because treasure-seekers have turned up enough earth out there over the years to build an entirely new island of their own. Some of them had begun their quest with the appropriate rites, sacrificing a rooster and shaking his blood over the spot, and so forth, but even that hadn't worked. Then, so the story goes, the usual ancient stranger arrived at Jewell one day in the last century, carrying the usual map and giving the usual tale; no one paid much attention to him except to allow that here was another of those treasure-mad derelicts. He said he was from St. John, New Brunswick, and had received the map from Captain Kidd's loyal Negro servant, who had been at his master's deathbed and been given the map by Kidd himself. And when *he* was dying he gave the map to the man from St. John. (How this deathbed scene squared with the fact that Kidd was executed for piracy was of no concern to treasure-seekers.)

It seems that the man from St. John couldn't start looking for the treasure at once, because he needed an accurate compass; strange that he didn't bring one, and stranger still that nobody on the island had one except a certain Captain Chase, who was away at the time, probably on a smuggling mission. When Chase came back he and the old man struck up a partnership, and then disappeared into the woods before anyone knew what was up and could follow them.

A few days later the captain returned alone and went out on another voyage. After a while people began to wonder what had become of the stranger, and went to look for him. They didn't find him, but on a lonely part of the shore, well away from the village, they found a deep hole, freshly dug, in the bottom of which they saw clearly the impression of a trunk or a chest that had been just removed. They decided that the treasure-seeker had been successful and had left the island without any fanfare, so they stopped wondering what had happened to him. But there was probably a lot of breast-beating at the thought that the treasure had been there all the time.

Captain Chase flourished. He became rich and, what's more, respectable. By the time he died, he had become in retrospect a dear old chap, a genuine old-time sea captain. But as if fate were waiting for the proper time to reveal the macabre joke, just a little while after Chase's funeral a berry-picker found a skeleton tucked away among the rocks not far from the treasure pit. The only identifiable mark was a silver ring which some of the old men remembered; they had last seen it long ago on the finger of the stranger from St. John.

The story takes on a more fantastic tone as the islanders searched the captain's house and found secret doors and subterranean tunnels leading to a hidden chamber where, according to Bisbee's *State o' Maine Scrap Book*, "undisputed evidence was unearthed that the stranger had indeed been murdered and that Captain Chase had stolen his treasure." One would like to know just what the "undisputed evidence" was.

The finale abandons all pretense of being only cold hard fact. It is a very satisfactory conclusion in its own way. With a fine sense of poetic justice the islanders buried the poor old skeleton with full honors beside the captain's grave. But a little while after this people began to see and hear weird lights and sounds in the Chase mansion. And one night an islander—whose reasons for being away from the village all by himself in the dark might be even more interesting than what he told—rushed home to describe events he had witnessed at the treasure pit: he had seen two men digging away at the site, illuminated by fitful blue lights, then heard a cry and agonized groans. Everybody went out to the spot by daylight, and found it looked the same as usual, well overgrown with alders and bay. But they decided it wasn't a very healthy place after dark, and neither was Captain Chase's house. The treasure pit practically disappeared into the underbrush, and eventually the Chase house collapsed into rubble from neglect.

After such picturesque goings-on, Jewell became in 1894 the property of the McKeen family, direct descendants of the first president of Bowdoin College. The family has owned it ever since, some of them spending several winters there; three of the present generation were born there, and it is still the family summer home.

During World War II the Government took over half the island and built an observation tower there. So the history of Jewell comes full circle. As the Merryconeag settlers built a garrison there to watch for their enemies the Indians, so 265 years later men watched for enemies to come by sea.

MACKWORTH ISLAND

THE LITTLE hundred-acre island lying a half-mile off Falmouth, at the mouth of the Presumpscot, was once a part of the Indians' lost paradise. In summer those Indians who lived along the Presumpscot came in their canoes down between the wooded banks to spend the warm months on the island. In those far-off Mays and Junes the only sounds as they traveled would be the faint ripples from the paddles, birdsong from the virgin forest that came down to the water's edge on either side, and, when they reached the river mouth, the splash of surf and the endless seething of the sea wind in the great pines that made them name the point Menikoe.

Today we can find an approximation of this vast and glistening summer quiet only on the outer islands, and even then it is broken by the hum of high-powered engines as lobstermen haul their traps in coves where once the Indians hunted fish with bow and arrow.

By the time Arthur Mackworth, Gentleman, received the island as part of his grant on the northeast side of the Presumpscot's mouth, in 1634, progress had begun its irrevocable course, and the Indians knew it. It was a long time since their sachem—he with the delightful name Skitterygusset, that suggests a breezy day in spring—had led the way to the summer encampment. But perhaps they did not resent Arthur Mackworth too much; he seems to have been a true Gentleman, greatly respected both by whites and Indians.

He came out from England in 1630 with some of his friends: Richard Vines, Sir Ferdinando Gorges' agent; Robert Snakey; and Samuel and Jane Andrews. At first he lived on the mainland, on the point nearest the island, the Indians' Menickoe, which of course became known as Mackworth's Point. It is probable that his first wife died there, and his friend Samuel Andrews; Mackworth later married Samuel's widow, Jane. The Presumpscot was the broad highway between Sebago Lake and Casco Bay. Thus there was a constant traffic past Mackworth's house at the mouth of the river, as Indians went on their way to the trading post at Richmond Island, and as a magistrate he came to know those who would consent to friendship with a white man.

Four years after their arrival in America Richard Vines, acting for Gorges, gave Mackworth his grant, including the island, and as soon as a new house was ready he moved across the half-mile of water and became an islander. At first he called the island Newton, after his home in England, but it came to be called Mackworth's, Mackey's, Mussey's, and, later, Mackworth's again. After he married Jane Andrews in 1637 he started to raise a family; eventually they had two sons and four daughters.

Again and again we are struck by the crowded, vigorous life which these islands once knew, back in a time when mere existence was a matter of chance. If one survived babyhood there were still wars, plagues, and Indians to dodge. And in the midst of perils we see someone like Arthur Mackworth, Gentleman, raising his children, being a public official, trading with the Indians, curing fish, raising corn and grinding it on the same rock the Indians had used, keeping up his religious life. He lived his years with a fullness and serenity that make him stand out among all the others.

Even when he was dying he showed what he was; Robert Jordan, of Richmond Island, testified that Mackworth on his deathbed stated "that his full will and testament was that his wife, Mrs. Jane Mackworth, should by her wisdom dispose of his whole estate, equally, as near as might be, between her former husband's children and the children between them, and in case any shortness was on either side, it should rather be on his own children's side." It is clear from this what devotion and trust there were between him and his wife, and what a strong tie there was among the children; there is no record of any complaint about their mother's division of the property. She seems to have settled land on each one as he or she married.

By 1657, when Arthur Mackworth died, there was already bad blood between the settlers and the Indians, who were being driven by civilization farther and farther back into the woods, away from the fishing grounds that had been theirs since long before the oldest men in the tribes could remember. It was the same all along the coast, down into Massachusetts. Nothing improved in the next eighteen years, and perhaps the holocaust of King Philip's War was inevitable. Mrs. Mackworth, who by this time had conveyed all her property to her children, and the island itself to her son-in-law Abraham Adams, moved to Boston before the bloody business struck her part of the world. One family of islanders, the Wakeleys, were all killed except for an eleven-year-old girl who was carried into captivity. Between the first of August and the end of November, 1675, about fifty English settlers were killed by the Indians.

There was always trouble after that, continual attacks by the Indians, who killed off livestock, again and again attacked the fort at New Casco, and actually captured Fort Loyal at Falmouth. Eventually those of the settlers who were left, their farms gone, retreated westward to the larger towns, leaving the territory to the wilderness, the wild animals, and the Indians.

Several attempts were made to resettle the area. Some courageous men brought their families back to the protection of the enlarged and reinforced fort at New Casco; some of the Mackworth heirs were among this group. But by now the French were helping the Indians and egging them on, and the settlers had to run again; Baron Castine made a slaughterhouse of the area and was considered even more savage than his Indians.

In 1703 the Mackworth granddaughters sold the island out of the family. From then on ownership of the island passed through many hands. Two of the most prominent owners were Jedediah Preble, who also owned Cushing, and later Richmond, in 1756, and James Deering, who in 1808 sold the island to James Rennie.

Rennie was one of those oddly enchanting characters for whom there is no room in the world today, which is a pity. He was a ventriloquist and a practical joker, but what makes him something really rich and strange is the great secret which he claimed to possess. He said it was a family thing, passed down from father to eldest son. It was a way of taming the wildest or most vicious horse. Apparently Rennie's claim was true, for he was successful enough to be known as "the Whisperer."

The last horse Rennie tamed had a reputation for biting his owner every time the man went near him. Rennie said he could tame the animal and waved away an offer to tie the horse's head up first. "No occasion," he said confidently. "He won't bite me."

He disappeared into the barn, and shut the door. The men waited anxiously outside, doubtless expecting a wild drumming of hoofs, frantic squealing of an enraged horse, and Rennie's cries for help. Nothing happened, except that in a few minutes he called that he was all through and they could come in. They ran in and found, to their everlasting astonishment, the vicious horse lying on his back, playing like a kitten with the Whisperer, who was sitting on the floor beside him. Both horse and man seemed exhausted, but the horse was perfectly tame and gentle, and as far as anyone knows he stayed that way.

Rennie's disappearance from the world of Mackworth Island and Falmouth is of a piece with his mysterious gift. He soon left the island and the two-story home which he had built there, and sailed for Jamaica; he was never heard of again. Creditors moved in, all his property was confiscated, and Theodore Mussey of Standish bought the island at a bankruptcy sale. Rennie had had it less than a year, but had left his mark on it in a gayer, lighter (but none the less memorable) way than any earlier or later owners.

Mackworth now became Mussey's and later Mackey's Island. It passed through several more changes of ownership, and during the Civil War soldiers were camped there. The training camp was called Camp Berry for Major-General Hiram G. Berry, who was killed at the battle of Chancellorsville. Some of the trees were cut to build barracks and supply wood for the soldiers' fires, but still the island was not burned barren, as so many islands had been. Arthur Mackworth would have been pleased at that.

The Union Bank of Brunswick owned the island next, until Lemuel Cushing, owner of the hotel on Cushing, bought it in 1884. In 1888 his widow sold it to the Hon. James P. Baxter of Portland. Luckier than some, whose ruined forests, alder-swamped pastures and cellar holes are silent but tragic reminders of what was once the realization of some man's dream, Mackworth Island (as it is now called again) has been almost constantly in use. Later it moved into another phase of its existence, as a summer home for a large family in that long, leisurely golden afternoon of the Victorian and Edwardian periods.

In 1914 Mr. Baxter built a bridge from the island to the Falmouth shore. When the family saddle horses were brought over to the island for the summer, they wore leather boots to keep their shoes from splitting the planks. The sight of the Baxter horses running the island pastures in the sea wind, or being ridden through the groves of pines and American walnut trees, with the Baxter Irish setters ranging ahead, must have been a memorable one.

Until 1914, springs and a windmill supplied the island with water, but in that year pipes were laid across the island and under the bay to take Sebago water out to Great Diamond Island. Civilization moved in also with electricity, and in 1916 the Baxters built a large house. Now Mackworth Island became the scene of large happy parties, as guests arrived by the steamer that went on to Cousins Island. Mr. Baxter was president of the Maine Historical Society for many years, and its annual picnics, and those of the Genealogical Society, were held on Mackworth.

James Baxter's son Percival, governor of Maine from 1921 to 1925, succeeded him as owner. In 1921 he began setting out a hundred thousand pine and spruce trees, and the island has been declared a bird sanctuary by legislative act. In a tranquil spot near one of the beaches a stone wall surrounds a cemetery where nineteen Irish setters are buried. A large boulder carries a bronze plaque with the name of each dog on it.

Governor Baxter presented Mackworth Island to the State of Maine in 1953, to be used as the site for a new State School for the Deaf, the older school having become obsolete and inadequate. To help the project along, the governor gave the state approximately $740,000 toward the cost of construction, and a new bridge to replace the one his father had built many years ago, over which the horses used to come in their leather boots. The Ninety-Sixth Legislature appropriated $440,00 to supplement the governor's gift.

Thus windows on a new and lovely world have been opened to these handicapped children for, as Rachel Field puts it: "If once you have slept on an island/You'll never be quite the same."

COUSINS ISLAND

CASUALLY, CARELESSLY, we say the names of islands; syllables which stand in our minds as symbols for a certain rock formation, the shape of a clump of woods against the sky, the way the surf breaks in a particular cove. We are so taken up with the island itself and its position in our experience of the moment, or its significance in the larger scene—as Cousins has today an enormous significance for a great many people who have never set foot on it—that we rarely think back along the clear sharp line of continuity.

John Cousins was more than the rocks and surf that make up his island. He was born in England in 1596, and when he had got his growth and his schooling, and reached his majority, he decided that the England of the Stuarts was not for him. Soon we find him in America. He was young, strong, and normally adventurous, and the fact that he wasn't at Boston with the Puritans suggests that he was probably Anglican. He settled first on the Royal River at Yarmouth, with George Felt and William Royal.

By 1645, when he was forty-nine years old and a man of substance and good reputation, he must have felt that the mainland was becoming impossibly crowded; or perhaps he was simply ready at last to achieve a lifelong desire to have a great deal of land around him. In any case, he bought Hog Island, about six hundred luxuriantly wooded acres lying half a mile off the projection of land that ends in Parker Point to the northeast and Prince Point to the southwest. The island lies in the same direction as the rest of the Casco fleet. The Indians called it Sequeson but the colonists called it Hog, as they called some thirteen other islands along the coast. Now it was to be called Cousins, though in later legal papers some diehards still insisted on calling it Hog. The Cousins River, which joins the Royal above Parker Point, is also named for John Cousins.

Cousins shows up from the first as a man of some stature and great powers of persuasion. He was able to buy the island outright from Sir Ferdinando Gorges' agent Richard Vines. This didn't happen often; Sir Ferdinando preferred to lease the land he held, through the Plymouth Company, for an unspecified number of years, collecting annual rent. Our clever Cousins made sure there would be no claims on his island from Gorges' rivals, the Rigbys. They were represented by George Cleeves of Portland, and Cleeves's long litigation with John Winter, who represented the Trelawny estates (Richmond Island, and so forth), was well known and probably provided a lot of juicy talk at the fireside on cold evenings. John Cousins evidently determined on not getting into any of *those* scrapes, as the old bachelor said when he refused to tie the pretty schoolmarm's shoe-lace. He talked George Cleeves into giving him a deed for the island, too.

Cousins appears often in records of the time. He was not only clever, but was regarded as a man of honor. He held several important posts in the affairs of the vicinity. He was for three terms a juror. He acted as an agent for Cleeves in several matters, and appeared as a witness many times. In 1665 he appeared before the grand jury in his capacity as constable in a case of thievery; he was a witness in a case concerning the abuse of an Indian, and also in Mrs. John Winter's famous slander suit, when she accused George Cleeves of speaking disrespectfully of her.

One William Haynes of Bustin's Island, with nothing better to do and perhaps a grudge against the prosperous, affable, highly regarded squire of Cousins Island, reported to the court that he had seen Cousins playing cards on Sunday. The long arm of the Massachusetts Bay Colony had reached all the way up the coast into the more free-wheeling Church of England settlements of Maine. But Cousins proved himself innocent, then had Haynes arrested as a common liar.

There are divided opinions about the location of John Cousins' house on his island. Some say it was about halfway along the western shore, facing the mainland. Others are sure it was between Blaney's Point and the Cornfield. The latter is at the northeast end of the island, and has been under continuous cultivation for many hundreds of years, some of them long before the white men arrived, to judge from the number of artifacts that have been turned up by the ploughs of later farmers.

Two years after he bought the entire island, with his two deeds from rival owners, Cousins sold half of it to Richard Bray, who later sold his half to George Peterson. Cousins continued to live in his "mansion or dwelling house," farming and raising stock on his 300 acres, being an active, useful member of the community formed by the island and mainland settlements. There is no mention of a wife and children. When King Philip's War began, the Indian raids drove the settlers of all the Casco islands farther out into the bay, to Jewell Island. From there they later escaped to the mainland and scattered to safety for the duration. John Cousins, by then an old man, went to York, where a lady named Mary Hayward took care of him until he died at the age of eighty-seven.

When the Indian wars were over, some of the original owners and the descendants of others came back to reclaim their holdings. Then it was discovered that "John Cossons" had conveyed to Mary Hayward his island property. Years later her heirs sold the land to Jonathan Preble.

Innocent of further wars to come, and ambitious, the new islanders set out to make a good life for themselves. Cornfield Point rustled with corn in the August breezes, and the big cod, split and salted, were dried on the Point's fish flakes for winter eating, good with stir-about and milk when the northeast blizzards howled down over the island. Cornfield Point had other crops too, gruesome ones, but to be expected: bodies of drowned seamen washed ashore from a shipwreck and left at the tidemark on the beach.

Fishing was of course the chief business of the times. Among the islands, and particularly just off Chebeague, which is about two miles from Cousins, the fish ran thick, and the small boats could do a good day's work all within a short distance of home.

At one time there were two small shipyards on the island, building sloops, ketches, wherrys, and yawls. One was at the place now called Sandy Point, at the northeastern tip, near Cornfield Point, and another was at the other end, at what is now Birch Point. There was also a blacksmith shop.

Of all the early settlers, the buyers and sellers of Cousins land, the name of Blaney alone remains on the island, at Blaney's Point. Oh yes, someone else was left. Workmen digging the foundation for a cottage out on a little point on the island found themselves working into an ancient shell heap or midden, and came upon the skeleton of a tall man: a young man, by his teeth. A long rapier or officer's sword, almost eaten away by rust, lay across the skeleton. There are no records as to what befell the island in the French and Indian Wars, but investigators were sure this man died then.

Of the later islanders, Drinkwater Point on the Yarmouth shore recalls the phenomenal Drinkwater family of Cousins Island. Joseph Drinkwater married Jennie Leighton, and they raised nine sons and two daughters. All the sons went to sea and became masters of their own ships. At one time they were all at anchor in New York harbor, which created a justifiable confusion on the part of port authorities, who believed themselves to be the victims of some sort of hoax.

Another islander who was to make his mark was Ebenezer Cleaves. There were always Cleaveses on the island, but Ebenezer really gave the islanders the most exciting time of all. And how grateful they must have been for all the endless and fascinating speculation they could engage in about him, over dishes of tea in their kitchens, or hot buttered rum in some bachelor's shack.

Ebenezer's first wife, the mother of all his children, had died, and suddenly, some time before 1887, Ebenezer married Emily-from-California, who sounds like the gayest of adventuresses. Emily's origins are doubtful. Surely for a girl to come east to make her fortune is a refreshing switch on the usual version, but Emily did come, Ebenezer met her (perhaps on a visit to the mainland), and no doubt wooed her with stories of his extensive island holdings. Perhaps she thought he was a rich sea captain. And he thought she was enchanting in her rustling silks, her perfume, her parasol, and—doubtless—paint.

But island life wasn't for Emily; at least, not on Cousins Island. She left with her trunks full of loot bought for her by besotted Ebenezer, and went to Chebeague—which suggests more interesting possibilities. Why another fishing island instead of Portland or Boston? But Chebeague was prospering, with her stone sloopers and all, and perhaps Emily had already met someone from there who looked well-to-do, and dashing to boot; or at least amenable. Anyway, after a divorce she married Jack Hamilton of Chebeague, and whether he or she ever repented the act, who knows?

Ebenezer composed a poem about her and wanted to call a public meeting and have someone read his ode. But perhaps Emily had champions who would have defended her honor; in any case, no one wanted to become involved. Nobody would read the poem, which began:

> The old she-devil has gone to roost
> In all her plumage gay,
> The all of which my money bought,
> Before she went away.

In our own time, abruptly, the face of the island and its place in the scheme of the civilization around it have been altered in a way that John Cousins could never understand or even believe. After working out certain amiable adjustments with the town of Yarmouth, the Central Maine Power Company has built its newest and potentially largest steam plant on Birch Point, at the southern end of the island.

Seen from the mainland the view is not greatly altered, for the main building is on the easterly side, and a grove of oak trees helps to landscape the installation. But there is a new bridge and the great colliers and tankers cut massively through the waters where Indian sea canoes went, and where later the winged sailing vessels beat their way up to Royal River from the open sea.

Cousins was selected for the station because it is close to heavily populated and industrial areas, it has a deep and protected anchorage, sea water may be used for cooling the vast condensers, and there is plenty of room for expansion. The energy magically conjured here from steam passes along transmission lines on great steel towers to the mainland, feeding into the Central Maine's network, which in turn connects with the other Maine electric companies and the New England power pool. At present the plant's current capacity is 80,000 kilowatts, but it is capable of producing 100,000 kilowatts, and future expansions on the site are planned to generate 500,000 kilowatts.

It is a tremendous project, in operation since 1958. In its own way it is as much of a pioneering event as the landing of the first settlers, for it forms the threshold of a new world. It would have staggered those early Cousins Islanders, remembering how laboriously they cleared their fields, to see some 10,000 cubic yards of earth and 12,000 of ledge being moved from one place to be used somewhere else. Where the early settlers depended on springs or dug wells, the Central Maine Power Company drilled a number of wells on the island for their necessary 125,000 gallons of fresh water a day. The company also built the 440-foot steel and concrete dock where the tankers come. At one time 326 men worked on the project, talented men with skills undreamed of three hundred years ago. They ranged all the way from engineers to tree experts.

As surely as John Cousins came pioneering on his island, this William F. Wyman Station is also a pioneer, for it may be only the beginning of a great future in hydro generation. The bridge and the presence of industry may make Cousins somewhat less of an island, but it has its vivid and lively past and now an extremely lively present and future; at least it will never be left to its ghosts and its cellar holes; it will be *used*, and that is just what John Cousins expected it to be.

HARPSWELL'S ISLANDS

HARPSWELL IS A WATERY TOWN, a Yankee Venice whose broad sea avenues on a summer afternoon present to the traveler-by-boat vista after vista of glistening beauty, each one opening into another more lovely than the last. The only part of the town connected to the mainland is Harpswell Neck, and the Neck tries hard to be an island too, and almost succeeds; it thrusts ten narrow miles out southerly into Casco Bay, and is all but surrounded by its more than forty islands of every imaginable size.

Once Harpswell was known as Merryconeag, and was a part of North Yarmouth. In 1740 Merryconeag Neck was annexed to Brunswick. But in 1758 we have the Neck and its surrounding archipelago incorporated as the town of Harpswell. It is likely that the town was named for the one in England from which some of the first settlers migrated.

Like all the islands, those later to be known as Harpswell were deserted during the Indian wars in the late 1600's. But as the first families came back, and new settlers were drawn to the region, an energetic life began which has never ceased, though its shape and form have often changed. Who in those days ever heard of summer visitors, of tuna tournaments, of Arctic explorers? Who dreamed of poets' and novelists' finding inspiration on the islands, or of artists' coming there to find beauty where these pioneers built their ships and fished for the giant cod of days gone by?

Some things remain unchanged: the roar of the rote on the ledges when a storm is building up, the way the wind sounds in the spruces, and the scent of a spruce wood in hot summer sunshine; the flowering of island meadows; the cry of a loon at dusk, the piping of a hovering osprey, the spring songs of the warblers, and the high and effortless soaring of bald eagles. All these must have been a part of the first islanders' life as they are a part of the Harpswell present.

Sebascodegan

Sebascodegan, lying to the east of the Neck, is the largest of the islands of Harpswell. With its fascinating shape, humped in places and deeply hollowed in others, and an island-spangled harbor of its own, it is a little Venice in itself, with fifty miles of waterways. It contains 5,790 acres, for those who wish to be exact.

There are many explanations for its name, which, by the way, is that by which it has always been known. One source says it means "great measure." Another translates the name as "long carry," because of the long portage connecting Casco Bay with the New Meadows River. A third suggestion is that it means a low marshy place for gunning (probably game birds). If this is so, the island must have been named after the Indians found out about guns.

Today it has about 360 year-round residents. But in its wild green past, its history starts with Captain Martin Pring, an excellent navigator who in 1603 established a trading post on the island near the mouth of the New Meadows River. He was seeking something a little out of the ordinary; not furs, or new fishing grounds for English vessels, but medicinal herbs to take back to England. The Indians may have brought him rare plants from secret places and told him what they knew of cures for sores and pains and fevers, in return for trade goods. Pring's voyage to America had been backed by wealthy Bristol merchants and approved of by Sir Walter Raleigh, who at that time still had strong claims with regard to American colonization.

In 1632 the Council of Plymouth granted to Thomas Purchase and George Way a patent including Sebascodegan and adjoining islands; in fact, it included all the islands between Maquoit and Small Point. Then Richard Wharton, who was a prosperous merchant in Boston —a Puritan, no doubt, because who else could prosper in Boston then?—bought Purchase's interest in 1639, and in 1683 George Way's son sold his share of the Way grant to Wharton for a hundred pounds. It is not known if the Purchases and Ways ever lived on the island, or why Richard Wharton, snug in Boston, wanted it; but want it he did, and his eagerness survived over forty-five years.

At one time during this period part of the island belonged to Major Nicholas Shapleigh, and was settled by Francis and Elizabeth Small of Kittery; theirs was the first white child born on the island. But a deed dated 1657 shows Small buying some land for himself elsewhere, from an Indian of some importance, so he must have left Sebascodegan. In 1683 John Shapleigh sold his interests to Richard Wharton when Eleazar Way sold his. Wharton had it all at last, but this was at the time of the Indian troubles, so the Indians happily took possession and lived there for a number of years, catching fish, seals, and porpoises.

According to the records there was, during these years, a lot of indiscriminate selling of the island that had nothing to do with Richard Wharton and his deeds. In fact it looks as if selling Sebascodegan was quite a hobby with both Indians and white men. One sharp redskin leased it to a John Parker for "one beaver skin received and the yearly rental of one bushel of corn and one quart of liquor to be paid on or before the 25th of December."

Back and forth the ownership was tossed like a bright-colored ball; Nicholas Cole and John Purrington bought it and other property from two Indians, Sagettawan and Robin Hood. Harvard College claimed it because of an old title, but this was denied. In 1684 the General Court of Massachusetts granted the island as a reward for "great pains and good service" to Thomas Danforth and Sumner Nowell. No mention of Richard Wharton. In fact, we do not hear of him again. Were lifetime feuds started because of the confusion of ownership? Did men use up their fortunes, large or small, in useless litigation? Did someone go embittered to his grave, wishing he had never heard of Sebascodegan Island? We'll never know.

In 1720 a Samuel Boone of Rhode Island bought half the Neck, half of Sebascodegan, sometimes known as Great, and half of Great Chebeague, from Nicholas Cole and Samuel Littlefield. But Boone didn't settle there, and in 1733 we find the island belonging to the Pejepscot Proprietors, a company which had been formed earlier to develop and divide the Merryconeag territory.

They leased the island to William Cady and his associates, but reserved the mineral and fishery rights. William Condy was one of the associates, and Cundy's Harbor may be named for him. By 1737 there were about twenty families settled on Sebascodegan, but again Indian activities drove them off. Nathaniel Donnell of York tried it again, unsuccessfully. But by 1755 there was a strong, vigorous, permanent settlement.

Judith Howard belongs to this period. It is not sure whether she was a real person or a legend, but either way she deserves a spot in the island's history. She was one of those independent females who crop up now and then, homesteading by themselves and minding their own business. Of course there was always someone to suspect such rugged individuality. Besides, Judith had a special gift which some of her neighbors were too ungracious to appreciate. With her knowledge of herbs and roots, and the marvelously healing teas she brewed and salves she mixed, she must have taken the pain and infection from many a burn or ulcer, and driven the chills out of racked bones and the fever from tormented flesh. But she was so successful in her cures that these apparently pious neighbors suggested that her gift came not from the logical place, Heaven, but from Satan. Judith, they whispered, was a witch.

She must have known what they thought. Perhaps she had a good time of it, making them nervous. Anyway, she seems to have had a rather gruesome sense of humor. She told people quite often that they must *not* bury her near Old Lambo; if they did, she promised them solemnly, she'd haunt them. Old Lambo was an Indian buried at Cundy's Harbor. What his particular reason for fame was, and why Judith thought it possible that she might be buried beside him, the story doesn't tell. It does tell that when Judith died the unkind neighbors promptly buried her beside Old Lambo.

But none of them slept that night. They were kept awake by weird manifestations, and not only that night but every night, until they haggardly got together and decided they'd done wrong and Judith would never let them be. The bravest of them set their jaws and probably warmed their cold courage with rum, took a yoke of oxen and a sledge, and went to open Judith's grave. They carried her more than two miles up the island and buried her on the west side of the main road, and went home to sleep in peace that night and thereafter.

An Irishman named Millet lived on the island during the Revolution; he has gone down in history as the man who knew how to get salt from sea water at a time when salt was very scarce. He formed a company which bought the necessary equipment. They produced about sixty bushels of salt a week and shipped it to Boston, where it sold for two dollars a bushel. A good price in those days; the company did exceedingly well, by the standards of the economy of 1775.

Shepard's Point is a rather sad memorial of the Revolutionary War. Colonel Purrington of the island had organized the militia, and when a British privateer began harassing the coast he took to sea in a fourteen-ton schooner, *America*. There was a short skirmish and he captured the privateer, the *Picaroon*. There was one casualty, Shepard, helmsman of the *Picaroon*. The fact that there was only one death makes that death all the more tragic, somehow. The rest lived to go home or to become settlers as so many British soldiers and seamen did, but Shepard was buried on the point; like Rupert

Brooke's soldier, this young man has made some corner of a foreign field forever England.

Orr's Island

Orr's Island is so close to Sebascodegan that it looks almost to be a part of the larger island until one sees the tiny strip of bridge that joins them. There are 290 year-round Orr's Islanders now, and many more in the summer; and whole generations of girls who have never set foot on the island have identified themselves with Harriet Beecher Stowe's character in her *Pearl of Orr's Island*. But in the days when the island was Little Sebascodegan, no one had heard of it except those who bought and sold it for one reason or another; Richard Jaques of North Yarmouth; William Tailer and Elisha Cook of Boston; and then two Scottish brothers, Joseph and Clement Orr.

The Orrs had come to America for a freedom to think and worship which they didn't find in the Old World. They were skilled weavers and had no trouble supporting themselves. They bought eventually a good amount of land on Merryconeag Neck and settled there, but Joseph thought he would like to live on an island—there is a magic about islands older than history—and he bought the whole of Little Sebascodegan from the Cook and Tailer heirs in 1748. It is said he paid about two shillings an acre. (Shore property today sells for twenty-five dollars a foot and upward. There's something to be said in favor of the good old days; now only the well-to-do can afford to settle on the coast of Maine.)

Joseph and Clement Orr built a garrison on the island to keep off the Indians. It didn't keep off another kind of trouble; Joseph had forgotten to get the signature on his deed of one of William Tailer's daughters, now Mrs. Matthew Byles of Boston. The fact that he bought the island in 1748 and did not settle the affair until 1760 suggests quite a bit of argument and litigation, but we can't be sure. He gave Mrs. Byles one-tenth of the island and received a quitclaim deed for the rest. Today this tenth of the island is still known as "Byleses."

After a while the island became Orr's Island. The family multiplied mightily, for there are Orrs all over the township of Harpswell. The chief businesses of the area were lumbering, fishing, and shipbuilding. Much of the hardwood went to Boston for firewood, and one day when Joseph Orr's coastwise schooner arrived in the city with a load of wood he met on the docks a young Irishman with a strange story.

Michael Sinnett, known also in the records as Micah Sinnot, was born at Wexford, Ireland, in 1730. He became a glovemaker. One day he and a friend fell victim to a particularly fiendish little scheme. Spending their holiday in Dublin, wearing their best clothes and sauntering as young bloods will along the waterfront, the two boys were invited aboard a vessel, just to look it over, by a sailor with the tongue of a charmer. While they were below decks the lines were cast off and the boys were on their way to the colonies. Whatever their treatment was aboard the ship, the most vicious part came at the end when they docked at Boston, and the two penniless and kidnaped young men were held up for the price of their passage.

We don't know how Joseph Orr met them; perhaps his boat was tied up at the same dock. He was a kindly man and took pity on young Sinnett. Some other good-hearted person must have helped the other young man, because it isn't likely Orr would have turned his back on one and helped the other. He took a great fancy to Sinnett, in any event, and said he'd pay his passage; Michael could come to Orr's Island and work out the sum. Joseph had no son of his own, and so the arrangement turned out well for them both.

As Orr's man, Michael sailed often to Boston with wood, and on one of these trips he met Mary Ward of Hingham. Michael must have been an attractive fellow, with a delightful trace of brogue and a lively eye. He won Mary's heart, and they married as soon as he was free of his debt to Joseph Orr. They settled in Boothbay.

But he was destiny's man and was again kidnaped, probably during the French and Indian War, because he was carried off by French raiders to Montreal. Mary was visiting in Boston. When she came home and found him gone, she made her way to his benefactors on Orr's Island and was sheltered by them. When you look at Boothbay on the chart, and follow with your finger around to Orr's Island, you can see what a long, dangerous, and desperate journey it must have been for a woman alone.

Now Michael escaped and somehow got back to Boothbay, either on foot or by boat. His wife was gone, and so he too went to Orr's

Island. The story of his return is a charming one. He reached the house just at milking time; he went to the barn, saw his wife milking, walked quietly to her, and put his hand on her shoulder. There is no record of his ever being kidnaped again.

Mrs. Stowe, who brought literary fame to Orr's Island, spent a good deal of time there during the period when she lived in Brunswick. She used to write out-of-doors, overlooking the sea from The Grotto, a niche in the rocks near the steamboat landing. Perhaps from there she watched sometimes the exciting chase and capture of the huge horse mackerel, now euphoniously called tuna.

Nowadays they are pursued as game fish and caught with rod and reel; it is a great sport. Then, though it was still a great sport, it was the necessary slaughter of predators, for the big bluefins loved —and fed on—the mackerel and whiting that the fishermen caught for a living. The men needed no tuna chairs, pulpits, or special rods. A man required only a punt about ten feet long, both ends square, but with the bow a little narrower than the stern; a harpoon, plenty of warp, and a pole. When the wild chase was over and the bluefin dragged ashore, everybody gathered to look at it and make bets about the weight.

The only part of the fish that had commercial value in those days was the oil. The livers were left in open barrels in the sun until there was enough oil standing to pour off. They got the rest by trying out the liver and meat in kettles. When the oil was refined, it was used in medicines, paints, and gun lubricants.

But the islanders knew a good thing when they saw it, and before the rest of the country knew tuna for what it is, they were glad to help themselves to all they wanted of meat from the catch; to fry delicious steaks for that day's dinner or salt down heavy "junks" for winter.

It was a summer resident in the islands, James Seymour of New Jersey, who first wondered just how much fun a sportsman could have going after tuna with a rod. In the winter he fished for tarpon in warm waters and wanted to keep up his sport in summer over the sparkling blue sea off the Maine coast. He started after tuna in 1910, in an open-cockpit, hampton-type boat, *The Newark*, built at Wilson's Boat Yard on Orr's Island. Her skipper was Henry Orr, and John Boyce went along as crew. They fished for five years before Seymour proved that a tuna could be taken by rod and reel. This first tuna was treated as a gallant adversary; after everyone saw the catch, and Seymour's hunch was vindicated, the fish was towed out to sea and cut loose.

BAILEY ISLAND

Between Orr's and Bailey there is a narrow passage where the tides rush hard and fast; in winter it is often clogged with great chunks of salt ice. Will's Cut, it is called, or Will's Gut, or, more elegantly, Will's Strait. Today the tides hurry through under the picturesque and unique cobwork bridge that connects the two islands, and what used to be at times a forbidding stretch of white water or crushing ice is now safely crossed at any time of year and in any weather, on foot or by car. But the name which was given to it around 1750 hasn't changed. It is a memorial to what must have been a heartbreaking experience for a family of early islanders who loved their island with the peculiar passion that islands seem to arouse.

Long ago Bailey was called Newwaggin, and the two islands together, Orr's and Bailey, were called The Twins. Then Will Black, a trader from Kittery, settled on the island and homesteaded at Mackerel Cove. The family lived there for over twenty years, and probably had quite a comfortable establishment, farming the fertile fields, fishing, perhaps building their own boats; in those days men could turn their hands to anything. The children of the island, born there, growing up to know every inch of the forest and the shore as they knew each other's faces, would not have been able to imagine any other existence, in any other place. One of the sons, young Will, filed a claim and received title to the island, which was then known as Will's Island.

Now comes Hannah Curtis, the second wife of Deacon Timothy Bailey of Hanover, Massachusetts, who, whatever her virtues, appears as an interfering and unfeeling woman; so she must have seemed to the Blacks. Why she decided that she wanted to move to North Yarmouth we don't know, unless she had come from that place. She *did* decide, and she worked on influential friends until she got the Deacon appointed to the parish there. But with all the space there must have been in 1750, Hannah still felt crowded on the mainland; she yearned for an island of her own (though it is hard to see how Deacon Timothy was going to carry on his parish duties from way out in the bay) and she wanted Will's Island. It was the only one for her. She bought it from the North Yarmouth Land Proprietors for one pound of tobacco and one gallon of rum. (Looking over these old transactions, one can only come to the conclusion that some people would do anything for a drink.)

So the Blacks, after more than twenty years of thinking they were in their own home, were thus dispossessed. There is a whole world of drama in the dry and simple words. As they moved across the strait that now carries Will's name, the mother must have looked back toward the garden she had coaxed to grow, the wild flowering shrubs she'd tamed in her dooryard and now must abandon, and the father must have thought regretfully of the pastures he had cleared from the wilderness. The older children, especially young Will who had received title to the island, perhaps reflected bitterly on the homes they had built from logs they cut, and the younger children remembered their secret playhouses in the woods and the special rocks from which they had fished for cunners.

The Blacks settled on Orr's Island, but Orr's was like a crowded city compared to what they had left, and besides, it was not their own; nothing was their own on it. They had left good parts of themselves back on the island that must always afterward have been "Will's Island" to them even when others began to call it Bailey for the deacon and his aggressive wife.

Deacon Bailey built a home at the north end of the island, near Garrison Cove. He was very friendly with the Indians, local history says; but so must the Blacks have been, to have lived comfortably there for over twenty years only to be dispossessed by white people, not by red. Other people settled on the island eventually—Merrymans, Alexanders, Sinnetts, Johnsons, Gardners, and Orrs—but it is the Blacks who have left their mark, in the name of the passage between the islands, and on our compassionate hearts.

POND ISLAND

Pond Island lies to the east of Bailey and to the southeast of Orr's; a small island, unimpressive on the charts. Its name comes prosaically enough from a fresh-water pond that used to be there and has long since dried up. It has been uninhabited most of the time. Altogether it seems hardly worth notice. But just as a very ordinary-looking person walking down the street might carry behind his quiet face the memories of an incredible life, so has Pond Island had an extremely lively history.

For one thing, it has always been haunted. When the pirate Lowe dumped his treasure in the pond he gave the future population of the Harpswells a far more valuable legacy than mere golden doubloons, because if a haunted island isn't a treasure to brighten anyone's life, what is? Just think of the generations of Harpswell children growing up with this delightful situation in their dooryard. Think of all the expeditions by Harpswell boys to dare the ghosts and dig for the treasure, and then wonder how many of the expeditions broke up in a violent rush for the boat because somebody *heard* something.

Lowe was supposed to have brought to the island three kettles of bar silver and a chest of gold and jewels from the Spanish galleon *Don Pedro del Montclova*. The story is detailed: the treasure was rowed ashore in three boats to the little cove at the north end of Pond Island, and then dropped into the pond. At that point the pirates began to fight among themselves, but the reason why has not been passed on with the rest of it. When the cutlasses and knives stopped flashing and the blood was wiped away, two men were dead, whom the others promptly hove into the pond along with the treasure. (We can only hope that nobody came along soon afterward looking for a refreshing drink of water.)

The now-dry bed of the pond and most of the island have been dug up and re-dug over the years, but no one has ever found anything. However, mysterious lights of strange hues shimmered over Pond Island, and odd noises were heard, explained by those in the know as the phantom squabblings of the spirits of the dead pirates, condemned to fight forever over the treasure. A white light was seen to lie over the island; it suggests the will o' the wisp of the marshes, but to the romantic and imaginative it meant something else.

All Harpswell was influenced by the goings-on at Pond Island. During the last part of the 1800's and the first part of this century, the islands and the Neck positively reverberated to spirit-rappings;

tables tipped, and walked, and things fell off shelves when no one was near, and there was a resident medium at Orr's Island who held séances considered successful. We wonder why they were, since nobody got any messages that led to the treasure. Perhaps their success lay in the fact that they gave everybody something new to talk about; those who believed and those who did not must have had some stimulating arguments over their mug-ups and trawl-baiting.

This is all within living memory. But back in 1763, when David Johnson was building a house on Orr's, he had the ingenious idea of collecting dry mussel shells from Pond and grinding them up to plaster his house; and unhappy spirits from Pond followed the mussel shells across the water and haunted Johnson's house with weird noises from then on.

In 1801 a unique personality appeared on Pond Island; the name his parents gave him is lost, but he is remembered as the "Acaraza Man," and "the Professor." It is astonishing to realize how näive some otherwise hard-headed Yankee businessmen could be, but even now notices in post offices warn against the Spanish Prisoner swindle, so perhaps it's not strange that the Professor was so successful in 1801. He convinced a group of well-heeled citizens that he could make silver out of morning dew, and they obligingly formed a corporation to back his enterprise.

The first batch of dew was gathered at Freeport and brought out to Pond Island. But after all the measuring and boiling, nothing happened except that the dew disappeared in steam. The Professor said it had not been properly gathered; the circumstances were not favorable. What the favorable circumstances were, and what the method of collecting the dew was, we are not informed. But the second boiling was successful, because the Professor thoughtfully dropped some melted coins into the kettle when no one was looking. As the others, greedily entranced by what was going on over the fire, were sure that they could make any amount of silver now with no help from the Professor, they were happy to pay his fee when he asked for it then and there, and thought they were well rid of him. So he went off to green fields and greener victims; there is no record of how long the corporation lasted after it was left holding the kettle.

From 1875 to 1880, Charles Sylvester, a Civil War veteran, ran a big poultry farm at Pond Island. Maybe he had been one of the boys to laugh at the ghosts and dig for the treasure; he doesn't seem to have been very nervous, because he did well on the island for five years. But one mild evening he saw something which undid his tranquil temperament. Sitting on his doorstep at sunset, enjoying his rest after a busy day, his spaniel beside him, Sylvester was justifiably startled to see a large phantom dog pass by. The spaniel was not only startled but horror-stricken; he rushed into the house and under the bed and stayed there. The phantom was the size of a year-old colt. It sounds to us like a deer, but Sylvester, a sensible man, not easily frightened, was disturbed enough to move himself, dog, and livestock over to Orr's Island the next day.

John Darling, known as the Hermit of Harpswell, lived on Pond Island once, and the ghosts were good to him, for he and his family did well there. The legend is that Darling was an incorrigible offender on the mainland and that the Harpswell selectmen gave him the choice of exile on Pond or State's Prison, and that he chose the island; and that, tragically, he was so neglected in his old age that he eventually froze to death.

The town records and some living persons contradict this. When he lived on Pond Island John was a healthy red-headed man in his prime, with a family of young children whom he rowed by dory to Orr's Island each day so they could go to school. He ran a string of lobster traps. Whenever a large vessel put in at Orr's Island, which was often because Orr's was an important port-of-call for the big fishing boats in those days, John made himself useful helping to unload and load. He worked seasonally for a large fish-buying concern, salting down the fresh-caught cod.

When his wife died, the family was broken up. John did as well as he could, but when the town felt he needed to be taken care of he was given a one-room cabin on Sebascodegan Island. A neighbor looked after him. When he fell seriously ill he was taken to the Maine General Hospital in Portland, and there he died, on January 15, 1918. He was brought to Orr's Island for burial, and the service was held in the Union Meeting House.

Pond Island was owned for years by the family of the late Robert P. Tristram Coffin. The poet's grandfather lived on it at one time, and apparently was driven off not by the ghosts but by his insatiable desire to live on as many islands as possible in his lifetime. In Coffin's *Yankee Coast* his daughter Peggy tells of the Pond Island picnics that were institutions in the family.

HASKELL ISLAND

Haskell, lying off Harpswell Neck with Little Mark Island, Whale Rock, and Eagle Island like a bodyguard between it and Casco Bay, was once called New Damariscove Island; it was where the Merryconeag fishermen had their fish flakes. Richard Potts, whose name is connected also with Jewell Island, lived there in 1672; the point at the southern end of what was then Merryconeag Neck is still called Potts Point, and there is still a Potts Harbor, though Richard went to Pennsylvania, as we have said, during the Indian wars and never came back to Maine.

Later some imaginative person called the island Pulpit, because he thought the high cliff on the south side looked like one. Then one Haskell, master of a coasting vessel, bought the island, either because he simply wanted an island, or because he had some business scheme in mind—we'll never know—and then it was called Haskell.

Whether he lived there or not we don't know, either. Perhaps his wife objected, the way some women object now to moving to the suburbs. Perhaps the thing was a romantic gesture on his part, to be regretted afterward. There is nothing romantic about the slaughtering business carried on to process the sheep and cattle that were pastured there.

The island made its brief bow to history one day during the Civil War when Albert Bibber and Eldridge Titcomb, fishing off the island, were captured by the rebel privateer *Archer*. Yankee and Southern accents twanged and drawled acrimoniously, but in the end Bibber, with a Confederate pistol in his ribs, had to pilot the *Archer* into Portland harbor.

The other story of Haskell Island, of the rats who ate old Humphrey, and of the subsequent arrival of the Mills brothers with their ferocious cats who attacked strangers, is apocryphal, though with a grain of truth. The story has been handed down with various alterations, some more gruesome than others. Briefly, it tells how an old lobsterman named Humphrey lived alone on the island, which was infested by rats. He was found dead, and mostly eaten by rats. Two young fishermen, brothers named Mills, moved onto the island and into Humphrey's shack then, but they brought along a dozen or so cats who took care of the rats in no time at all, and then started in on the birds. The cats increased, as cats left strictly to nature will do, and the brothers were kept pretty well occupied in catching enough fish to feed their pets.

These pets were so fierce that they threatened strangers. Captain Haskell wanted to sell the island for a summer place, and he told the boys to control their cats—in fact he suggested an outright purge —but they refused, only to wake up one morning and find all the cats had been poisoned during the night.

Mrs. Robert M. Driver, in the magazine *Down East*, says it's all a big leg-pull perpetrated on an innocent public by generations of mischievous natives. When she was a child her family spent summers on the island, and she knew the surviving brother of the pair who had the cats. Their name was Douglas, not Mills; their cats did not bother the rest of the year-round inhabitants. The latter are left out of the Humphrey story. In fact, says Mrs. Driver, there never was a Humphrey, and there were only a normal number of rats on the island.

When Mrs. Driver was on Haskell the surviving brother, Oliver Douglas, was a kindly man with three or four cats for pets, and the children called him "the hermit." The boys liked to hear his stories of the old Harpswell days. Eventually people stopped living on the island all year round, and Oliver lived there alone, except when the summer people came. A Mr. Charles Bibber, who made periodic trips over from South Harpswell to look after the summer cottages during the winter, always checked on Oliver's welfare whenever he came to the island. One day he found the old man dead, but the rats had found him first. "I came out of there a lot faster than I went in," Mr. Bibber said afterward.

Oliver was decently buried and the old shack was torn down. There is no trace of it or the Douglas brothers left, except in the legend, which has made Haskell Island famous in a rather ghastly way.

Malaga Island

Unnamed on the charts, little Malaga Island lies a mile southeast of Cundy's Harbor in Harpswell. Seen from the shore today it looks like any island along the Maine coast. Its early history is unknown; for instance, we don't know what Indians came there, and what white man named it for a Spanish port which we always associate with grapes and wine.

But it has a sort of fame after all, as having been the stage for a somewhat squalid drama that made people all through Maine associate the name Malaga not with grapes and wine but with some of the wildest tales of degeneration, miscegenation, incest, and general nastiness that were ever fabricated. The legend was far worse than the reality.

Malaga seems always to have had a bad reputation locally, as far back as people could remember. But in the first years of this century the island suddenly burst into public notice. The stories spread like a particularly disagreeable epidemic. Everyone had his yarn directly from Someone Who Knew for a Fact. The least of the tales said that the people on Malaga lived underground like animals and were dying by the score from starvation. This seemed to arouse more horrified fascination than pity.

The reason for the sudden publicity was the angry attempt of Phippsburg, on the mainland, to get the island off the town pauper account by claiming that Malaga should really have been a part of Harpswell. The truth was, nobody wanted the island. There was not even a personal landlord to claim it as his private property, and no town wanted the responsibility of the thirty-odd islanders.

What is known of those islanders is scant. For instance, only two facts are definitely known about James McKenney, who was called "King of Malaga" at the time when the scandal broke, between 1903 and 1905: he was of Scottish descent, and was born in Phippsburg. It is said that he ruled his people like a dictator. The Malagans themselves were supposed to be of mixed Negro, Indian, and white blood; the former strain probably came from a family of Negroes who had settled on nearby Horse Island a long time before, though one exotic story says Yankee sailing masters used to drop their African concubines off on Malaga before they sailed into their home ports.

However, James McKenney—"King Jim"—always said that the colored people came from "down south," and this is logical, because the underground railway ran this way long before the Civil War. There were also Negroes in Maine who had come first as servants and slaves, well before the Revolutionary War. Before 1742 there were Negroes on Bailey's Island.

Why the Malagans degenerated into such a sad state is easy to understand. Misfits on the mainland, rejected by society for one reason or another, withdrew to the nearby island, and in time it became a sort of salt-water Skid Row. The derelicts clung together without any moral guidance; their children grew up uneducated. Intermarriage was common, and so was no marriage. After a time there was a large percentage of mentally retarded and physically unfit islanders.

Whatever natural resources the island had once had, had by 1900 long been exhausted. The place was by then hardly more than rock with a scanty soil covering which produced only scrub growth and one sad little vegetable garden. Some soul not completely without hope tried to keep this going, and there were a dozen or so scrawny hens.

There had once been plenty of clams for the digging, but the flats were becoming exhausted. In summer the men went lobstering, and caught and sold herring. At least they ate well in summer if not in the winter, when they also froze. They burned for fuel anything they could find, and were sometimes reduced to using brush. One woman died of pneumonia, lying close to a pathetic fire of brush. Broken windows were stuffed with anything handy. There was no money for soap, and rubbish was simply thrown out beside the door.

This was the situation when Phippsburg, which had been allotted the island in 1841 when Georgetown was divided into three parts—Phippsburg, Arrowsic, and Winnegance—took her troubles to the Maine Legislature. People passed on the newest Malaga yarns, and the newspapers pointed shocked fingers and dug out stories of other such depressed communities elsewhere in the state.

Phippsburg won her battle; in its 1905 session the Legislature relieved her of responsibility for the islands of Malaga, Bear, and Wood. Now no one owned Malaga officially, but there was no chance of its slipping back into oblivion. It had received too much notice, and the public conscience was aroused.

Someone had to take responsibility for the island, that was plain, but nobody wanted it. Meanwhile the Malagans deteriorated still further in mind and body, many of them probably oppressed by sheer hopelessness, malnutrition, and the knowledge that they could not alone pull themselves out of their wretched state.

Finally someone did something besides talk. Captain and Mrs. George Lane, of Malden, Massachusetts, had a summer home on Horse Island, and during the summer Captain Lane used to sail along the coast and anchor in little coves to preach, starting Sunday schools in isolated communities. The almost total illiteracy on Malaga was one of the evils that could be attacked at once, he felt. There were children growing up there who might not be as retarded as they seemed. Captain Lane approached the State Superintendent of Schools, Mr. Payson Smith, who said the state could not provide funds for school buildings on Malaga, but would send a teacher if there was a school for her to teach in.

On the first of June in 1908 the Lanes came to Malaga. They found the islanders in even worse condition than before. Clamming was very poor, and several new families had moved onto the island, which could not even take care of those already there. But there were children, and that was what mattered to the Lanes.

James McKenney must not have been too brutal a ruler, for he allowed the Lanes to set up a school in his house. It was said that a couple of adults on the island knew how to read and write; perhaps King Jim was one of them. A Boston woman had given the Lanes chairs and desks for their school. All through June, July, and August of 1908 the Lanes' daughter Cora rowed across from Horse Island on every good day to teach the children. She started them off with singing lessons and thus aroused their interest and enthusiasm.

On July 6 Malaga had a flag-raising ceremony, which must have stirred pride and hope in minds long dulled by misery, on the site of a new schoolhouse. By August 1 the men had laid the frame. Now help began to come in from everyone whom the Lanes could interest. Massachusetts people sent money. The Maine Federation of Women's Clubs took a hand. Fraternal orders helped. Captain Ridley of the schooner *Sebasco* worked long and hard. Major John

Gould of Portland managed the legal arrangements. The firm of Loring, Short, and Harmon contributed wallpaper. Hiram Ricker and Sons furnished drinking water.

By October the results of the Lanes' practical well-doing was a little red schoolhouse, and a home for the teacher. Supplies of all sorts had been donated, and a teacher and a practical helper were engaged. In an astonishingly short time the children of Malaga could read and write well enough to send letters of thanks to those who had helped them. Girls were learning to sew and boys applied their carpentry lessons to making improvements on their homes.

The whole community began to look up, to take pride in itself and interest in a life which until then must have been a uniformly depressing dark gray. By the next summer there were more gardens growing from the poor soil, and James McKenney's son-in-law, Jerry Murphy, who succeeded him as King, bragged that the island children wrote and read as well as those in Bath.

Spiritually and emotionally, life was better on Malaga than it had been for a long time. But there were still the bitter winters, still the worry over supporting an increasing population. Now that the state was interested in the island that had so long been neglected, it faced up to its duties. When Governor Plaisted and the Executive Council visited the island in July, 1911, it had been tidied up for the occasion, but its best was still rather dismaying. The governor suggested drilling an artesian well for a decent water supply, burning down the shacks, and building new homes.

There was a practical but painful alternative: the islanders could be moved somewhere else. There was no sustenance left in the soil, and the unrestricted clamming and lobstering practices of the times had depleted the surrounding flats and sea. But nobody wanted the Malagans, and they didn't want to go. Some had fled from contempt and cruelties on the mainland, and didn't want to go back, and some had never known any other home but the island. They wept pitifully at the idea of being moved, even when they were told they would have more comfortable homes. They were islanders first and foremost, and the mainland must have seemed like a wilderness or jungle to them, full of unknown risks and terrors.

Then someone raised the legal question; was it right and proper to remove human beings from their homes by force? They could be evicted, it was established, if a landlord could be found.

Various claimants to the property appeared, no doubt expecting to sell to the state and make a little profit. Finally the state bought the island from the heirs of one Perry, as their story was the most valid of all those presented. The price was four hundred dollars and the legal fees.

By July 1 of 1912 everyone was to be off Malaga. The evacuation was supervised by a Doctor Kildore. It must have been a bad time in many ways, but the children whose minds had been opened and aroused by school surely looked forward to life on the mainland as if to a new world. A sum of $1,350 was divided among the people by the Executive Council. Those who could not fend for themselves were taken care of, and the rest put down roots on the mainland and eventually became self-respecting citizens.

In January 1913 the state put Malaga up for sale. All the buildings on the island but the schoolhouse were torn down. The little red schoolhouse was given to the Maine Sea Coast Mission; carefully taken apart, it was shipped to Loud's Island in Muscongus Bay and reassembled, for use as a church.

Today Malaga is owned privately, and has happily lived down its sad history.

Ragged Island

"Rugged," it is called on the early charts of Casco Bay, and rugged it is as well as ragged: fifty acres, off Phippsburg, that must have been exceedingly hard to get to, surrounded by ledges, one of which is poetically named the White Bull, giving rise to charming mythological fancies. If only some classical scholar of those days had named a nearby ledge Europa.

Ragged has only one tiny harbor, and there is no record of an early settlement, only of fish flakes. Perhaps when the fishermen came in from the sea they stopped there, split and cleaned their big codfish, and laid them out to dry on Ragged Island in the sparkling summer winds. Still, someone stayed there long enough to name the Devil's Wall and the Ghost Cliff, on the westerly shore; but in these names may be found another explanation for the fact that it wasn't a very popular island.

One man who loved it was the Reverend Elijah Kellogg, who is as important a part of the Harpswells' history as the saga of its shipyards and seafaring men. He was a talented and high-spirited man who lived every instant of his life in the fullest sense of the word; born in 1813, at thirteen he was at sea, determined to be a sailor, and though he didn't become one after all, he used those exciting boyhood experiences for his books. Something in him always remained a boy and thus he was an especially understanding friend to boys.

He came to the Harpswell Center Congregational Parish in 1844. He must have explored the surrounding bays until he knew them as the gulls and medricks and seals did. It would not be surprising if he had had his own catboat or yawl, remembering his experience as a sailor. And he was a very energetic and imaginative young man.

Ragged Island was one of the places Kellogg loved best. When he built his home on Harpswell Neck, he brought stones for the foundation and hearth from Ragged Island, and on that island he cut the timber for his house. Later he set the sights and sounds and scents of the island down in his Elm Island and Pleasant Cove scenes; and boys today can read stories that began in Elijah Kellogg's brain as he sailed among the islands and climbed the Ghost Cliff over a hundred years ago.

Ragged Island had the same fascination for the poet Edna St. Vincent Millay; it was her summer home until she died. She was unmistakably a part of her time, as Kellogg was of his; but on the other hand they belong to every time, because they are of the clan who love wild and lonely outflung islands. They would have had much to say to each other, those two.

It is reassuring to know that some others are left who love Ragged Island enough to spend summers there.

The Smaller Harpswell Islands

Most of the tiny Harpswell islands are summer residences or uninhabited. Each has an undeniable personal significance for someone, each has its own beauty. Necessarily we mention only those which have a bearing on the wider history of the coast: Birch Island, for instance, settled by Walter Merriman, the ancestor of all the Harpswell Merrimans. He was an Irishman, kidnaped in Dublin as Michael

Sinnett was, and brought to Boston. He was sold for his fare to a Simonton of Cape Elizabeth. When Walter finished his indenture, he went to Birch.

In the early 1800's there was a thriving village of salt-water farmers on Birch, which lies far up in Middle Bay between the Neck and Mere Point. There were forty-eight children in the school, a sizable group for an island. There was no reason to suppose the islanders would ever uproot themselves; yet, in 1849, when the news came of gold in California, everyone left. They cleaned themselves out as efficiently as a hurricane or an epidemic. Nothing is left of them but their cellar holes. One wonders how many reached California and how many found gold, and how many stopped along the way and were thus responsible for scattering old Maine names across the nation.

Eagle Island, lying off the southwest point of Haskell, is a tiny island once known as Sawungun, and once as Heron, because of the great blue herons that built their big untidy nests of sticks in the spruces there. There must have been eagles there too, to give it its present name; the bald eagle of the coast who can be seen on summer days high above the highest-soaring gulls, lazily gliding in great and effortless circles.

But Eagle's fame comes from another sort of eagle; the late Admiral Robert E. Peary, discover of the North Pole, whose summer home it was. He bought the island while he was a student at Bowdoin College. His daughter, Mrs. Marie Peary Stafford, the "Snow Baby," and other members of the Admiral's family still maintain their summer home on Eagle, and the house is filled with trophies and souvenirs from all over the world.

Bombazeen, a small island between Brunswick and Great or Sebascodegan Island, was the home of Bombazeen, the Indian sagamore. He was killed one August day in 1724, while he was crossing the Kennebec, by Captain Moulton's men on their way to Norridgewalk.

In 1775 one Granny Young fought a private war off Bombazeen. She had paddled over there in her canoe to pick berries, having only a stave for a paddle, and when she was on her way home she found herself followed by a black bear. According to the story Granny stunned the swimming bear with her stave and held his head under water until he was dead. Then, to crown her exploit, she towed his body home.

The Cedar Ledges, seven or more of them lying east of Ram Island and southeast of Orr's, don't seem to have been classed as islands big enough to be visited by pirates; probably since the earliest days men have hunted seabirds there, and that was their peculiar value. But they deserve special notice, because someone actually did find treasure on one of them. Captain John Wilson of Orr's Island, hunting birds on a frosty Thanksgiving morning in the 1850's —*not* on the track of treasure guided by spirit messages or personal hunches, but engaged in a forthright no-nonsense occupation— stumbled somehow on three caches of silver Spanish coins.

Captain Wilson's find amounted to about $16,000, in those days quite a fortune, and with no income-tax bite. He bought two houses on Orr's Island and a woodlot on Sebascodegan. A woodlot was money in the bank, and still is a handy little thing to have. The captain also bought two vessels and fitted them out to take wood to Boston. His discovery of pirate loot while he was looking for seabirds is a perfect example of serendipity, and he used his find wisely, and took great and lasting joy from it.

Flag Island is near South Harpswell. Its name suggests colorful standards blowing in the wind, but it really comes from the cattails that grow there, called flags. The story is that Captain Mowatt of the British Navy and his five warships anchored off Flag on their way to burn Falmouth in 1775. This vicious and senseless act, which reduced a town of four hundred houses to ashes in a deliberate daylong holocaust, give Flag Island an indirect sort of immortality.

Little Mark Island, south of Great Mark, took its name back in 1827, when the Government built a fifty-foot stone tower there as a day mark for ships entering the lower harbor. But just before World War II a beacon was installed there, so now it serves as a night mark as well. What makes it different from other beacons is the twenty-foot-square room in the base of the tower, meant to be a refuge for shipwrecked sailors. It would be interesting to know if it was ever used as such; we do know that it has been used as a sheepfold, and doubtless the sheep appreciated it.

Eastern Mark Island, or Woody Mark Island, was once the hideout and workshop of counterfeiters, around the end of the last century. This is one of those facts we're better off not knowing, because it gives rise to an irrepressible and tormenting curiosity; in this case one would rather know nothing if one can't know all. The same with Big Hen, eastward of North Yarmouth Island, where one Dan Wilson was found shot to death in his cabin.

Very small Shelter Island, in Middle Bay, once gave refuge to settlers who were driven from Mere Point by Indian hostilities. It also has a local fame as a place where smugglers bringing goods in from British territory hid their illicit cargo; that is, if they were smart enough to get past the Coast Guard which had been formed for the very purpose of stopping them.

Some of the other little islands have names which make a poem in themselves: Irony and Little Irony, the Goose islands and the Goslings; Rogue, Turnip, and Uncle Zeke.

The Dead Ship of Harpswell

No account of the Harpswells is complete without the most colorful legend of them all.

On a summer day in the 1880's, when the sea and its islands were as lovely in their deep blue and gold and green as the Aegean and the Grecian islands could ever be, a visitor at the Harpswell House strolled out onto the verandah in time to see a breathtaking sight: a full-rigged ship was sailing into the Sound, her sails gleaming in the sun, a bone in her teeth. He called the others to look, and in the instant he took his eyes from the vision it disappeared.

This was the last authenticated appearance of the famous Dead Ship of Harpswell. Why has she never been seen since? To those who saw her, or those who, never having seen her, still implicitly believed in her, the explanation was obvious; she had found her harbor at last. All the long years of weary voyaging over the seas, the futile attempts to make Potts Harbor, surely came to an end on that golden afternoon, and though the summer visitor could not see her after that one shimmering glimpse, she and her phantom crew had returned to their home anchorage for all time.

Some rational souls have tried to argue that the Dead Ship was simply a drifting derelict. But according to those who sighted her she was truly a ghost vessel, usually seen in the hour after sundown and before twilight, always under full sail, heading straight for harbor no matter which way the wind was blowing or the tide flowing. Here is where the wonderful power of longing takes over in the human mind: she was never seen twice as the same ship, but always the one that was expected or long overdue. She came bearing down on the wharf and then, as the watcher stiffened in horror, waiting for the crash, she disappeared; first a shimmer or quiver began at the top of the mast and ran through the whole ship, then it vanished. Others told of her coming up Merryconeag Sound and being blotted out by an unexpected cloud of fog before she reached the shore.

Inevitably her appearance stood for death; it was believed that whoever saw her would shortly die, or that someone close to that person would die. Robert P. Tristram Coffin used the legend in *John Dawn*, where the ghost ship foretells the passing of each member of the family. As a Harpswell man, Coffin had known of the ship all his life, he had heard her story from his uncles and from very old people who had actually seen her. She was sighted several times off the Lookout at Harpswell Center, and to the eastward and westward of Bailey and Orr's Island.

Phantom ships are almost as common in sea mythology as buried treasure, and yet there is something *un*commonly stirring about them. The sight of a sailing ship under full sail is inexpressibly moving; how much more so the thought of a phantom ship guided by phantom hands, sailing forever in search of the lost treasure, the lost captain, the lost port. As *The Flying Dutchman* is a classic example of the myth, so the Dead Ship of Harpswell has become an integral part of Atlantic folklore. John Greenleaf Whittier's poem about her sends the authentic chill along the spine and makes one half-wish, half-fear, to see her:

> What weary doom of baffled guest,
>   Thou sad sea-ghost, is thine?
> What makes thee in the haunts of home
>   A wonder and a sign?
> No foot is on thy silent deck,
>   Upon the helm no hand;
> No ripple hath the soundless wind
>   That smites thee from the land!

Whittier's version is, if anything, a little more tragic than the others, for his ship, after her gallant approach, drifts helplessly out to sea again, stern-first. The ship of his poem is supposed to have been the Privateer *Dash*, built in Freeport in 1813 for Seward and Samuel Porter of Portland. But in the Harpswell-Freeport area, the ship is the *Sarah*. Here is the story they tell in these parts:

In the year 1812, George Leverett was twenty-one and Charles Jose a year older. They had great plans; with the backing of George's father and Charles's uncle they were going to order a ship built for the West Indian trade. George was to be captain. Even a pair of boys could grow rich in those days taking salt cod, pine boards, shooks and barrel staves to the southern islands, bringing back molasses, rum, coffee, and cane sugar to sell at home. These two Portland boys, setting out on horseback one spring morning for the Soule yard at South Freeport, had no reason to dream of anything but a glorious future. They did not know that before the trip was over their friendship was to end in a violent quarrel.

In South Freeport they met pretty Sarah Soule, and both fell wildly in love with her at first sight. But George went on to the shipyard, while Charles, pretending he felt ill, stayed behind and made passionate love to Sarah. But she would have nothing to do with him; his Spanish blood made him seem far too urgent for her. George was the lad she preferred, and she showed it. George responded by suggesting "Sarah" as the name for the new vessel. Meanwhile, Charles smoldered with Latin intensity.

The keel of their ship was laid two days later, and then the two boys rode back to Portland. Evidently they fought all the way; Charles accused George of foul play in winning Sarah, and tried to force George's horse off the Yarmouth bridge into the wild Royal River. Afterwards Charles backed out of the deal and went away by himself to make his fortune.

The *Sarah* was ready to be launched in the early autumn; after Sarah christened the ship, she and George were to be married. It was a big day in Freeport, and the town was crowded for the double event.

There was nothing about the launching to suggest bad luck. So on to the wedding. But Freeport's First Church was found to be too small for the crowd, so on the spur of the moment the ceremony was postponed and the decorations of fall flowers and leaves transferred to the huge planing loft at the shipyard. Here is the first hint of an ill omen. The older people worried about that. And yet another change: for some reason or other, the bride's own minister couldn't perform the marriage at the new time. Someone was sent to Yarmouth and he returned with a clergyman, but by now the wedding had been put off till sundown, and there were three things for the old ladies to worry about: change of place, time, and preacher. It was a terrible way to begin a marriage.

They were right. George, now officially Captain Leverett, had a hard time getting a crew. Weird tales of bad luck were going around, losing nothing in the telling but gaining a great deal with every repetition. He finally signed on his officers in Portland, and found enough seamen from the Neck and the islands of Harpswell who weren't afraid to sail with a master whose original partner had quarreled with him over a girl and cleared out, and whose wedding had suffered a few last-minute changes.

About now a foreign barque, painted black and flying no flag, was seen here and there between Cape Elizabeth and the mouth of the Kennebec. The fishermen who saw her said that she was pierced for cannon. Strange, but what with smugglers busy it didn't pay to ask too many questions or look too closely. Then she sailed boldly enough into Portland harbor at the very time that the *Sarah* arrived there from Freeport to load her cargo for the West Indies. Captain Leverett's wife and mother-in-law had come along for the sail.

The foreign barque turned out to be the *Don Pedro Salazar*, and her master was, of all people, Charles Jose; her crew were a tough, hard-bitten lot of Cubans. Charles wished simply to register her in the port where he was born. He'd been wandering around, he said, since he left home, and in Havana he had found the *Don Pedro Salazar* on a reef. He had bought her as a wreck, got papers from the American Consul, recruited himself a crew, and had come home to register her. He didn't explain why he'd been lurking about in Casco Bay for so long instead of coming straight into Portland harbor; he didn't explain why he chose to come in on the day the *Sarah* came.

If Captain Leverett was at all disturbed by Charles's reappearance, remembering the bitter quarrel on the bridge over the raging stream, he didn't show it. He was about to clear for Matanzas with his load of lumber, salt cod, butter, and bayberry candles, and had booked passage for his wife and her party back to Freeport on the packet *Bunganac*. But someone in the group became sick, and they decided to go home by stage.

The packet, sailing without them, reported a most extraordinary incident. Just outside Clapboard Island she was halted by a whaleboat manned by foreign seamen. An officer boarded the packet, peremptorily lined up the passengers, ignored incredulous and angry protests, and desired suspiciously to know where Mrs. Leverett was. When he was finally convinced that she wasn't *there*, he went back aboard the whaleboat. This strange and disturbing event was reported, but that is as far as it went. Nobody investigated.

The *Don Pedro Salazar* cleared for Boston two days before the *Sarah* sailed. But the *Sarah* had got no farther than Halfway Rock when the Spanish barque appeared on her beam. She gave no sign of recognizing the other ship. She flew no ensign, and ignored signals. But always she was there, and like an evil shadow she followed the *Sarah* south.

At Hole-in-the-Wall, a landmark on Abaco Island in the Bahamas, Captain Leverett had a grim decision to make. If he kept on as he was going, on the regular course to Matanzas, he would sail through the Florida Strait, which was infested with pirates. By now his crew were pretty uncomfortable with their shadow, and they were relieved when he chose to head straight for Nassau, to report to the British Admiralty the actions of the *Don Pedro Salazar*.

Offshore the black barque waited like a vulture; and when she saw the *Sarah* heading for Nassau she hoisted the Jolly Roger and ran down the merchant ship. The Harpswell men and the Portland officers put up a good fight, but they were no match for an armored barque carrying heavy cannon. They were all killed in the short battle—all but Captain Leverett, whom Charles Jose had saved for a different, more leisurely, death. After the *Sarah* was looted, the pirates tied the captain to the foot of her mainmast, and roped down the helm so that the vessel would stand out into the open ocean. They went back aboard the black barque, probably after Jose had his say to the helpless Leverett, and sailed quickly away.

Then, through his daze of horror, the captain felt his ship come alive beneath him. His dead crew rose up. The sails were braced about and the helm put up. Dead men, not living, turned the *Sarah* toward her home. Captain Leverett lost consciousness.

Far from these blue-green tropical seas, in the Harpswells on a late November day the island meadows were brown and the sea had a wintry look. The people on Potts Point saw a full-rigged ship coming. She found her way along the unmarked channel between the Point and Haskell's Island.

She ignored the harbor pilot who came out to guide her. He saw no one aboard but the helmsman, who took the ship along the dangerous, tricky course with uncanny accuracy. Gazing up in astonishment and now something very like awe, the pilot saw that the ship's name was defaced by battle damage. The sails were tattered by shot. The superstructure had been blasted away. She was a tragic wreck of a ship, but she reached Potts Harbor and came to a stop, though she dropped no anchor. A strange and silent crew lowered the one undamaged boat, rowed Captain Leverett's unconscious body ashore, deposited it on the grass, and returned to the ship.

Suddenly, before anyone could reach the vessel or even see it clearly, a heavy fog came out of nowhere and settled blindingly over the harbor. When it lifted the ship was gone, but Captain Leverett still lay on the grass, and his log book had been left at his side. The last item in the log showed a change of course for Nassau.

It was a long time before this young man was able to tell anything that had happened, and his last memory was of being deserted aboard his shattered vessel among his dead crew, and of feeling his ship come to life under his feet. He knew nothing of the return trip; it was like a long and dreamless sleep.

He never went to sea again.

[III]

The Middle Coast

CAPE SMALL TO PORT CLYDE

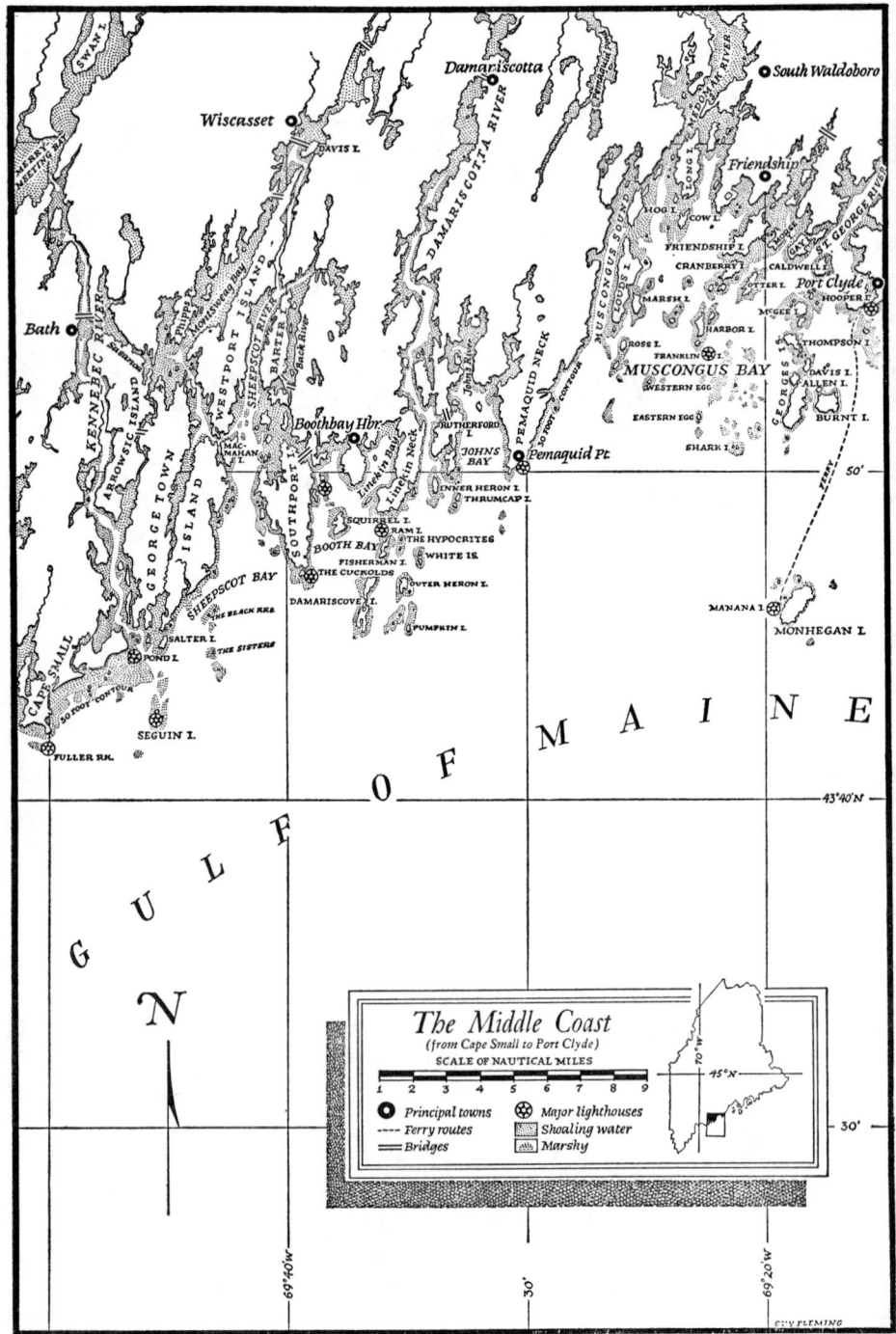

SWAN ISLAND

Swan island in the Kennebec rests its southeastern end in Merrymeeting Bay, and beyond that it is almost completely landlocked; in comparison to the unprotected position of the outer islands, what a delightful situation this must have seemed to explorers from Popham's Colony in 1607. Captain John Smith visited it, of course—in 1614. Was there any island he did not visit? Even then it was called Swan Island. One pleasing idea is that there were wild swans there, but a more realistic theory is that the name derives from some Indian word. There was a little while in 1719 when it had another equally evocative name: Garden Island, given it by its probable owner at that time, Adam Winthrop of Boston. That it should have been called thus suggests that it was always lush and fruitful, a walled garden of an island.

Swan is about four miles long, a little less than a mile wide at its widest part, and half a mile at its narrowest. All in all it has 1,600 acres of land, which have been treated kindly in its history of occupancy. The town of Richmond lies on the west side of the river, and Dresden on the east side. Little Swan (why not Cygnet?) lies, thirty acres of it, snug against the easterly side. Its early name of Calf Island could have come from the fact that it snuggles up to the larger island like a calf to its mother; or perhaps someone pastured calves on it.

Farther north lies a ledge with a few weathered trees, named Spaulding Island for Ann Spaulding, Spinster, who settled on the Dresden shore under the Plymouth Company. Every locality has its familiar spirit, and Ann Spaulding should be the one for this region. Was she young and hopeful and adventurous, using some small inheritance to finance her way, sailing to America because she had too fine and free a spirit to be caged in an English village in the early 1600's? Or did she come perhaps expecting to marry a man who had come over earlier, and find him dead or taken by someone else, so that she, stubborn in her pride, went homesteading by herself? It is disappointing to know no more about Ann than the ledge carrying her name. One can only hope she didn't die violently in an Indian attack but lived to a vigorous old age.

Swan Island has been almost continuously lived upon, changing hands often until 1750, when we find only one family of settlers there. Captain James Whidden then lived on the south end of the island with his daughter Abigail, her husband Lazarus Noble, and their children.

Until that time Swan's history had been unusually peaceful. It was a fertile island, a sheltered one, and those who lived there seem destined for fortunate lives. Even when, in an act of revenge for the murder of a sleeping Indian by white hoodlums at Wiscasset, the Indians raided the island and seized the Noble family to carry to Canada, they seem to have treated their captives with unusual kindness on the long journey north. Some members of the family were freed when they reached Montreal; the children who were kept behind survived. One married and settled in Canada, another stayed with the Indians, apparently from choice, and fortunate little Fanny, who must have been a husky three-year-old to survive a trip when other Indians knocked infants on the head rather than be bothered with so much excess luggage, was ransomed by a wealthy French family. They reared her with such great love that she had to be forcibly restored to her original family, being practically kidnaped from the convent where she was a pupil. Later she married John Shute from New Hampshire.

The aristocratic Dumaresqs of Boston settled on Swan Island soon after the Whiddens and Nobles. The house they built in 1758 still stands today. But the good fortune of Swan Island did not favor the Dumaresqs. Like a dark stream through a green and gold summer landscape runs the doom that touched each generation. Young Philip, while serving in the Royal Navy, was drowned at Southampton, England. James Dumaresq was drowned on October 30, 1826, when a boat capsized in a gale just below Gardiner. The wife of his son Philip, with her little daughter and a Miss Sarah Richards of

The Middle Coast · 111

Gardiner, were drowned in 1855 in the little channel between Swan and Little Swan, directly in front of the family house. From then on Philip did not come back to the island, and he did not talk about it. His own death by drowning in Long Island Sound in 1861 rounds out the series of tragic coincidences. One wonders at the pattern. But who can guess why one house on Swan was cursed and another blessed?

James Dumaresq's daughter, Jane Frances Rebecca, married Colonel Thomas H. Perkins of Boston on May 14, 1820. Colonel Perkins became the sponsor of a pioneering institution for the blind at South Boston, which was named for him. He spent many summers on Swan Island, and was so highly regarded by the islanders that when the island separated from Dresden in 1847 the new town was named for him. He had worked to help the town get its charter from the state.

The Barkers settled on Swan Island in 1772. They were formerly a Nantucket family, which suggests an affinity for islands. (Of course the fact that all these people were of English origin may explain their attraction to the insular life.)

Young Jacob Barker, son of a Nantucket Quaker mother and Robert Barker, was born on Swan Island on a wintry night in 1779. Robert died the following April: a world of tragedy in five words. The beginnings of the island spring, the return of the birds, the thoughts of the plowing and planting, the first lambs and calves, must have given an especial edge to his wife's grief. But she stayed on until another April five years later, and then took her children back to Nantucket.

Mrs. Barker brought her children up as Quakers and educated them with Quaker thoroughness. Jacob went from school in New Bedford to clerking in a store, thence to a brokerage office in New York. Then we find him a successful merchant in New Orleans in the 1830's. What greater contrast could be imagined to the place and time of his birth fifty-six years before? What material here for a historical novel!

Buying, shipping, trading, bargaining, Jacob was always in the forefront of the battle. He was a business associate of Albert Gallatin; he owned the steam engine which was later sold to Robert Fulton for his steamboat on the Hudson. During the War of 1812 he negotiated government loans amounting to ten million dollars. From his experiences in New Orleans he learned a great deal about slavery and didn't approve of the slave market, but suggested that slaves, on the whole, had a better life than laborers in the north. He died at his son's home in Philadelphia after a long, crowded, eager, and creative life. He was another of Swan's fortunate children.

The Barker house on Swan Island later was called the Harward house, after a Mr. Harward bought it in 1796. Mr. Harward lived in the house for nearly seventy years. His grandson George Harward, farmer and fisherman, was a selectman when the island was a part of Dresden, and was in the Maine Legislature as late as 1931. He died in Richmond. Thus in one leap we spring from Revolutionary times to the present.

The following description of the old Harward house, written by Mrs. Louisa Hatch Maxwell, who was once a Swan Islander, is included because it expresses so well the particular grace brought to island living in so many instances:

> At the lower end of Swan Island there stood for many years a large square colonial house that was built in 1776 by Robert Barker. In the upper story of this house were portholes for defense, when it was used as a garrison, as was sometimes necessary. It could be seen far down the river and served as a landmark for incoming craft to steer by. Glistening Merrymeeting Bay was spread out before it and five towns could be seen in the distance. The front door, with its bronze knocker, faced the south, and outside were purple lilacs and golden-hearted lilies. In the hall hung a copper warming-pan, its cover perforated with the figure of a peacock. In the corner of the living room stood an old clock that was brought from Holland. A Sheraton sewing table, with drawers having brass handles, was at the east window. On it lay an ancient prayer book, with quaint illustrations, of early date. The paper on the wall had a parrot, a poppy, and a shepherdess—many times repeated. A niece of Mr. Harward's, Miss Mary Morrell, was married in this room with the picturesque paper upon the wall to Mr. Samuel Reed of Woolwich. Miss Jane Reed, of Richmond, is a descendant of this family. The old clock, the Sheraton table, the copper warming-pan, and a sample of the wallpaper, are treasured possessions in her home.

When life in the Harward house and on Swan Island was in full bloom seines were set all about the island to trap the great schools

The Middle Coast · 113

of shad and alewives, in catches so heavy sometimes the men could hardly land them. Mr. Harward was here, there, everywhere, lending a hand, pulling and hauling. From far up on the height of the island they could see the schools of fish moving upriver. Following the fish came the vessels from Newburyport and Rockport in Massachusetts, to buy the catch at three cents a pound.

There was always work on Swan Island for an able-bodied man, at the time when we were a nation of producers rather than consumers. Farming, fishing, lumbering, brickmaking, and the building of small ships kept everyone busy.

The land has always been fertile. The Reverend Jacob Bayley, who wrote a history of Dresden, tells how Captain Whidden raised fifty bushels of wheat from one bushel of seed. This island garden in its ideal sheltered position produced its own flax and sheep for linen and wool; winter and summer wheat; Indian corn on burnt-over land; immense quantities of potatoes. The wild berries grew with extravagant enthusiasm. Jacob Bayley tells in his journal of eighty-one varieties of flowers and vegetables that were grown at the time. Some of the rarer things grew only within his own mainland garden. He must have been quite a horticulturist, far in advance of his times; but the records show what was possible in those days and what must have been done on Swan Island across the river from him by devoted and dedicated farmer-fishermen.

In 1848 regular town and state elections were held on Swan Island for the first time; there were then about eighty-four persons on the island. In 1854 a new schoolhouse was built. For about ten years the teachers' pay averaged between $1.45 and $2.50 a week, but progress was running before the wind and wouldn't be halted; by 1867 a schoolmaster received $21 a month. The town paid $2.50 a cord for wood delivered to the schoolhouse. Men and oxen got ten cents an hour for work on the island's one road.

The end of the ferry service between Richmond, Swan Island, and Dresden left the islanders more or less stranded, not like those on the outer islands who traveled back and forth across the bays in their own boats. They began leaving the island, and gradually through direct or indirect ways their properties passed into the hands of the state of Maine. By 1940 only summer people came to Swan; the last summer resident was Mr. M. C. Priest of Brookline,

Massachusetts. After his death Mrs. Priest sold the property to the state, and eventually the whole island became the Swan Island Game Management Area.

Somehow it seems entirely appropriate that Swan Island, which provided sustenance first to the Indians and then to white men who meticulously guarded, cultivated, and preserved it, should now offer food and shelter to wild life. Sometimes there are more than two hundred deer roaming freely in the woods, living in the winter on hay put out for them. In the spring there is the heart-stopping spectacle of from eight to ten thousand Canada geese resting in safety about the island's shores. Fields that once held the farmers' crops or grazed sheep produce Ladino clover and grain for the geese.

Swan Island serves as a laboratory; here a successful deer repellant has been developed, for instance, and many other experiments in wild-life conservation have been carried on. The farmland is operated under standard soil-conservation practices. Naturally the island is closed to hunters, but it is possible to shoot waterfowl during the open season below high-water mark on the tide flats, except at Maxwell Cove, which is kept closed to provide a constant feeding and resting place for the fowl.

Many people would like to see the old colonial Dumaresq house restored and preserved, and perhaps also the one that was built by Major Tubbs, who fought in the Revolution. One particularly appealing idea is to turn the Dumaresq house into a guest house to accommodate visitors who would like to spend several days on the island and explore it thoroughly. It would not only be a mistake but a tragedy to let these houses rot and crumble into their cellar holes, for their past is ours.

THE BOOTHBAY ISLANDS

THE NAMES OF THE ISLANDS in Sheepscot and Booth Bays challenge the imagination. For whom was Seguin named? Who named some deceptive rocks The Cuckolds? Was it someone fresh from England in the robust and bawdy Elizabethan times? Herons must have nested on the Heron islands, but Pumpkin isn't shaped like a pumpkin. The Hypocrites tease our fancy. Thrumcap is another odd name.

Some islands with quieter names are unique for what has happened on them or is happening now. Some, after a bloody history, have become summer resorts, some preserve their continuity with fishermen and salt-water farmers, some, after a crowded and exciting past, are now barren and deserted. And some offer silent, protected retreats for thoughtful men.

SOUTHPORT

Southport, a long triangle of an island, perhaps four miles in length and two miles wide at the apex of the triangle, lies between Sheepscot Bay and Booth Bay; it is close to Georgetown and Arrowsic on the west; Boothbay Harbor is to the northeast. The long end of it, tipped by Cape Newagen, points like a finger to the south.

To many people Newagen is a more familiar name than Southport. Newagen is an ancient name, intimately involved with the history of the state. The settlement by that name had been established at least two years before Christopher Levett visited it in 1623 and reported that the Indians came there to trade their furs to an Englishman named Coke.

On old charts the entire island is called Cape Newagen, or Cape Newagen Island, and so it was known for years; sometimes it is referred to in old documents as Newaggon, Nekrangan, and even

Bona-waggon. Its early history is much like that of the other islands in the vicinity. When Levett visited, it was a center for the Wawenocks, those intelligent and industrious Indians—the tribe of Samoset—of whom early travelers speak with admiration. Today traces of their huge shell heaps, relics of many happy years of eating clams, are still to be found on Southport, and there is also a burial ground.

After the comparatively peaceful days of the white men's early occupancy, the usual Indian troubles cleaned out Southport as they cleaned out the other settlements, and on Cape Island, a few hundred yards off Cape Newagen, there are still the ruins of the fort to which the islanders and Sheepscot settlers hurried for refuge after the massacres at Arrowsic.

It was not until after the Revolution that Southport—still known as Cape Newagen Island—emerged from the composite picture of the coast into her own individuality. We find Captain Jonathan Pierce at Marr's Harbor, now Hendrick's Harbor, on the westerly side; he was a genuine tycoon of the codfishing industry, commanding a large fleet of bankers—vessels that went out to the great deep-water banks to fish. Today yachts lie at anchor where once the sturdy and hard-working fishing boats lay, and Captain Pierce's homestead belongs to the Southport Yacht Club. If his ghost ever walks it must be endlessly astonished by the fact that now men sail for pleasure. (And even more by the fact that men have so much time for pleasure.)

The island had a brush with the War of 1812 when the British frigate, *Bulwark*, with seventy-four guns, sailed up the Sheepscot and put six bargeloads of marines ashore at Marr's, or Hendrick's, Harbor. But the militia was ready for them, and beat them back in what must have been a woeful surprise for His Majesty's Marines. Superbly trained fighting men, what a blow to their collective ego to be driven off by Yankee yokels! The Old Pine marks the landing site. Those islanders who weren't fighting in the militia had taken the island boats farther up the river to hide them in secluded coves and inlets.

After this the island enjoyed such a period of calm and prosperity as to make us insecure moderns look back in envy. The fishing was good wherever one went, and the island had its great fleet of bankers that went after cod, and mackerel vessels that shared in the wealth and excitement. Every man and boy on the island had work; those who didn't go fishing built boats for those who did.

Until 1842 the island was a part of Boothbay, but in that year it was set off and incorporated as a town called Townsend. The name was changed to Southport in 1850, but the earlier name still remains in Townsend Gut, where one passes from the mainland to the island over a drawbridge.

The Civil War, which we usually think of in terms of land fighting, made veterans out of a handful of Southport fishermen; they were the crew of the banker *Archer*, belonging to Ebeneezer and William Decker of Decker's Cove on the easterly side. The *Archer* was captured by a rebel privateer, and her crew held prisoner for a long time. More recently Decker's Cove has been the home anchorage for Commander Donald MacMillan's Arctic schooner *Bowdoin*.

From 1850 to 1900 the menhaden or porgy-oil business was an important industry on Southport, as it was all along the coast. Besides that, the Southport men were the first in Maine to take to fishing from a dory with hand lines, for cod, in 1858. And they were also the first to use a purse seine to net mackerel, in 1865.

But the old breed of deep-water fishermen was slowly dying out, and lobstering was coming in; a man could live at home, go out every day in a small boat, and still make a good living. Still, there were a few survivals from the old days and there are some today—men who go like gulls or seals searching for the schools of herring and mackerel and whiting; who travel in the dark as easily as in the daylight, and who, in spite of modern equipment that makes their work easier (and more expensive), are still spiritually kin to their prototypes of seventy-five or a hundred or two hundred years ago.

On the whole, however, the face of Southport kept changing—not all at once but gradually, until now it is an island of lobstermen and summer people. There is still one big boat yard; there are also stores, and three year-round post offices marking out the points of the triangle. There is a fire house near Hendrick's Harbor, and a town hall at Ebenecook Harbor. There is a good elementary school, a Methodist church that is active all year round, and there is an

Episcopal church in the summer. Newagen Inn is the principal summer hotel.

Southport's lighthouses are The Cuckolds, off the Cape, and Hendrick's Head, which looks over toward Five Islands and down past Georgetown (and Reid State Park) to the open sea. Squirrel and Mouse Islands, on the Boothbay side, are part of the town of Southport. There are 340 names on the Southport voting list, standing for 340 individuals who find their island life a good one in all particulars.

Squirrel Island

Squirrel Island was the first organized summer resort in Maine; all the others followed after the birth of a brilliant idea conceived on a July day in 1870, when the Ham and Dingley families, out for a picnic, hired a fisherman to sail them to a rocky, spruce-crested island just outside Boothbay Harbor, between Southport and Linekin Neck. They had heard of the island and its spring water; by the time they had spent the day on it, they were in love with it, and that is how it all began.

But these picnickers in their post-Civil War clothes, sailing leisurely out of Boothbay Harbor in a fisherman's yawl, were only a small part of an endless procession that had been coming to Squirrel Island over the years. First, there were Indians, who came as they always did to the islands in the summer for the fishing and hunting and the meetings with other tribes; then the name of the island was a secret and significant thing, known only to them. And the explorers came—Dutch, French, Spanish, and English. In 1583 a vessel called *Little Squirrel* was wrecked on the island and perhaps that gave it the name by which Captain John Smith knew it, and the white settlement that was known to be there in 1622.

Like so many other islands, Squirrel drops into oblivion at the time of the Indian wars. The hard-won pastures were swallowed up by the woods and the cabins crumbled where they stood. In 1739 Colonel David Dunbar came from Scotland with new settlers. But the fighting kept up, with harassment by both Indians and Spaniards, and full-scale violence in the French and Indian Wars. By the time the Revolution began, the islands had been pillaged, bloodied, and burned again and again for over a century. Still, nothing spoiled the Squirrel Island spring, and the island was a common stopping place for all kinds of vessels.

A new wave of pioneers came from England after the Revolution. One was Colonel Samuel Ball, first recorded owner of Squirrel Island. He began clearing the island as fast as he could; he needed the timber, and besides, deep woods could hide Indians. Eventually the lovely bird-haunted forests were completely gone, the great groves of white and yellow birches only a memory. But as always, through everything, the spring kept its purity; the white sand glittered in the island's two coves, and the ocean about it was still crowded with fish.

Amos Gray married Samuel Ball's daughter and later inherited the entire island. In 1820 he traded Squirrel for a farm in Starks. The new owner of the island was William Greenleaf, a highly intelligent and original personality. He was skilled in the finding and use of healing herbs and roots; he had been educated at Waterville College (now Colby); he was a teacher and he had married a woman who was also intelligent and well educated. Squire Greenleaf and his wife were exactly the right sort of people to take over an island and get a great deal out of it. "King William," as people at once began to call him, is still remembered as an ardent admirer of Henry Clay; he admired Clay so much that he wore the same sort of beaver hat and broadcloth coat with brass buttons, and he drank the same kind of brandy.

Greenleaf eventually sold the island to Mr. Ham, one of the picnickers who'd fallen in love with it that July day, and moved to the mainland. He died shortly afterward. It was his wish that he be buried in the shining white sand of Davenport Cove on Squirrel Island, and therein lies a tale:

The crew that was sent with a scow to get the proper sand thought it was all pretty silly. Sand was sand, wasn't it? So they got their load at the handiest place, which wasn't Davenport Cove, and started back. Out of nowhere a squall blew up, the sky got black as slate and the sea the same color under the furious white crests; the crew thought they were all going to the bottom, and they were sure of it when they spotted King William's ghostly figure scudding over the waves and making all kinds of threatening gestures. In a frenzy they shoveled their traitorous sand overboard, every grain, and then looked up to see the rocks of Squirrel Island looming over them. They had blown all the way back again.

Of course they went straight around to Davenport Cove and loaded up with fresh sand. Immediately the sun came out, the sea flattened, and they went home across summery blue waters with the white sand shining on the scow. And nobody ever saw King William's ghost again, though the present caretaker of the island lives in his house.

All this provides a nice contrast with the sedate trips out to the island of prospective buyers, aboard the steamer *Spray*, to choose lots for summer cottages. Ethan Allen Chase, who with Mr. Ham and others was one of the original proprietors of the island in its new incarnation as a summer resort, has left an account of those peaceful, idyllic days when the Civil War was over at last, and no one had yet heard of the atom bomb. He tells of the party taken out from Bath to inspect the island, and of dinner at the Greenleaf house, the only house on the island. After the meal there was an auction of house lots, with land going for only a few dollars a lot.

In 1871 the Maine Legislature allowed twenty-two persons to incorporate under the name of the Squirrel Island Association. A constitution was drawn up, calling for town meetings at which women not only were to be present, but could vote. The constitution also proclaimed the glories of the simple outdoor life, always on a high plane; for instance there was to be no boating on Sundays, no intoxicating liquor *ever*, no spooning. At least there was not supposed to be any spooning, but youth is youth, and summer on the coast of Maine is an exhilarating affair. One Squirrel Islander reflected some years later in the island newspaper that there was more kissing done to the square inch on Squirrel's wharf than in any other place in the world.

Cottage construction was to be kept cheap and plain. It was even better, more in keeping with the aims of the Association, if you camped out on your lot in a tent. No wonder that when Ethan Chase said he was having his lumber planed Mr. Dingley replied with disapproval, "You are too much of an exquisite for the colony." In spite of this chilling reproof, Mr. Chase went right ahead and had his lumber planed, and doubtless his family had fewer splinters than any other on Squirrel.

At first there were serious problems to mar the summers. Mainland communities resented the island one, probably because of its exclusiveness, however innocent, and were reluctant to be helpful, especially in the matter of steamers. These were almost all owned and operated by Boothbay people who very much disliked this group that had come "from away," and set themselves up as a private little town. In those days summer people were not regarded as legitimate prey, so the steamer owners refused to make themselves necessary to the Squirrel people and thus earn a little extra money. At one time the members of the colony had to get off at Mouse and try to find fishing boats to sail them to Squirrel. On Squirrel a flag was run up as a signal when people wanted to leave for the mainland, but nine times out of ten the signal was ignored. But when the steamers did come all the way to Squirrel, one faction of the Association disapproved of Sunday landings and departures.

There was a long-standing argument about taxes between the island and Southport. The summer people felt they were being taxed within an inch of their lives. But that was settled in time, and nowadays part of the island taxes are returned to the corporation.

Soon the famous spring no longer provided enough water for the community, and in the early 1900's the island began getting its water from the Boothbay system. The last ten years of the nineteenth century and the first decade of the twentieth encompassed a rapid succession of changes. There was not only the difference in the water supply; there was telegraph communication with the mainland, to be replaced by the telephone in 1910. A chapel had been built and furnished, there was a post office, a bowling alley, a casino—not for roulette, but for socials and dancing. The island now had concrete walks, a steamboat wharf, and a hotel called the Chase House.

Croquet was played with passionate intensity, as a later generation was to play tennis. Everyone lived outdoors, and the young people lived principally on the sea, swimming, sailing, racing their boats, or rowing the three miles into Boothbay Harbor just for the fun of it. Baseball was a popular sport, and the *avant-garde* faction was introducing golf.

Early in 1900 Frank Dingley, of the Dingley family that picnicked on the island with the Hams that prophetic day, founded the island newspaper, *The Squid*. Principally because of his wit the paper became famous all over the state. Mr. J. B. Ham, Nelson Dingley, and Judge Percival Bonney all contributed largely to the intelligent expansion and development of the colony. Albert Davenport provided its memorial library.

Today the Squirrel Island Association still exists, still holds its annual meetings at which every property owner, man or woman, is entitled to vote. There is a daily boat, and the Squirrel Inn, the present hotel, is open to newcomers. One doesn't have to belong to the Association to visit the island. But today the vision the picnickers saw as they wandered over the ledges and white coves of a bare and almost deserted island is no longer a vision, but something that has been intensely alive for seventy-eight years, during which generation after generation of children has been inoculated for life with the love of islands.

Mouse Island

Tiny Mouse Island, two thousand feet off Juniper Point and a mile out of Boothbay Harbor, has sixteen acres. No one knows whether it is so called because it is so tiny, or because it once had a lot of field mice. It still keeps its forests, when so many islands have lost theirs. Perhaps one reason is that the island has always been loved. A John Adams of Ipswich, Massachusetts, is the first recorded owner. He settled in Boothbay in 1784, and when he died his son inherited the island and promptly moved out there to live. His was the first house on the island, and until 1864 the island was Adams property.

At a later time it was a summer colony. Three Skowhegan men built the Samoset House there in 1877. Until the hotel burned in 1913 the Eastern Steamship Company had a regular stop at Mouse, and the tiny island was the center of the water-bound community around it.

With the hotel gone, the island changed its personality. It was bought by two island-lovers who turned it into a family place. One of them was Mr. Harold Gilpatrick, and the other the noted clergyman Dr. Harry Emerson Fosdick. When Mr. Gilpatrick died, Mr. G. Ellsworth Huggins bought his property. Since then the Huggins and Fosdick families have been neighbors and the sole owners of the island, and here, in a study on the shore, Dr. Fosdick has written many of his books.

The island is not left alone in the winter; there are year-round caretakers, and besides them, the keeper of the light on the island.

RAM ISLAND

Ram is a five-acre scrap of island lying off Linekin Neck in Boothbay Harbor, easily overlooked on the chart among the larger islands, and its common name is overshadowed by that provocative one of the ledges so close by, The Hypocrites. What makes this bit of turf and rock significant is the history of its lighthouse.

Once Ram was simply a very small part of a group that formed a graveyard for many a ship, the archipelago of Fisherman's, Heron, White, Damariscove, and The Hypocrites, and as such its surf drowned its quota of men and pounded to pieces its share of vessels. Then, one night, a lobsterman coming home after dark nearly ran ashore on Ram, but saved himself. After that, in thanksgiving for his second chance at life, he went out to Ram late every afternoon and lit a lantern which he had lashed firmly to some sort of strong support. It was a weak beam, but its tiny spark gave adequate warning through the darkness. He tended his light for a year before he died, not knowing that on the very last night the lantern burned another fisherman was saved by it.

This man took over the job. He improved on the light by building a glass-sided box to hold the lamp. For several years he tended the light until he moved away from that part of the coast. Then a new volunteer hung the lantern high from a dory mast, lighting it at night on his way home from fishing, and extinguishing it when he reached the island on his way out in the morning.

But it wasn't much help in the dense Atlantic fogs, and one morning the solitary man who lived on Fisherman's Island, across the bar, saw through the thinning mist that someone was on Ram. He went across and found a dazed seaman, the only survivor of a ship that had been dashed to pieces on the rocks. The bodies of the rest of the crew were strewn around in the rockweed, a frightful sight which had sent the survivor into a state of shock. He couldn't tell either his name or that of the ship.

It was one more thing to add to the stories of Ram Island, both legendary and true. A whole series of phenomena was reported: the sight of a woman in white holding a lighted torch above her head; the burst of flames as from a burning ship that warned away another vessel, though no charred remains were ever found; the mysterious roar of phantom surf sounding over tranquil seas to let a helmsman know he was too close to the ledges, and the ghostly whistle sounding through a blizzard, and the flash of lightning out of a calm sky to show a skipper the deadly rocks ahead. Over the years many a sober man swore he had received one or more of these weird warnings.

In 1883 the Government established a permanent lighthouse on Ram, and one or two men are stationed there. From the top of its shaft the light shines thirty-six feet above the average high tide, eastward by Pemaquid Point toward Muscongus Bay, southward down between Damariscove and The Cuckolds toward Seguin, northwestward into the approaches to Boothbay Harbor. But the devotion of those solitary men a hundred years and more ago has never been forgotten, and never should be.

Fisherman's Island

Fisherman's Island, lying between Ram and The Hypocrites, was once a densely wooded and fruitful place which some scholarly traveler named Hypocras, or Hippocras, for its spiced and aromatic wine. This suggests an abundance of wild grapes. There must have been game too, swimming out from the nearest mainland point; and white-shelled clams for the digging, lobsters to be found under the rockweed at low tide, and fish wherever a net or line was dropped.

John Smith knew this island, and so did the other English explorers. Myles Standish visited it. The great chief Samoset once owned it. His name for it is long forgotten, but the name Hypocras has not quite disappeared along with the forests and the grapes and the game; it lives today in the name of the nearby ledges, The Hypocrites.

Today Fisherman's Island has only a few spruces, and above the surf breaking on the granite ledges the daisies dance in June. The island is dominated by a massive gray house built of stone collected on the island, and made to resemble a medieval Scottish manor house. It would look familiar to the early European travelers, if they should suddenly materialize. They would never recognize their beloved Hypocras, but they might think their compass had gone mad in mid-ocean and led them back to the Hebrides, and a glimpse of some island chief's stronghold.

This establishment is known as Greystones Hall, and it is the summer residence of Dr. John Henry Wilson, a Unitarian minister from New Hampshire. At least, it is used as such during July and August. But in May, June, and September it serves quite another purpose, whose story begins some time before 1925.

Dr. Wilson had been studying the monastic orders in this country and in Europe. He believed fervently that Protestant clergymen needed a place in which to find healing solitude and new spiritual strength for the demands of their ministry. Dr. Wilson knew the Boothbay Harbor area well, and he knew that Fisherman's Island lay deserted, except for one man whom he had known for years; Tom MacAfee, who lived alone on the island in his family's 200-year-old house, and went lobstering from there. Dr. Wilson bought Fisherman's Island in 1925, thinking not only of a summer home for his growing family but of an ideal spot in which to conduct interdenominational retreats.

He felt that Protestant clergyman would not only find rest there, but, in his own words, "a greater understanding and profounder appreciation for and of each other in their common parish work in the great work they were doing for human souls." With this in mind, he had Greystones Hall built, in 1929 and 1930, and held the first Retreat in September of 1930, with a dozen clergymen present.

Since then over 220 clergymen, of various Protestant denominations, have come to Fisherman's Island to find what Dr. Wilson hoped they would find. There have been seventy-three Retreats in all. An order called the Brothers of the Way was founded in 1935 by seventeen ministers, with Dr. Wilson as the first prior. There must be a Brother present at each Retreat, though the clergymen who come need not belong to the order.

Tom MacAfee, the last lobsterman on Fisherman's Island, had an important place in Dr. Wilson's scheme. He was the first bell-ringer of the Retreat, sounding the old ship's bell to call the men together for prayer, music, talk, or food. The bell still rings today, and the necessary chores are shared by all.

Damariscove

The world of Captain John Smith and of the Pilgrims knew a certain group of islands lying west of the mouth of the Damariscotta River as Damarill's Isles. It included the islands now known as Fisherman's, Outer and Inner Heron, and Big and Little White, and Damariscove. Damarill's Isles suffered a sea change into Damariscove, the name borne today by one long, slim, and barren island. Humphrey Damarill, who once owned the group, died in Boston around 1650. The records say nothing about him, beyond the date of his death and the fact that he was a seaman. It is likely that he came over from England in the wave of exploration that swept these shores in the first decade of the 1600's, and bought this group of islands from friendly Indians.

It is certain that the island of Damariscove was a trading center for English, French, and Dutch vessels long before the arrival of the *Mayflower*. John Smith found it a busy place when he stopped there on his voyage to New England in 1614. In 1622, Edward Winslow came up the Maine coast from Plymouth looking for help for the hungry Pilgrims. Damariscove must have had a thriving white settlement, for he wrote of his visit: "I found kind entertainment and good respect with a willingness to supply our wants and would not take any bills for same but did what they could freely."

As children we absorbed a picture of the Pilgrims stepping ashore to face a wilderness absolutely untouched except at Jamestown. In reality there were a number of established and quite prosperous settlements to the north, founded by men who go quite unnoticed in the history books, but who were glad to give aid and comfort to the struggling little group at Plymouth. Winslow met the same hospitable and open-handed attitude everywhere on his trip north. On this same trip he received from Samoset a good supply of the corn his tribe had stored at Pemaquid; the Indians seem to have given help as freely as the white men did.

Massachusetts took over the entire Province of Maine in 1658; in 1672 fifteen Damariscove men were among the ninety-six signers of a petition to the Massachusetts General Court, praying for a little

The Middle Coast · 127

more attention. They were being neglected and slighted up there to the north, they said, in favor of the newer settlements around Massachusetts Bay. They wanted their children educated, a clergyman provided, a market for their fish. They received a little help, being allowed to form a county of their own called Devon, with the court and county seat at Pemaquid, but they still felt cut off from the mainstream of benefits, and continued to agitate for their rights until the terrible year of 1675, when the Indians decided to make a clean sweep.

As Woolwich and Arrowsic burned, the coastal colonists took to their boats, fleeing out from Sheepscot, Damariscotta, Pemaquid, and Corbin's Sound. Monhegan would be safe, they thought, but the winds were wrong, and the small boats could not get out by Damariscove. Other refugees, from Newagen (now Southport) and Arrowsic, had already reached the island, and soon there were three hundred people clustered on the shores, bereft of all their possessions, not knowing if the Indians would come out there after them or not, and all the time gazing back with stunned eyes at the blaze that was devouring their homes.

No one knows why the Indians did not come out to Damariscove; perhaps they thought three hundred persons were too many to tackle, especially since the men would have taken their muskets along if nothing else. The other islands were raided, and the Damariscove refugees found on them burned homes and dead bodies. Later the group moved southward to Massachusetts and beyond. But there were settlers again on Damariscove as soon as the French and Indian Wars were over: some were descendants of the first.

From Damariscove, men watched the battle of the British frigate *Boxer* and the American ship *Enterprise* on September 5, 1814. The British ship surrendered after a thirty-five-minute battle, and both young captains died in what seems a tragic waste of the finest material. The English commander, Blythe, died first; the American, Burroughs, who had never before been under fire, lived long enough to receive the sword of the dead Englishman. The two young men were buried with all honors side by side in Portland.

The island of Damariscove has changed a good deal since John Smith saw it. It was once heavily wooded, with nut trees and grapevines bearing plentifully in their seasons. A few hundred years of sea-action have worn it down to the granite skeleton in many places, so that it becomes two islands at high tide, and is only a quarter of a mile in width to its two-mile length. However, the fresh-water pond from which the settlers probably fetched their drinking water home is still there, with pond lilies floating on it today. Several old houses are left.

Nowadays no one lives on the island. Nine men are stationed there at Coast Guard Life Boat Station Number Eight, manning the lookout tower twenty-four hours a day, but they cannot be said to be residents. Transient lobstermen live there by spells; they know about the cranberries that cover the ground in autumn, about the seabirds sheltering in the quiet coves, and about the dawn and dusk silences. They also know that it is hard to land on Damariscove for those who don't know the way. The reef called The Motions, on the westerly side, is enough to frighten anyone when there is any sea at all. The reef lies just off the harbor, in which an old stone wharf is the single monument to the early and exciting days when Damariscove thrived.

Many an ignorant seafarer is supposed to have drowned off The Motions, only to go on screaming forever out of the surf when the wind is from a certain quarter. All this goes with the stories about the pond, supposedly bottomless, into which Captain Kidd dropped his treasure, and the heavy chain he put across the harbor mouth to keep people out. If a pirate did actually visit Damariscove and toss his loot into the pond, it might have been Lowe or Lattimore, or Dixey Bull. The latter, an English gentleman, came originally to New England to help develop Gorges' York patent. He turned pirate in 1632 as an act of revenge for a French attack on his schooner, and later began to attack English ships as well as French ones. His crowning exploit was to sack the town of Pemaquid, and he could very well have visited Damariscove at that time, but it is doubtful whether he would have bothered to unload any of his plunder here.

There *are* ghosts on Damariscove, however: a woman with flowing fair hair has been seen walking into the pond, and a headless man occasionally sits down beside someone who is peacefully contemplating the sea. The innocent contemplative (in one instance a workman on the Coast Guard project there) becomes conscious that someone has joined him; he looks around to nod pleasantly and discovers that his companion has no head. Sometimes the headless man has a dog with him. He is said to be Captain Richard Pattishall, who was killed by Indians aboard his own ship on August 2, 1689. His body was beheaded and thrown into the sea, and his dog jumped in after the body. Since Pattishall owned Damariscove after the death of Humphrey Damarill in 1650, it is entirely appropriate that he and his dog should have been guarding the island for almost three hundred years; but to share a log with him would be unnerving.

THE ISLANDS OF MUSCONGUS BAY

IF THE IMAGINARY BOUNDARIES of Muscongus Bay were to be squared, the compass points would be: Port Clyde to the east, Monhegan to the south, Pemaquid to the west, and Waldoboro to the north. In this square lie more than forty islands, large and small, inhabited and deserted. Some of the names have an odd charm: Hungry, Cranberry, Thief, Friendship, Haddock, and Wreck. And let's not forget Jones Garden, and Otter Island. One of these rare, playful, intelligent little animals was seen recently on Gay's Island, which is close enough to Otter to give body to the supposition that once there were many sea-otters in the neighborhood.

Then there are the island names that are memorials to long-ago settlers (who still have many descendants in the region); Morse, Franklin, Davis, Hall, Hooper, Allen, Caldwell, Teel, Ross, Barter, Thompson, McGee, Seavey, Gay's. Some of these last-named are called the Georges Islands, because they stream southward from the mouth of the St. George River. It was this river, unnamed then of course, up which Captain George Weymouth sailed in 1605, on a voyage of exploration. He had been sent out in his ship the *Archangel* by the Earl of Southampton.

The *Archangel* anchored in Muscongus Bay, probably off Allen's Island, early in May, and a Whitsunday service was held on the island, the first Anglican service in New England. Later Weymouth went exploring among the islands and up the river in a smaller boat, and his scribe, James Rosier, wrote glowingly of this lovely bay. A cross called the Weymouth Cross has been placed on Allen's Island.

Harbor Island is marked by an old stone house where at a later time Mistress McCobb beat off some looting English sailors with a beanpole. They went, too. Her husband Samuel, who had built the house, was away at the time as a soldier in the Continental Army. They say there is treasure on Caldwell; and on Teel Island, where one ancient oak tree towers against the sky, Andrew Wyeth painted old Henry Teel looking seaward from his kitchen windows. The Teels had held their island since George II granted it to Adam Teel, and it has just recently gone out of the family. After Henry, known as "Hen," died, none of the young ones wanted to live there.

There stood until recently on Gay's Island a house said to have been built in 1694. Garrison Island once had a garrison on it, protecting Friendship. To the westward Bremen attracts yachtsmen. There is a thriving weir at Cranberry, and on most of the islands lobstermen live, with only a small lacing of summer people among them. Muscongus Bay is not a popular summer place, and in many ways it has kept incorruptible its essential character.

Loud's Island

Loud's Island is one of those islands which has never forgotten its history. Cellar holes on some of the islands are a silent reproach to those who pick blueberries around them without knowing or caring who was born there or who may have died in this very spot under Indian tomahawks. But Loud's Island knows its place in Time. Once it was called Samoset's Island, for it was that great chief's home. Later it was known as Muscongus Island.

Captain George Weymouth's useful voyage of exploration for

the Earl of Southampton ended rather disgracefully when he kidnaped five Indians who had approached him in all innocence and friendship. Three of them he handed over to Sir Ferdinando Gorges, back in England, and one of the three is believed to have been Samoset. Captain John Smith described the Wawenocks, the tribe of the Muscongus region to which Samoset belonged, as strong, healthy, active, mentally superior to other tribes, and very witty. With all these natural gifts Samoset made the most of his enforced stay in England, learning English and studying the peculiar habits of the white men. He made friends, too, and found men whom he could respect as equals. He was well treated and eventually returned to America, and forever afterward was a friend to the English.

When he became sachem of the tribes in the Muscongus region, he kept the peace so well between his people and the settlers, and his integrity was so well known, that Muscongus Island seems to have been spared the massacres that decimated the settlements on other islands or wiped them out altogether. Samoset and another chief sold a large parcel of land, including the island, to John Brown of New Harbor in 1625, but he continued to live there off and on, and he is buried there.

After the French and Indian Wars, new people began to flock to Maine. One of them was a retired British naval officer named William Loud, who came to Muscongus with a Mr. Bishop, and found this forested island beautiful and good. It is a lovely island today, in the contours of its land, the ins and outs of its rocky shores, and with its view out over a bay starred with islands as its meadows are starred with wild flowers in summer. So imagine it in 1750, when there were still remnants of great groves of hardwoods that must have made Loud think of the English woods he had known.

His deed to Muscongus Island from Shem Drowne is still on record, and a descendant still has Loud's commission from Governor Shirley. But his grave is unmarked on the island, and it is his son who is remembered almost as vividly as if he had died just the other day.

William Solomon Loud grew up on the island, fished, and eventually had his own ship. He seems to have been a healthy, handsome extrovert who sang at the top of his lungs when he stood at the wheel of the *Laughing Mary*. Everyone knew when William Solomon was coming up to his home anchorage after a good sale of wood in Boston; if the wind was right they could hear him for miles.

Eventually he was the father of four sons and five daughters, and was known as Captain Sol. On one of his trips he stopped at Portsmouth and hired a young carpenter named Robert Oram to come to the island to build a house for him. His was to be the first frame house on the island. This was about the year 1800, and evidently the islanders were still living in log houses at that time.

Something else develops from Robert Oram's arrival on Loud's Island: the fact that the island belonged to no mainland town and by some slip-up had been left off official maps of the time. There it lay off Bristol, a complete little continental nation in itself, much amused by the whole business. "Did ye ever set foot on foreign sile before?" one old man dryly asked Robert Oram.

Young Oram found plenty of work to do there, for then as now carpenters were hard to come by. He stayed on the island, married Captain Sol's daughter Mary, and raised ten children. Oram was what used to be called a man of parts. He was well educated, so that he could teach school when there was no teacher. He was a deacon in the church. He was a thoughtful and progressive farmer.

Robert Oram hated liquor. Though many a house he planned, including Captain Sol's, went up on a tide of rum, he refused to raise his own house thus. And the neighbors refused to help without rum. There was great firmness on both sides for over a year, but finally the deacon won out and the house went up, probably on deep refreshing draughts of non-alcoholic switchel. At least the helpers were spared headaches the next morning.

The Baptist church was organized about 1794, and Elder Edward Dunbar is believed to have been the first pastor on the island. But interest in religion slacked off, other denominations rose and fell, and by the time of the Civil War there was practically no church activity. There was instead a great and all-consuming interest in the war, complicated by the island's peculiar political status.

As an island without a country, Muscongus had nevertheless good-naturedly paid taxes to Bristol and voted there until the presidential election of 1860. For some reason, which delights us as a demonstration of rugged individualism, Muscongus turned in a solidly Democratic vote which appalled solidly Republican Bristol. So the Bristol selectmen performed one of those feats of legerdemain in which politicians have always exhibited such artistic skill, and decided that if Muscongus wasn't on the maps it did not exist, and therefore its vote did not exist either. The Muscongus ballots went into the fire, Bristol remained incorruptibly Republican, and Muscongus began talking loudly about taxation without representation and recalling the Stamp Act and the Boston Tea Party. However, rather than set up as a new nation, the islanders decided to ignore Bristol and still be loyal to the United States.

Bristol, after nonchalantly throwing out Muscongus's vote, just as nonchalantly drew heavily on the island's men to fill out her draft quota for the Union Army. In fact, the choice was so much out of proportion that it caused deep suspicion on Muscongus. Nine men from the island, out of forty-five for the whole district? It didn't look like an innocent slip-up in somebody's arithmetic.

A uniformed major was landed on the island to pick up the nine men, who had failed to show up in Bristol. The first name on his list was Carter. He was directed to Carter's house, probably by someone who followed along to see the fun. Carter was out fishing, but Mrs. Carter was cooking potatoes. The major made himself known and demanded Carter, whereupon Mrs. Carter lobbed a hot potato at him, and then another and another. The major returned to his boat, and left the island. No one came back from Bristol to collect the nine.

In the meantime the island hired lawyer Chamberlain to go to Augusta and find out what was what. He discovered that Bristol had no right to draft Loud's Islanders, so they had a draft among themselves and chose three men, who in turn bought substitutes. It constitutes some sort of record for a Yankee community that no islander enlisted during the war, and that all those drafted bought substitutes instead. Not strange, perhaps, when we consider that almost solid Democratic vote, which meant they were not Lincoln men. Yet they said they were loyal to the United States.

Stateless, they had to struggle to provide a school and teacher for their children. This had been their chief expense until the Civil War, met by renting fishing privileges to fishermen from New London. The first schoolhouse was roughly built of stones, the next was of brick; here Robert Oram taught his own children and the others. In 1871 the first frame schoolhouse was built, and it is still *the* school.

One of the memorable teachers in this school was the Reverend Hannah Powell. She was also the first pastor of the non-denominational "Brotherhood Church" and laid the cornerstone when the church was erected on the hill in 1913. The church has an interesting history, which we have mentioned earlier; for it was the former schoolhouse on Malaga, built through the efforts of the Lane family on the promise of the state to send a teacher to that unhappy island. When the islanders of Malaga were taken to the mainland to live, Alexander MacDonald of the Maine Sea Coast Mission asked the state for the schoolhouse. It was gladly given, and in two days the building had been taken down, loaded on a schooner, and brought to Loud's Island. The men of the island turned to with their horses and oxen to do the heavy work of rebuilding. Soon Loud's Island had a church on the hill, with living quarters for the minister. Hannah Powell, energetic and much beloved, remained for a number of years as both pastor and teacher.

For many years after her departure Mrs. Lettie Prior taught the school, simultaneously raising a large family in a big house on the northern end of the island. She is retired from teaching now, but continues her civic service as postmistress. Her son, Cecil Prior, carries passengers, mail, and other essentials back and forth in his lobster boat between the island and Round Pond on the mainland.

Now Muscongus, or Loud's Island—post office, Loudville—definitely belongs to the "cont'nent." Maine has adopted it as unorganized territory, and thus the school is supported by the state, which looks after its schools very well indeed. Officially the island is a part of Lincoln County, and records its births and deaths and other important events in Bristol. But it pays its taxes in Augusta. Once more the islanders vote in Bristol at national and state elections, but have no part in the local elections.

In 1917 it was suggested by the Maine State Board of Assessors that the islanders might like to form a municipal government, but they didn't think so. They had been getting along peaceably for several hundred years without a government; why borrow trouble? And so they've continued to get along, tranquilly and co-operatively, the Louds, Pryors, Orams, Carters, Polands, Hoffses, Osiers, and the rest, maintaining the island's reputation for self-containment and self-sufficiency, looking after each other and keeping their own and the state's laws.

Hog Island

Hog Island lies in the upper part of Muscongus Bay, a few minutes' row off Hockamock Point at the northern end, and with Loud's Island lying off the southern end. It is a mile and a half long, and the greatest elevation is ninety feet. Sometimes the granite bones of the island show in lichen-scaled ledges out in the open, or in mosy rock formations in the ferny woods that look like something to be found in a Japanese temple garden. Its woods of spruce, pine, and balsam are deep and unspoiled. Birds and animals are the chief citizens, and the only shooting is done with a camera. The paradoxical thing is that thousands of persons from all over the United States, Canada, and some foreign countries know more about the island than most of the people in the State of Maine. For in spite of its graceless name, Hog is a lovely and unspoiled wilderness area, the Todd Wildlife Sanctuary, maintained by the Audubon Society.

The vision that saw Hog as a small but perfect sea-bounded Eden appeared first to Mrs. David Todd. On a summer day in 1908, the Todd family were cruising the Maine coast, and put in at Hog Island. They were appalled to see that a forty-acre strip had just been cut through the woodland, leaving a wasteland of stumps and dead brush, dispossessing crowds of birds and small animals. It was said that the whole island was to be cleared. Mrs. Todd felt the tragedy of this with a particular poignancy, and bought a part of the island to keep at least one section of it unviolated.

Mr. Todd was a professor of astronomy at Amherst College, and as a teacher he could move his family to Hog Island each summer, where they lived in a cabin and were as close to nature as modern man can be. After 1919, when the inn on the island closed, the Todds spent their summers there alone. Mrs. Todd studied the crowded, varied life of wood and seashore. Their small daughter knew the birds even before she could read and write, and wandered the woods as familiarly as the birds themselves. When Mrs. Todd died in 1932 she was just finishing a book, *The Epic of Hog*.

After her death, her daughter, now Mrs. Bingham, owned, with

Dr. James M. Todd of New York, three-quarters of the island. She wanted others to enjoy and love it as she did, but for a long time her dream of preserving it for the public seemed a hopeless one. The people who owned the inn and the disused bungalows were willing to sell, but Mrs. Bingham could find no one to buy. Maine bird clubs and natural history societies were eager, but none had any money. Dr. James Todd offered to buy the property and give it to any organization that would use it, but the cost of repairing the buildings would have been prohibitive; nobody could afford to accept the offer.

Then the owners of the unsold land decided to clean off their trees and realize what they could for them. Mrs. Bingham, to whom each part of the woods was dear and familiar, made one last passionate effort. She talked to Dr. Robert Cushman Murphy of the American Museum of Natural History. Dr. Murphy had an idea. He brought together Mrs. Bingham and John Hopkinson Baker, executive director of the National Audubon Society.

"Just what I want," said Mr. Baker at once. He too had a dream, it seemed—a dream of a camp where teachers and non-professional adults could come and study nature, in groups of fifty, for two weeks at a time throughout the summer. Mrs. Bingham, seeing her mother's dream and her own so close to coming true, used her mother's insurance money to buy the last quarter of the island. She leased all her part of the land to the Society for a dollar a year, and Dr. Todd gave his land outright. In just a few weeks the dream was truly realized; the Todd Wildlife Sanctuary was established.

In 1936 the camp opened. Two hundred and twenty-three persons came that first summer, ranging in age between seventeen and seventy. Since then more than five thousand people have come, from all the states, from many Canadian provinces, and from foreign countries. The Hog Island camp has been a pioneer; because of its success, the Society has started three more camps in other parts of the country.

Because a cruising boat stopped at Hog Island on one significant day, because a woman was appalled by destruction and then determined, in the way of women, that there should be no more destruction if *she* could help it, and because a daughter dreamed her mother's dream, Hog Island is what it is today, more than just an island in the geographical sense, but a spiritual island, where a man can remember humbly and with wonder his original kinship with the natural world around him.

MONHEGAN

When John Smith landed on Monhegan in 1614, this island lying at an almost equal distance from New Harbor to the northwest and Port Clyde to the north was already well known to seafaring men. If the rocky heights of the island and the adjacent hump of Manana could give out all the voices they have heard over the years as men made anchorage in the harbor, climbed the slopes, and walked the cliffs, made maps of the area, caught and dried fish, built ships, grew gardens, and wrote in their journals, the air would be filled with the babel of Norse, Basque, Breton, Spanish, Portuguese, English, and, before them all, a mixture of Indian dialects. For like all the islands, this one which they called "Island of the Sea" was a part of the Indians' lost paradise.

Though one school of thought maintains that the Vikings never touched anywhere in Maine, but sailed by to Massachusetts on their voyages around 1000 A.D., there are runic figures carved on Manana's ledges that are believed to be a sort of Norse version of "Kilroy was here." Anyway, seeing the narrow slot of harbor between Monhegan and Manana on a blustery day, with the southeast wind blowing up through and tossing the boats at their heavy moorings, it is easy to imagine a long ship run ashore on a steep bit of beach, the great square sail furled and the oarsmen swarming up the steep slopes where now island dooryards brim with civilized flowers, and the artists outnumber the fishermen.

John Cabot dropped anchor in this harbor in 1497. The Italian navigator Verrazano, working for France, knew it well in 1524. A Spaniard, Gomez, lay in its lee in 1525. An Englishman named Rut, a French priest named André Thevet, Sir Humphrey Gilbert, Bartholomew Gosnold, Champlain, and Captain George Weymouth had all visited the island by 1605. They were interested in trading with the Indians for furs; in the fishing; and, at least in the case of the Englishmen, in the prospects for colonization.

By 1611 Monhegan was a well-known landmark to seafaring men, and a well-known name to men in England who, like Ferdinando Gorges, had their hearts in the New World even though by some ironic circumstance they were never to set foot on that romantic soil. Monhegan was general headquarters for exploring expeditions, a place where European fishermen came to spend the summers catching and drying the huge cod, and where traders waited to buy furs from the Indians of the bay, who came in their sea canoes to paddle among the anchored vessels and do business with the bearded, jack-booted Englishmen. Those white men who had learned some of the Indian language asked questions about the life and customs of the red men, and sent home written reports to English scholars for whom the savage races of America held a never-ending fascination. Of course they also sent home business reports to their sponsors, men like Gorges and the Earl of Southampton, the first Earl of Stirling, and companies formed of wealthy merchants.

In 1614 came the greatest publicity man of them all, John Smith, sailing up into the North Atlantic on a typical grand search—"for gold and whales"; but he would settle for a shipload of Monhegan cod. Smith writes a good deal about Monhegan, mentions "Monanis" as close by it—how did that ever come to be Manana, unless it was the Spanish or Portuguese influence?—and one charming note, which shows "Captain Jack" had not forgotten that his father was a farmer, says: "I made a garden on the top of the rocky isle of Monhegan in May that grew so well that it served for sallets in June and July."

We still plant in May for our summer sallets, as John Smith did. Some things never change; the fish flakes still stand open to the sky on the island slopes as they did three hundred years and more ago.

John Smith had seven ships built at Monhegan, in addition to growing sallets. In 1619 the first permanent settlement of the island

The Middle Coast · 139

was begun, and was well established and comfortably fixed when Edward Winslow came up from Plymouth in 1622, seeking aid from the older settlements for the Pilgrims. As the other islanders, such as the Damariscove men, had done before them, the Monhegan men gave freely and refused payment. The next year they helped the Weymouth (Massachusetts) colony in the same way.

On the petition which the settlers along the coast and on the islands east of the Kennebec sent to the Massachusetts General Court on May 18, 1672, asking for help, eighteen of the ninety-six signers' names belong to Monhegan men; when the Devon county court was set up at Pemaquid, Monhegan had nine officers out of the appointed thirty-three. This alone shows the size and importance of the Monhegan settlement.

The island must have seemed a sophisticated center of trade and travel in those days, what with the constant arrival of ships from England that made this their first stop, the busy traffic of smaller vessels for whom Monhegan was home port, the shipbuilding and the fur trading and the fisheries.

Until the 1670's the settlement had had nothing to do but grow. Even when the Indian troubles broke out on the mainland and adjacent islands, Monhegan seemed safe. Settlers with nowhere to flee from Indian attack but seaward sailed out to Monhegan for sanctuary. But at last the terror threatened to reach Monhegan, and in 1676 the settlement was broken up. The islanders sailed west to Salem and Boston.

It was almost a hundred years before the island came to life again. In 1770 the Bickford family of Beverly, Massachusetts, bought it for 160 pounds from Thomas Drowne, son of the Shem Drowne who sold Muscongus Island to William Loud in 1750. In 1790 the Bickfords sold the island to Henry Trefethren of Kittery, the son of Welsh or Cornish emigrants. He gave the island to his son, and young Henry went there to live. He got his two brothers-in-law to move their families out there too. These three who came to the island as young men—and how they must have loved it—owned it between them for years, and today the descendants of Henry Trefethren, Francis Horn (Orne), and Josiah Starling still own parts of Monhegan.

Monhegan has had its great houses; one is the Trefethrens', elegantly square and dignified. And then there was the Pink House. Josiah Starling, Jr., was the jolly and reckless person who painted his house pink. (Monhegan must have been destined for an artists' colony from the very first.) The Pink House stood in its pinkness until it was partly torn down and rebuilt into the Island Inn. The lobby of the Inn is a room from the original house. The first clapboard house on the Island, built in 1800, is still there, used as a summer home.

In the old part of the cemetery are still other links with Monhegan's past: the graves of the Starlings, Horns, and Trefethrens, including the inevitable and pathetic markers for babies like Phebe Starling, aged one month, and Mary Starling, who grew to be two years and six months old.

The Monhegan library, which is a busy spot, for reading is not a lost art on islands, has a rather poignant origin. The wife of a former Governor of Maine, Mrs. John Fremont Hill, started the foundation fund in memory of two children who were swept off the rocks by the surf on August 10, 1926. They were Jacqueline Stewart Barstow, ten years old, and Edward Winslow Vaughn, who was fourteen. The book plate which is placed in each juvenile book reads, "Jackie and Edward's library to the children of Monhegan."

In 1941 the Monhegan men imposed a six months' closed season upon their lobstering business, beginning in June. From then through December they go hand-lining, trawling, or seining. "Trap Day," the opening of the lobster season, is on or about the first of January, depending on the weather, and it is one of the high occasions of the year.

The fishermen of Monhegan maintain their own artistic integrity, and are very much themselves despite the exotic invasion every summer. *Exotic* is the correct word, to judge from the picturesque raiment and the number of beards—not of the John Smith variety—seen about the wharf when the boat is due, or at the boardinghouse called "The Trailing Yew," rallying point for the abstractionists who have discovered Monhegan. In times past George Bellows, Robert Henri, and Rockwell Kent, to name only a few, lived and painted on Monhegan; recently Andrew Winter, who had for a long time lived all year round on the island, died. These men found an unending source of subject matter in the constantly changing pattern of man, rock, and ocean. Today if one sees an artist working at an easel on the rocks, now and then squinting professionally at the horizon, he is likely to be painting things never yet seen on land or sea.

In the winter the village narrows down to about sixty-four natives. School affairs and the services at the church keep life from getting dull. Social activity in any season centers around the Odums' store, and the wharf when Captain Earl Field's mailboat, the *Laura B.*, is due from Port Clyde. She makes two trips a day in summer, one daily in spring and fall, and three trips a week in winter. With her arrival, everyone then moves to the post office, another important spot on the island.

Nearby Manana is fortunate enough to have a genuine hermit who enjoys a tranquil existence tending his sheep. Ray Phillips is a cheerful personality about whom many stories are told. He is remarkably photogenic, and serves as the inspiration for a charming book by Yolla Niclas, *The Island Shepherd*. It is more than a children's book, for the photographs show the magnificent sweep and scope of the Monhegan setting.

Botanists say there are over six hundred varieties of wild flowers on thousand-acre Monhegan. More than two hundred bird species have been logged. Like all islands it has plenty of edible berries growing wild, but supposedly unique to Monhegan is the plant called the trailing yew, which is really a variety of cedar.

Monhegan's light, set in a tower of granite on the height of the island, where Captain Jack and the other early travelers climbed to look out to sea for the first glimpse of ships from home, had always had a resident keeper until 1959, when it was made automatic, and is now controlled from the Coast Guard station on Manana, where there is a foghorn and a radio beacon. And now the unsheltered harbor, little more than a gash between Monhegan and Manana, where tremendously heavy moorings have always been necessary, is to have a breakwater.

On the east the cliffs, Black Head and White Head, rise to a hundred and sixty feet. There is always surf there. A woman disappeared off those cliffs a few years ago, and in 1958 a small child and two women died here, and a third woman nearly died as she tried to save them.

The village of Monhegan lies over on the west side, away from the wild windswept fields and precipitate rocks of the east, with Manana to help break the wind. In between are the Cathedral Woods. They are deep and quiet, as their name implies, and yet if you stand still and listen long enough you will know that the silence is really made up of many things; the thin, distant crying of gulls, the slow seething of the wind through the trees, and the far-off rote of the sea on the shores. And if you wait and listen a little longer, you will think of all the others who have heard the same sounds, from the Indians and the Norsemen to the Basque and Breton fishermen, from the Elizabethan adventurers to young Henry Trefethren, and they will no longer be names in a book but your brothers.

[IV]

Penobscot Bay

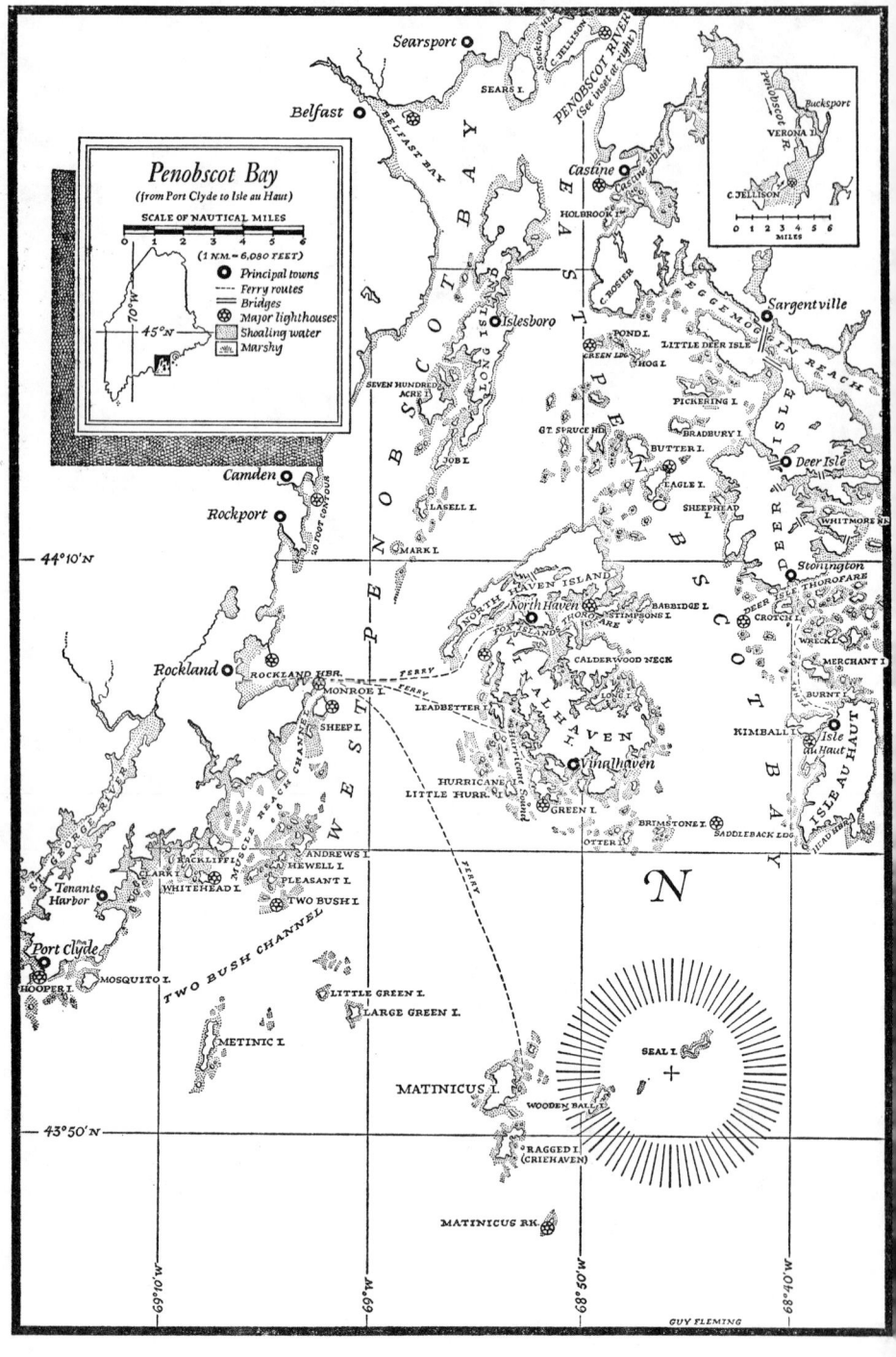

MATINICUS

Matinicus lies twenty miles south of Rockland, a vile trip in a gale, when Penobscot Bay is a hissing, tumbling white hell for those who must head straight toward the outermost limits to get home. Not that the trip is always a stormy one. On a calm, sunny morning the bay is a poetically blue sea fringed by shimmering green islands, reminiscent of the isles of Greece, rising like enchanted mountaintops—which, of course, they are—out of the shining water.

Making that trip no matter what the weather, there is always an emotional upswing for the traveler when at last he sees the wooded shape of Matinicus looming dimly through the spray and rain over the plunging bow of the *Mary A*. It used to be the *Calista D. Morrill*; and she was only one of the procession of boats, large and small but all bold, that went straight out into the biggest bay of them all: snows, pinks, schooners, sloops, mail packets, steamboats, naphtha launches.

From about 1920 you made the trip with Captain Stuart Ames, himself a Matinicus man; and no matter how wild the bay looked from either Rockland harbor or Matinicus, you knew that if Stuart thought it was all right to go, it *would* be all right. You'd make it. Something might happen halfway, like the time the *Calista* broke down and drifted all night in the fog. She was carrying children bound for school on the mainland, and a number of adults who watched with horrified fascination as the great searchlight of the Boston boat bore down on them out of the fog. All shouted as one to augment the reedy bleat of the boat's horn till the steamer sheered off, leaving the drifting *Calista* rocking in her wake. But you would make it eventually and with a whole, if wet, skin. Stuart never lost a trip. Now Stuart, Jr., in the *Mary A.*, is vainly trying to outgrow being called "little Stuart."

The name Matinicus, says one school, means "Place of Many Turkeys." Another says it was orginally Manasquesicook, meaning "A collection of grassy islands." Well, there might once have been wild turkeys on Matinicus, in the bright morning of the world when there was plenty of everything; and on the other hand Matinicus certainly was once one of a cluster of grassy islands, even if by now great fires and constant nesting of cormorants and gulls have killed off the vegetation of some of the little islands in this group at the entrance to Penobscot Bay.

The Vikings may have landed on Matinicus looking for fresh water and seabirds; French fishermen were there in the sixteenth century, leaving behind them remains of stone huts. But the first definite mention of the island is in John Josselyn's journals.

This English traveler came to America first as a young man in 1638 to visit his brother Henry (who later became Lieutenant-Governor of the Province of Maine). John lived in Scarboro with his brother for a year, and then went home, but he returned again a long time later, in 1663. He stayed for eight years this time, traveled widely, talked, listened, observed, and set down the sum of his impressions in a book called *New Englands Rareties*. Unfortunately this book put him in bad odor with the Puritans at Boston because of some of his remarks about them, so it was impossible to obtain his book in this country. Also, since he recorded a good many legends, superstitions, and ancient remedies, and described flora and fauna that were never heard of—except by the people who told him about them—he has been in bad repute with more modern authorities. But some of his tall tales have been proved to be not so tall at that. A great deal of his work describes actual places and events; he visited Matinicus in 1671, and wrote that the island was "well supplied with homes, cattle, arable land, and marshes."

Many others besides Josselyn visited the island. In 1728 William Vaughan of Damariscotta established a fishing station there. Vaughan is famous in New England history for having persuaded Governor Shirley of Massachusetts to send out the 1745 expedition against the fortress of Louisbourg which William Pepperell of Appledore and Kittery led. Vaughan had a stake in the expedition, for French privateers, based at Louisbourg were ranging the coast making trouble for his fishing fleet.

All through this period the Indians came out to the Matinicus group regularly to fish, kill birds, and collect eggs, apparently on a peaceful basis. But by 1757 Vaughan's fishing station had seemingly disappeared and there was only one family on the island—enough to invite a full-fledged massacre (of one man).

Ebenezer Hall of Portland had settled on Matinicus in 1751, building himself a stone house. He had married the widow Green, who had a son Daniel, fourteen. There were two little girls in the home also, either Hall's daughters or his wife's. Hall's grown son by his first wife, young Ebenezer, was off fishing outside Halifax, Nova Scotia, at the time of the massacre.

A party of Indians landed on the island in June, 1757, besieged Hall's stone house, and finally killed him. Daniel had been put out a back window by his stepfather, with three loaded guns. Hall intended to get out too, thinking he and the boy could surprise the Indians at their evening meal and kill them all. But Mrs. Hall held on to her husband in terror, and the result was the death of Ebenezer, while his wife and the little girls were taken into captivity. The boy hid in the woods, and after the Indians had gone he came out and was eventually able to signal a passing schooner. The men helped him bury his stepfather, and then took him to their home port in the Fox Islands.

There are two theories about the affair. One is that the raiders were Tarratines out for scalps, for which the French paid bounty. But if so, why didn't they scalp Mrs. Hall and the two girls? The mother was back home, after long travels and adventures, by 1765; she married again, and lived to be eighty-nine. She never did locate her daughters, though one source says their brother later found them living quite contentedly with the Indians, and that they preferred to stay where they were.

The other theory, substantiated by a letter, is that the Indians were Penobscots who felt they had a right to their fowling and egg-gathering on the islands around Matinicus, but were being driven off by Hall, who kept burning over the fields to improve the hay crop. He had also tried to keep them from their fishing and sealing.

So, after a number of attempts to regain their rights—at first their relations with Hall had been good—they wrote a civil letter to the governor. It was signed by four Indians, Cosemes, Modobt, Chebnood, and Mugdumbawit, on behalf of the Penobscot tribe. Still no one paid any attention to them, so at last they did what they had warned they would do. They took things into their own hands.

Young Ebenezer Hall eventually returned to Matinicus with a wife, after the Treaty of Paris ended the French and Indian Wars in 1763. They raised fifteen children. Mrs. Hall was a Young, and Daniel married her sister. A little family feud shows up here; Daniel asked his stepbrother for part of Matinicus, but Ebenezer offered him such a small bit that Daniel refused, and moved his family to a good-sized island just off the southeast of Vinalhaven. Naturally it became known as Green's Island.

Other Youngs moved out to Matinicus and soon there were so many of them it was said that if you went out and shouted the name "Young!" from the top of Mt. Ararat, overlooking the harbor, practically everyone on the island would answer. Other names have joined this one over the years: Ames, Tolman, Fernald, Condon, Burgess, Marshall, Abbott, Ring, Wallace, Philbrook.

For a long time the early settlement was a part of Vinalhaven. The Matinicus men paid their taxes and voted there, and recorded births, deaths, and marriages. In 1840 the Matinicus Plantation came into existence, including Ragged Island, which was called South Matinicus at the time, or the South Island, and Matinicus Rock.

In those early days there must have been fine farms to make the islanders self-sufficient, but the great industry was codfishing. They caught other fish too, haddock, mackerel, herring—the "silver darlings" that are still the quicksilver wealth of the weirs and the stopped-off coves—and the menhaden, or porgy. But the squires of Matinicus grew well-to-do on cod, dried, salted, and taken away in coasting vessels.

Nowadays there are no farms as such; they are all fishermen on Matinicus, of the rare deep-sea breed who, in spite of fast modern boats with powerful engines, short-wave radios, radio telephones, and Fathometers, would have a great deal in common with those Basque, Breton, Portuguese, and English fishermen who crossed great oceans as casually as we cross streets.

The first schoolhouse on the island was built in 1800, the money raised by subscription. One stratum of the community regarded the teacher as an honored guest and respected his brains; but there seems to have been a rowdy element as well, according to a story of the time when the young men, primed with potent West Indian rum, manhandled the schoolmaster and auctioned him off to the highest bidder.

Matinicus had her share of the West Indies trade, building and outfitting ships to carry salt fish, lumber, and other things that brought a good price in the southern islands. That they brought back rum among other goods and that there was probably a grog shop at the harbor is a perfectly natural fact of the times; rum was as common a drink then as Coca-Cola is now.

There are no written records of an early church on the island, but it is known that the Baptists started a branch there in 1808. No one knows the names of any of the preachers, however, until that of Abram Plummer appears in 1850, when the Methodist Home Missionary Society decided that Matinicus presented fertile ground for any seeds they might sow. The present church was built in 1905. Services are conducted there by ministers in the service of the Maine Sea Coast Missionary Society, and usually there is a minister from the Society on the island for the whole summer.

Matinicus is nearly two and a half miles long and about a mile wide. The western side slopes to the water in long green fields, first cleared a hundred and fifty or more years ago. The eastern side is where the harbor is, and where Ebenezer Hall built his stone house.

Most of the homes on Matinicus now are comfortable and modern, but the past is not forgotten. It lies close enough to touch, in the granite ledge which concealed the Indians who killed Ebenezer Hall; in the old houses like Joseph Young's, built in 1800. Mrs. Scott Young lives in this house today. It is in the traditional Cape Cod style, but with its own particular touches of originality—the graining in the doors, for instance, representing bulrushes in one and a burning bush in another. (Did the builder have a particular fondness for Moses?) There is another door with an opening shaped like two hearts, and an old piano with mother-of-pearl keys, a rare and wondrous treasure, since there were only six more like it in the whole United States.

Matinicus men have always fought in the country's wars, usually volunteering, not waiting to be drafted. No buying of substitutes for *them* in the Civil War. Their island home must have looked particularly satisfying to them on their return; they must have felt, without putting it into words, that they had won it for themselves as surely as their ancestors had won it in the first place.

Matinicus Rock

The Rock: two syllables to stop you in your tracks, hard, uncompromising, final. Try it. The Rock. No one ever speaks of "the light." It's always The Rock, this outermost marker, not only for Penobscot Bay but for the coast of Maine. Thirty-two acres of granite ledge drop off in sheer cliffs on the southerly side, and on the north side is what is euphemistically called The Landing. Boats, which can come in for a landing only when the seas permit, must be hauled up a slip.

The Rock lies five miles south of Matinicus. Seen from a distance it rides the horizon like a heavily armored, antique dreadnought; in other lights, across a calm and pastel sea, it could be a medieval castle built on a high crag. The wind always blows, or so it seems, at Matinicus Rock, and with nothing to break the force of the Atlantic, spray can drench the whole ledge like a savage and blinding rain. In really wild storms surf tumbles over it in a flood.

Yet the birds find this a good safe place in which to raise their young, and the gulls and arctic terns that fly screaming wildly over the visitor's head return the Rock's hospitality by supplying fertilizer when and where needed so that grass and wild flowers may flourish in the thin soil. And let's not forget the puffins of Matinicus Rock, which is the only island along our Atlantic coast where these little sea parrots nest and raise their young in their burrows. Ornithologists from all over the country make summer trips to the Rock to see the puffins—more often than not to be disappointed by not being able to land.

The first lighthouse at Matinicus Rock was built in 1827, a cobblestone dwelling with a wooden tower at each end. In 1847 these towers were taken down, and a granite building with semicircular towers replaced them. Until 1923 there were twin lights, but now there is only one, an electric beacon, where once a great lamp had to be carefully tended by hand. At the point where the light stands, the Rock rises fifty feet out of the sea, which lifts the tower to a soaring ninety-five feet; its light, sweeping the sky, is visible for fifteen miles.

With a head keeper and three assistants, the Rock was always a family station, with children growing up in the white houses washed by sun and spray, finding a dangerous but thrilling playground along the cliffs. In the old days schoolteachers went out to the Rock to live and hold classes, but in modern times the children have gone to the mainland for the school year.

The annals of the Lighthouse Service are full of heroic deeds and Matinicus Rock has its proper share. Abby Burgess in her day, and for as long afterward as her story was passed along by word of mouth, must have been the heroine of all the young girls on the coast. In January, 1856, Abby was seventeen. Her father, the keeper at the Rock, sailed across to Matinicus Island one day—probably one of those deceptively pleasant days that occur sometimes in midwinter. Abby was left alone with her invalid mother and four little sisters. That pleasant day was a weather-breeder, developing with frightening speed into a storm as terrible as that which swept away the tower on Minot's Ledge in 1851. Great seas rushed in from the open ocean, reared, and struck, pouring over the Rock in a tumbling and deadly cascade.

Abby's chicken coop was set among the boulders a little way from the house, and perhaps each little Burgess girl had a pet hen; anyway, Abby was not going to let those chickens be swept away. She waited for a lull between seas, rushed out through water that was swirling knee-deep around her, and managed to save all but one of the chickens. She'd just got back to the house and shut the door when a new sea brought down the old cobblestone building.

Now the granite house where they lived was threatened. The mother and five daughters, and the chickens, of course, took to the towers. There they stayed, with the wind roaring past, the seas thundering below, never knowing when their refuge would be shattered, until the storm quieted. Abby kept the lamps trimmed and burning. The seas stayed so high that Captain Burgess couldn't come back from Matinicus for four weeks, and Abby kept the light in that time.

When Captain Burgess retired, five years later, a Captain Grant succeeded him. Abby was left on the Rock to teach the Grants (father and son) the ropes, and in no time at all she and young Grant were engaged to be married. She was appointed assistant keeper, along with him, and in 1875, when he was made head keeper of White Head, she was again appointed assistant keeper.

Many a little girl going to sleep on Matinicus or Criehaven to the sound of the Rock foghorn, or watching the light sweep across her ceiling until her eyelids drooped, must have dreamed of being as valiant as Abby Burgess.

With the beginning of World War II, the Lighthouse Service as such ceased to exist; it became a part of the Coast Guard, and sailors lived on the Rock where once children had grown and played, and wives hung out their washings to snap in the constant breeze. Boys from Kansas, Utah, and Texas found a year's duty on the Rock a pretty desolating prospect—say from October to April, at least. Some of them, with great feeling, called it Alcatraz. They probably still do.

CRIEHAVEN

It is Ragged Island on the charts, but Criehaven is the name of the post office and the name by which the island is chiefly known, except by those who with Elizabethan gusto and rough affection still call it "Ragged Arse." The Indians knew it as Racketash, so the derivation is plain, at least from the phonetic point of view. It is also the "Bennett's Island" of Elizabeth Ogilvie's *Tide* trilogy.

Mr. Horace Beck in *The Folklore of Maine* dismisses it as an unattractive island, with a few scraggly trees; cucumber-shaped, too. He's wrong on both points. In the first place there's no such thing as an unattractive island along the Maine coast. Even those that are barren have their own charm, and Criehaven with its deep forests, its sunlit meadows, its old orchard blooming each year surrounded by tall dark spruces, its warm tawny stone that seems to shine almost rosily, and the exhilarating heights of Sou'west Point where one can *smell* the wild strawberries, growing so abundantly that one gathers them in ten-quart pails instead of a little quart dipper, is anything but barren. In the second place, it is not shaped like a cucumber, but has an enchanting variety of coves, headlands, and cliffs.

It is a small island, 300-odd acres, and its early history is undocumented, for the powder horn, the tomahawk, and the hundreds of arrowheads and spear points turned by the first settlers were tossed aside, or were handed around to be wondered at and then lost, to the fury of the children who heard about them in later years.

The Indians were probably the same who fished and hunted seals from Matinicus and the other islands; perhaps those who killed Ebenezer Hall hung out there until they decided to begin their attack. Indians sold the island to Henry Brookman, a Swede, and it was from Brookman that young Robert Crie of Matinicus bought it, piecemeal. In 1848 Robert was twenty-four. He married Harriet Hall of Camden and took her down to "South Matinicus," or "the south island," and set her up in a log cabin. She was nineteen; she must have been a courageous girl, very much in love, and superbly healthy.

Through the winter Robert cut logs and hewed out the planks for a house, and in 1849 he built the original Crie homestead, which not only overlooks the harbor but looks out to sea in the other direction. It is situated like a dignified presence at the top of a long rise.

Robert and Harriet raised five children on the island, and in 1896 all the children, now married and some with children of their own, lived on the island, making it truly Criehaven. In those days the fishing business was vigorous; cod and herring were processed and packed, cod livers were "tried out" in the sun in the big open hogsheads, coasting schooners came and went, and artists set up their easels at Schooner Head, Fern Cliff, the Eastern End, and Sou'west Point and contentedly painted the summers away.

The Crie interests also extended to sheep raising and farming. Men who came from the mainland to fish for the Cries gradually acquired land of their own and built houses back from the shore where they had lodged as young bachelors in little camps they would later use as workshops. They brought wives to the island, and children were born. Now Criehaven wanted its independence, to establish itself as a plantation.

But there were difficulties. To become a plantation it must have a post office, but before it could have a post office it must have a school, and there were not quite enough children on Criehaven for that. Over on Matinicus lived Carl Anderson, a Norwegian veteran who had spent his life on square-rigged sailing ships, with his wife and five children. Criehaven coveted those youngsters, so Carl was approached and offered a parcel of Crie land. He accepted, and moved across to Criehaven.

Now the school was a reality; then came the post office, and at last the right to hold town meetings was granted, making the island a self-governing community. As such she prospered from 1900 until the '20's, when the inhabitants asked the state to declare the island wild land, in order to lower the tax rate. Now, though it is no longer a plantation, it is a busy community and a pleasant one to look at.

One of Criehaven's charms for those who love this island is the mixture of racial types and accents among the fishermen. There were the three tall Simpson brothers, Herman, Fred, and Alfred, who came down the Penobscot from Bucksport in a dory, with a sail to assist the two pairs of oars as they made their way across the great bay to Criehaven, there to put down new roots and put out sons like leaves; there were Norwegian Carl Anderson and his Swedish wife Anna; the Ericksons, also from Sweden; Peter Mitchel, the Dane who had received his naval training on a Danish ship and who had crossed the Atlantic forty-five times when he worked on one of the big steamship lines. Peter went lobstering, but he was always building a boat, too. That was his art. And many a man grown, living far across the country, has handed down to his son or grandson a toy sloop or schooner that Peter built with the same loving skill that he put into his big boats.

There was Joe Alves, Portuguese; and Simon LeBlanc (Americanized to "Sam White") who with his boys mixed soft French-Canadian accents with down-east and Scandinavian. "Mike" Mac-Clure was of the same tall, rangy, ruddy Scottish stock as the Simpsons. There were others too, whose fathers or grandfathers, or they themselves, had come from some other country, seeking in one way or another the same things the men in 1605 or 1620 had sought: pilgrims all.

Criehaven has her share of mysteries. There was Ed Higgins, who went out in his dory one day to haul his lobster traps and never returned. No trace was ever found of him or the dory. Another was Captain Albert Hall, who set out for Tenant's Harbor in his sloop *Wild Rose;* he too was never seen again. A year later Judson Young of Matinicus was tending his lobster traps about two miles southwest of Criehaven, and discovered that the difficulty he had in hauling one trap was due to its being entangled in the rigging of the *Wild Rose.* There she was in twenty fathoms of water, but still no one ever found the captain himself.

And there was Harry Harbridge, who somehow drifted onto the island's shores, in a manner of speaking, and remained there until he died. Properly, Harbridge was not his name; he said he was brought up by Indians and didn't know his last name. He lived in a small house called Harbor Edge, shortened to something like "The Harborage," and so Harry comes down in history as Harbridge. Harry was famous for a number of things. One was the way he kept his fire going. He had a long stick projecting out into the room, with one end in the stove, and as that end burned, he pushed in a little more. A really gruesome recollection of Harry was the way he made his plum duff. He tied up the bottom of an old pants leg with a piece of twine—not bothering to wash the pants first, of course—poured his mixture in, tied up the top, steamed the luscious mess for hours, and probably enjoyed every mouthful. He never bothered to dress a fowl when one came his way for the pot. He tossed it into a kettle of water, guts, feathers, and all, as the saying goes, and grinned when anyone turned up a fastidious nose at his cooking.

Harry has long been gone, but there are young men on Criehaven, sons and grandsons of Simpsons and Andersons, who dug for Harry's treasure when they were boys. For Harry was supposed to have had a great deal of money buried in the woods or on Sou'west Point for safekeeping. At any rate, he showed a large amount once to a man of incorruptible character; but when Harry died the money was never found. Directions for its location have come from dreams, hunches, and even more occult sources, but wherever it is it remains secure.

At one time Criehaven and Matinicus kept contact with a mainland doctor, Doctor Edwin Gould, by carrier pigeon. One of Robert Crie's sons, Horatio, and his family took care of the pigeons on Criehaven, and in case of emergency a pigeon was sent off with a message. The bird could be depended upon to arrive in the doctor's loft, whereas in time of sail the mail packet was many times becalmed in the bay in summer, or held up by gales in winter. This message service attracted attention all over the world, and the doctor received inquiries from as far away as New Zealand.

Criehaven's woods are like Robert Frost's, "lovely, dark and deep," and make a good backdrop for the comfortable homes. The meadows still blaze with wild flowers, and migrating sea and land birds come in great flocks. In the summer there are still church services in the little white schoolhouse with the belfry, overlooking Seal Cove; the ministers are supplied now by the Maine Sea Coast Mission, where once they came from Tremont Temple in Boston to visit Mr. and Mrs. Fred Rhodes at Hillside Farm, back in the days when artists and writers, too, were summer boarders on Criehaven. Now not so many people know this outermost island, but those who do love it beyond telling.

MONROE'S ISLAND AND SHEEP ISLAND

SOMEONE COMING IN from Criehaven or Matinicus will, at the end of two hours, be said to be up by the Muscle Ridges. Or some shoal spot or ledge will be mentioned by fishermen as in around the Muscle Ridges. No one knows where the Muscle Ridge—or

Ridges, as it is known locally—got its name. "Mussel" would seem logical, but the charts say "Muscle" and so do most writers. At any rate, to everyone who knows Penobscot Bay, fishermen, Coast Guardsmen, yachtsmen, the names of Monroe's and Sheep Islands are practically synonymous with that of the Muscle Ridge.

Coming out of Rockland harbor by Owl's Head Light, which was commissioned in 1826 by John Quincy Adams, one faces the large rough square of Monroe's. Its thickly wooded area and ledgy shores hold a special glamour for everyone going out of the harbor on the way to a home island or a summer one; another kind of charm for those who for the first time in their lives approach the magnificent harbor in all its busy, exciting beauty on a summer afternoon.

Otherwise it is not an especially distinguished island. Picnickers enjoy certain sandy beaches, and once it was a great place for bootleggers, but so little is known of its history that it has a curiously expressionless aspect, like a face that keeps its owner's secrets. For Monroe's certainly has secrets; every island has.

The island is named for a Hugh Monroe, who lived on it once. That much is known, but not who Monroe was, what sort of man he was, and what his life was on the island. Indians went there, but that can be said about all other islands. British privateers lurked in its lee during the War of 1812, flying American colors to trap Yankee coasters, and local men gathered there and tried to shoot up the privateers. But the island did not come into prominence until an incident that took place in 1884.

In that year the big side-wheeler *City of Portland* took a short cut into Penobscot Bay through Fisherman's Passage. This channel leads from south of Sheep Island, which is south of Monroe's, into Owl's Head Bay, threading among a spotty outcropping of ledges and islets. The steamer came to a sad end, tearing a large hole in her hull on a bad ledge plainly marked by a spar buoy. The fog was thick, but the seas quiet. The *Portland* sank gently until quite a bit of her was under water. No one was in danger of drowning at once, but the passengers and most of the crew took to the boats and went to Monroe's Island. A lifeboat was coming up from White Head, by oar, but meanwhile small craft appeared out of the fog like products of spontaneous generation. Men boarded the steamer and swarmed over her, taking everything that wasn't nailed down. The officers, who naturally had stayed aboard, couldn't stop them.

It was the big event of the century, good for years of conversation as people showed off what they or Pa or Uncle Tim got from off the *Portland* that time. Perhaps some of the looters or their offspring still lingered on Monroe's in the early 1900's, when a dozen or so families were living there, under rather earthy conditions, scavenging sea and shore like gulls, jacking any deer that was foolish enough to swim out from the mainland, drinking hard and not being very discriminating about what they drank.

The story is that one night one of the exclusive little group died from bad liquor, and in a hurry to get rid of his body his companions —those who could still see—put him in a dory, rubber boots and all, rowed him to the mainland in the dark, and buried him. Why they didn't bury him on the island is a mystery, unless they didn't want anybody on the island to know about his death either. Anyway, of all the craft that have negotiated the channel between Owl's Head Light and Monroe's, that dory with its load of hard drinkers and one corpse must have been the weirdest.

There were only a few people left on the island in 1938, when it was bought by an individual of humane principles who, after the inhabitants had all gone, turned it into a sanctuary for deer. Now it is a state game preserve.

Monroe's has a sort of national importance, apart from its very special significance for deer who swim out from the mainland to get away from dogs or the sound of guns in November. On its northernmost tip there stands what is known familiarly as "the spindle," a tall frame structure with a peaked top. Exactly one nautical mile to the southwest, on the northern tip of the adjacent Sheep Island, stands another spindle. Each of these markers is matched by another spindle on the mainland, approximately a mile away. All four contain neon beacons.

In the sea off the island spindles, the measured nautical mile is set off by great markers illuminated at night by flashing lights. Here all United States warships built on the eastern coast have their trial runs. As this is the only trial course on the Atlantic coast, commercial ships come here too, to make their trial runs; but it is the sight of an aircraft carrier knifing through the waves and rolling her bow wave back in a roaring, glittering curl of white water that makes the heart stand still and then begin to beat twice as fast as normal.

Sheep Island, lying just a little way off Monroe's, is surrounded by ledges which, on the chart at least, have a bristling and hostile air, as if they've managed to keep people off for *this* long, and intend to keep on doing so.

There seems to be very little recorded history for this small island —74 acres to Monroe's 180. It has always been used as pasture for sheep, cows, and horses. The last owner had plans for starting a boys' camp, but wasn't able to carry them through. At the moment the island is for sale.

It is not a useless island, though. (No island ever is.) The birds and animals love it, finding it safe and private. Generations of boys have camped there. Owl's Head people have dug clams there for years. The first glimpse through rain and spray of the island's familiar outline with its neon-lighted marker is as welcome to a storm-caught fisherman as a friendly face, and the sound of its surf through the fog has told many a man where he was.

THE FOX ISLANDS

The islands still known as the Fox Islands were so named because in 1603 an explorer was intrigued by the number of silver-gray foxes that lived freely in their woods, and roamed the shores trying to catch fish. They lie where the land widens out from the mouth of the Penobscot into the great Gulf of Maine. They are

North Haven, Vinalhaven, Hurricane, Green's Island, and a great many more smaller islands; the whole group measures ten or eleven miles across. The passage called The Thoroughfare, between the two largest islands, was in prehistoric times a deep valley between mountains.

Many mariners have sailed Penobscot Bay: the Norsemen, Cabot, Verrazano, Estévan Gomez, who named the great river Rio de Gomez; they were all impressed by the beauty of the huge bay with its spatterings of islands and its range of blue mainland mountains. But no one singled out this particular group of islands for mention until Martin Pring's vessels, *Discoverer* and *Speedwell*, dropped anchor there in July, 1603. Pring had been collecting medicinal herbs from the Indians down the coast of Sebascodegan Island, but of all the places where he anchored and stayed for a little while these islands in Penobscot Bay enchanted him most of all. He named them the Fox Islands, and wrote an enthusiastic description for the Bristol merchants who had sent him out on his voyage of exploration.

For the next hundred and fifty years after Pring's visit, the islands' history matches that of the other islands on the coast. Men tried to settle and were killed or burned out by raiding Maliseets, Micmacs, and the Tarratines, whom even other Indians feared. The Thoroughfare was the stage for the murder of many an English fisherman. The Tilton brothers from Ipswich, with a boy to help, were fishing there when a group of Indians came out from shore, pretending to be friendly, and then attacked them. By a masterly piece of hard selling, one of the brothers persuaded an Indian to loosen his bonds, and then he set his brother free, and they fought the Indians in hand-to-hand combat and killed them. Badly wounded themselves, they were able to sail away before three canoes full of Indians could overtake them, and got safely out to Matinicus.

There were no attempts at a permanent settlement until the end of the French and Indian Wars.

Vinalhaven

Francis Coggswell ran a sawmill on Vinalhaven during the summer of 1765, and thereby gains some indirect glory. For he sold his land, about 700 acres, to Thaddeus Carver, who had come with his father and brother from Marshfield, Massachusetts, when Thaddeus was fifteen. His father and brother didn't stay long, but

Thaddeus went to work for Francis Coggswell. He married Hannah Hall of Matinicus, young Ebenezer's daughter, and they raised ten children. They began their married life in a log cabin, but in time a village grew up around it that was called Carver's Harbor, for him. When he died he left his wife well provided for, money to all his daughters, and land and buildings to his sons.

Thaddeus saw a great deal in those years between the time he started work for Coggswell, as an adolescent boy, and his death in his big house at the age of eighty-one, in 1832. He had known what it was for a handful of people to start a settlement haunted by the bloody events of the past hundred years, yet irresistibly drawn by the space, the freedom, and the abundance that the bay life offered them; he knew what it was to feel one's confidence grow as the lumber sold for a good price, the fish seemed to come flocking to the handlines, and the farms did well. He remembered too what it had been during the Revolution, by which time there were around eight hundred people on the Fox Islands, when it was impossible to salt fish to sell because it was impossible to get salt. No one wanted to buy the islands' wood and lumber, the produce of the farms fell off until some people were actually in want, and to add to it all they were constantly hectored by bands of Tories who went up and down the coast stealing what crops and stores the people had. Many Fox Island men went to fight for the colonies, and those who stayed behind petitioned the Congress for muskets as well as food.

While the British occupied Castine they raided the outer settlements periodically for forced labor battalions, and one hero of Vinalhaven history was John Smith, the father of fourteen children, who was taken away to work on the British fortifications at Castine. Every time he got a chance he pounded his ax on a rock so that he managed to spend most of his time grinding it.

When the Revolution ended, Thaddeus was one of those who signed a petition to the General Court, asking the Court to remember how these islanders suffered during the war for their patriotism, having their homes burnt and their crops and animals stolen; asking the Commonwealth to relinquish its claims on the islands to the petitioners and their heirs and assigns forever.

The Court obliged by granting the claims of all those who had settled on the islands before the first day of January, 1784, on the condition that they set aside 200 acres (of good land, the resolution says pointedly) for the use of the ministry, and 200 acres for the use of a grammar school, and that they pay the surveying expenses.

The name Vinal first appears in this period. Mr. John Vinal of Boston was hired to look after the islands' legal affairs, and William Vinal, Esquire, John's son, was one of the assessors chosen at the first town meeting. Some men have nothing before or after their names, some have "Captain" or "Mr.," but William Vinal was always "Esquire." His prominence was such that when the North and South Fox Islands were incorporated into a town, the town was named Vinal Haven, or Vinalhaven.

How did Thaddeus Carver like that, we wonder? But perhaps he was satisfied to have had a village named after him; Carver's Harbor was the community center of the island. And he must have been proud of the growth of the place. In 1789 the island men met to choose three selectmen for the North Island, and three for the South, whose first duty was to lay out roads and hire men and oxen to work on them. After that, town meetings were held alternately on the two islands, and the selectmen chosen the same way.

By the time Thaddeus died in 1832, his islands had weathered another war, and fought in it too. The British schooner *Fly*, lying off Owl's Head and flying American colors, in the summer of 1813, was brash enough to sail into the harbor of White Island, south of the Fox Islands, with three coasters she'd taken as prizes. In the silence after sunset, the privateer began loading the goods from two of the prizes on to the third. The captain thought the island was uninhabited. He felt perfectly safe in the warm, quiet, summer dusk, with the only sound from shore that of the birds. What he did not know was that the Fox Islanders knew he was there, and that through the night the men were gathering together, until the White Island woods were full of them, armed with every weapon they could collect—"musket, fusee, and fowling piece," says Eaton.

Quietly they watched operations in the cove, and in the morning someone pleasantly hailed the privateer, whose captain said she was the *Shearwater*, of Baltimore, and invited the hailer aboard. When the islanders opened fire the captain was killed at once and the rest of the crew, seventy-five of them, were driven below. But one of them crept out and managed to cut the cable, and with a favorable wind the *Fly* blew out of the cove, then hoisted her sails and went quickly away from there. The Fox Islanders were left with the three prize vessels and some prisoners, the crew of the *Fly*'s boat. The privateer had four Americans on board as prisoners, and these they released at Matinicus Rock.

Thaddeus Carver lived to see Maine become a state in 1820. We wonder how he would have felt about North Haven's being set off as a separate entity in 1846. Loving his island and his freedom as he did, he would have been enthusiastically recruiting in 1862, when the town went all out for Lincoln and the Union. There is no record of substitutes being bought for Vinalhaven men. About 180 men went to fight, and 23 of them were killed. A Lafayette Carver and a Thaddeus Carver were among those killed—probably Thaddeus's grandsons. His sons John and Reuben were carrying on in his place, busy men with a sense of community responsibility, as were the Calderwoods, the Vinals, the Areys, the Philbrooks, the Dyers, and the rest.

Vinalhaven's claim to uniqueness comes from its granite industry. A Mr. Tuck of New Hampshire first quarried granite at Arey's Harbor for building a jail in Massachusetts. From then on there was always quarrying somewhere on the island, though the Bodwell Granite Company is perhaps representative of the whole industry and was certainly the largest enterprise on the island. Suddenly there was a tremendous demand for granite. The list of destinations for the stone is unbelievable; it's probably safe to say that everyone in the country has at one time or another either walked on, looked at, or touched Vinalhaven granite.

As a quarry town in those great and golden days, Vinalhaven must have been as exciting as a Western village in the days of the Gold Rush. Quarrymen came from everywhere, bringing their own languages and cultures. They spent their spare time in athletic contests, and in keeping the lockup behind the cooper's shop well filled with brawling and alcoholic celebrants. On the other side of the coin, the Knights of Labor, the Granite Cutters' Union, and the unorganized granite workers too, helped to start the Vinalhaven Public Library.

Those were the days when the Bodwell Company had fifteen hundred men, and a hundred yoke of oxen, besides the teams of magnificently tended and groomed horses; at the Fourth of July parade in 1872 the Vinalhaven band was carried in chariots drawn by 72 yoke of oxen. Besides the quarrymen, and the animals who got the stone out, there were the craftsmen who shaped, and polished, and carved. These men worked out of granite blocks the great eagles for the post office in Buffalo, New York. "It's easy, ma'am," one explained. "The eagle was already in the stone and all I had to do was to chisel it out."

As all such exciting things must come to an end, so did Vinalhaven's granite boom, but it went out in a blaze of glory. Among the last great things the industry produced were the columns for the Cathedral of St. John the Divine in New York; when they were first removed from the quarry they were each sixty-four feet long, eight feet wide, and seven feet through, the longest stones to have been taken from any quarry anywhere in eighteen hundred years. Finished, they were plain polished columns. Three of the columns broke during the polishing and so the workmen began again, making the columns in sections of forty and twenty feet.

After the Bodwell Company went out of business, there were attempts to reactivate the quarries to supply stone for paving, bridge construction, and so forth, up into the 1930's, but nothing lasted for long. Still, the town does not forget the glorious past, which for a time turned it into a cosmopolitan sort of place and left it a whole new batch of memories to join with all the others.

All during the 1800's there was an active shipbuilding industry on Vinalhaven, of course, and the fishing industry thrived. Today it is principally a lobstering and fishing island, with a busy town life. It is loved by a good many summer people, and written about, most suitably, by its own poet, Harold Vinal.

North Haven

Officially North Haven and Vinalhaven were a unit until the northern island succeeded in getting itself set apart in 1846, and incorporating as a town by itself; but it is pretty sure that as North Islanders they had always felt themselves set apart by an insular pride in their location. And besides, the North Island had the first permanent settlement, and a larger population for quite a few years. In 1784 there were 68 taxpayers there, paying over 100 pounds in taxes, as compared to 42 taxpayers on the south island, paying 32 pounds and 2 shillings. What a lot of arguments there must have been whenever there was a question of raising money; what pointed remarks must have been shot back and forth like arrows across the Thoroughfare.

Most of the early settlers were from Massachusetts; some too were from New Hampshire, and one bright and shining star was Michael Bowen, of Cork, Ireland, who came there to teach. A brilliant graduate of Dublin University, who taught his boys well, he alternated his services between the north and south islands. Whenever a pupil advanced to the rule of three in mathematics, he celebrated by presenting his teacher with a gallon of rum.

North Haven men fought in every war that came along. Archibald MacMullen, for instance, was with Washington at Valley Forge. Those who went away to fight and were able to return, or those who came to the island as veterans to begin a new life, must have felt that the miseries and perils of battles with French, Indians, and British were worth enduring, if afterwards they could come to this: a free and self-sufficient life with a land to cultivate and seas to fish. The only things they wanted which they could not raise themselves were rum, raisins, and molasses; these they bought when they sold their fish in Boston, or sailed it down to the salt-fish-hungry West Indies.

All people who live by the sea, whether on islands or on the mainland, know the law of salvage, and islanders become dedicated beachcombers at an early age. A famous North Island lady beachcomber was Granny Robbins, who once found the carcass of a whale washed up by the tide. No doubt imagining the long succession of winter nights when her house would be lighted by whale oil, Granny made sure to put a mark of ownership on her whale by unraveling one of her woolen stockings, winding the yarn around the gigantic corpse as best she could, and tying one end to a tree. Then she went home for rope and help, knowing that nobody else would claim her prize. Her other claim to fame was that of having brought over a thousand babies into the world. Her father was John Newbury, one of the first settlers and a soldier in the Revolution.

North Haven was affected greatly in 1836 by the burning of the *Royal Tar*, a sidewheeler coming from New Brunswick and headed for Portland with ninety human passengers and a cargo of animals. A revenue cutter, *Veto*, was at North Haven at the time, commanded by Captain Howard Dyer of that island, and went immediately to the scene of the fire. Dyer and his crew saved as many as they could, taking them back to North Haven, where he and his neighbors took care of them. The horror of that occasion has passed down through the years by word of mouth, the horror not being dimmed in the slightest by time.

The fishing industry was the backbone of the North Island for years. There was a short venture into canning clams and lobsters, beginning in 1855, and ending in 1897 because of the high cost of operations. Boat-building became a major industry on North Haven in 1888 when J. O. Brown rented the old MacDonald fish house and began turning out almost every class of boat. In 1890 Charles Brown started his boat shop at Pulpit Harbor, branching out from small craft to fishing sloops and yachts.

In the 1880's North Haven discovered another industry; summer people. There are no hotels on the island, but there are the comfortable, unostentatious homes of summer residents like the Morrows, the Lamonts, the Saltonstalls, the Cabots, and the Strongs. The latter family brought over from Norway a log house and had it rebuilt above a quiet, spruce-guarded cove. Many of these families have been coming to the island for so long that it is in the very blood of their children, for whom a summer without "the island" would be equivalent to a year without any summer at all.

The church in one form or another has always been active. At the old church at Pulpit Harbor, built in 1804, the members used to loan books to one another. This worthy habit was kept up for years, the headquarters being moved from place to place until in 1898 the North Haven Library Association was formed, and a lending library set up in Mullin's Hall. (Mullin was an enterprising soul who, over a hundred years ago, enlarged his home into a public house and took paying guests; this venture blossomed over the years into the inn called The Havens which, regrettably, was closed a short time ago after a long and celebrity-starred history.) In 1939 the association received a bequest for the purpose of building a library from Cora A. Spaulding; the summer visitors helped too, and the old hall was torn down and a new library built.

North Haven does not seem to have been affected by the "granite rush" that struck Vinalhaven and also Hurricane, but to have kept on a serene and steady track, turning its hand to whatever came along and giving a good account of itself.

Hurricane

Hurricane's story is simply granite and nothing else. It is an island of granite, tiny as compared to Vinalhaven, off whose western shores it lies, but massively imposing when one considers it as what it really is, a monument rising out of the sea to remind the winds, the cold salt combers, and the perpetually wheeling gulls of a time when 850 people made a village on it: the granite workers and their families.

Where now there is only the wash of surf and the sough of wind through twisted trees seemingly rooted in granite, there used to be the stirring clamor of the quarries. Roads were paved with slabs of refuse from quarries. In the village those who couldn't live without gardens worked hard to find pockets of loam which they could carry into their dooryards.

The quarrymen spoke Norwegian, Swedish, Italian; they spoke with a Scottish burr, an Irish brogue, a Welsh lilt; they spoke with the intonations of the parts of England where quarrymen were bred, and with the varied accents of New England.

There was a bandstand for music on the summer nights, and a bowling green; racial groups got together for their own music so that Italian accordions sounded out nostalgically over northern seas, and Welshmen sang in the stone-cutting sheds. Labor groups met in Anarchy Hall to talk seriously about politics and reforming the world. There was a church, there was a school, there were boats coming and going. The barge *Jemima Leonard* carried away paving for New York streets, granite for the New York Custom House, the Library of Congress in Washington, and for many more places than there is space to name.

Artists brought images of men, birds, and animals out of the clear rosy granite, the hammers rang and the workmen sang; it looked as if the island which William Vinal had sold for fifty dollars in 1870 had turned into Eldorado, not only for General Davis Tillson ("Bombasto Furioso" to the Italians, and "Lord of the Isles" to the Scots) and his partners, but for those who came to work for him. General Tillson had other ventures; he started a canning factory on Hurricane, canning immense quantities of clams, mackerel, herring, and lobster, and this worked well until new laws governing the lobster catch put an end to it. He started a try works on nearby

Green's Island for the production of whale oil. But of all the things he turned his hand to, granite was the one that made money which looked to be as inexhaustible as the stone itself.

But then somebody discovered something cheaper than granite, and easier to come by: concrete. The contracts became fewer and fewer. Quarrymen, trying not to believe that they, as a class of craftsmen, were about to die, began to leave the island looking for work. In the 1890's life had been marvelous on Hurricane, but within ten years the gardens tended with love were gone, and cottages were sagging down onto their granite foundations. The bandstand was tottering, and the bowling green was overgrown; the stone-cutting sheds were haunted by the echoes of Welsh songs, and the hushed summer evenings remembered the Italians' homesick music.

Yet, according to one Hurricaner, what caused the sudden end of her industry and the rapid exodus of her people was the death of the general foreman, John Landers. He could not be replaced; he was a genuinely indispensable man, and so the owners had to close shop without filling the orders they had on hand.

To visit Hurricane now is to visit a ghost town, a cemetery where blocks and carven pillars of granite lie overgrown by grass and wild morning glories, where the church is a ruin. The paving of Broadway has a peculiar poignancy when one remembers the hundreds of feet that walked on it with confidence and vigor, and then walked down it to the wharf for the last time, slowly, heavily, dragged back at each step with regret, anxiety, and fear. It all comes up from the paving, in almost as tangible an emanation as the sea-scent and the warmth of a summer sun that makes the whole scene even more tragic.

Harold Vinal's long elegiac poem about Hurricane, addressed to his ancestor William Vinal, pictures the scene most vividly:

> If you could see your island now, my Sire,
> you'd see it very nearly as it was
> before you struck that wild, preposterous bargain.
> The marble has turned back to sleep again,
> the hammers in the wind at last are silent.

William Gaston of Connecticut owns the island now, but as yet has no plans for it.

ISLESBORO

GOING OUT OF PULPIT HARBOR on North Haven, sailing up the river and a little to the northeast with a nod to Mark, Lasell, and Job's islands on the left hand, the Rockport, Camden and Lincolnville shores showing in blue-green curves in the background, the traveler by boat comes to Islesboro, or Long Island. He can see Seven Hundred Acre Island out past Pendleton Point—a name that is synonymous along this part of the coast with that of the illustrator Charles Dana Gibson. He continues up the easterly shore of this truly long island, passing Dark Harbor on the way, and comes into Islesboro Harbor. Beyond this big bite out of the island's middle, there is as much more island as has already been covered. When Captain Benjamin Church chased the French and Indians off Seven Hundred Acre Island in 1692, they fled across the three miles to Long Island in their canoes; there they had plenty of space in which to hide from him. However, he did get to Islesboro eventually and stole their beaver and moose skins before he sailed away again.

Before the first permanent settlers came to Islesboro, then Long Island, in the year 1760 itinerant fishermen had known it for a long time. Block Island men made regular stops there for wood and water, and between 1750 and 1760 whaling crews made it their headquarters. At that time there were successful whale fisheries along the coast, run by Rhode Island and Connecticut companies. But it was the Block Islanders' acquaintance with Long Island that led to immigration from Massachusetts.

These early settlers suffered a good deal from the British occupation during the Revolution, but most of them remained good patriots in spite of the temptation to take the line of least resistance. Quite inadvertently the island suffered gunfire; a house at Pripet, the little village at the upper end of the island, has a hole in it made by a cannon ball during the big naval battle of 1779, when twenty-two American ships were destroyed by five British ships. They had been sent out as part of a force to clear the British out of Castine and put a stop to the activities of the "shaving mills," the small craft that went up and down the coast taking everything the Tory crews could lay hands on, from cattle to muskets, and handing the loot over to the British forces.

The Colonial forces that gathered in Penobscot Bay heavily outnumbered the defences at Castine, but instead of attacking at once the Americans waited for unnecessary reinforcements. (They never did show up.) Eventually the American fleet was trapped upriver by the arrival of five big British frigates. Trapped, they did not fight, but beached and burned their ships, and escaped into the woods, eventually getting back on foot to Boston and disgrace. The commanding officers were Captain Gurdon Saltonstall and General Lovell. Paul Revere was in charge of artillery, he was arrested for cowardice when he got back to Boston, by the way.

But Islesboro's real fame came on one of those sparkling Maine coast October days, in 1780. The British, at Castine, held the Bay. To the Islesboro colonists, restive under the occupation, anything that looked like a change was welcomed with high enthusiasm. On this day in October it was the sight of a small boat beating her way up the bay out of Camden, under a flag of truce, with a handful of Continental soldiers aboard, and a civilian.

Watching through telescopes, the settlers were astounded to see the boat come up alongside the British warship *Albany*, anchored outside Castine. What they did not know was that the civilian aboard was a young man named Fortescue Vernon, a Bachelor of Arts from Harvard College, who carried with him a letter from the Reverend Professor Williams of Harvard to the British commander at Penobscot. Representing the new American Academy of Arts and Sciences, Professor Williams in his letter requested permission for the expedition to enter the British territory immediately. "Our business," he wrote, "is solely to promote the interest of Science, which is the common interest of all mankind."

What the settlers saw that day really began back in the summer, when the Academy at Harvard College had voted to do something about securing an accurate observation of the eclipse of the sun to take place in October and be visible along the eastern part of the state, Maine then being a part of Massachusetts. Even today a total eclipse of the sun is an exciting event; scientists go halfway around the world to observe one. Back in 1780, war or no war, these scientists at Cambridge were not going to miss out on a total eclipse that was going to be clearly visible from their private section of the world.

Not only were the scientists determined; the people of Massachusetts felt a solemn obligation to regard such things, for their state was the Hub of the Universe. The Great and General Court passed a resolve ordering the Board of War to outfit the state sloop, *Lincoln Galley*, for Professor Williams and his assistants, to take them wherever he judged necessary.

They set out from Boston on October 9—Professor Williams; Stephen Sewall, Professor of Foreign Languages; James Winthrop, Librarian; Fortescue Vernon; and six undergraduates. The weather was bad and they did not land at Camden until the 14th. Here they received permission from General Peleg Wadsworth, the Continental commander, to send a flag of truce to the British commanders at Castine and ask for permission to enter their harbor.

The captain of the *Albany*, Henry Mowatt, was friendly and courteous, Colonel Campbell of the British forces gave grudging permission. "Come up ye Bay immediately," his orders read. "Anchor ye vessel in Williams' Cove on ye east side of Long Island, about 3 leagues from ye British Port. From thence go in your boat to ye *Albany* which lies near the Fort, before you shall land. Have no communication with ye inhabitants and depart on ye 28th day of ye month."

On the 17th the *Lincoln Galley* anchored in Williams's Cove. The party visited the *Albany* according to orders, and were again forbidden to communicate with the islanders. This made it pretty hard for the expedition, as they wanted to buy food, and rent a place to house their instruments. Then the fog shut in to harass them further. There was some difference of opinion between their charts and their instruments, so they were not sure of their latitude and longitude.

Here is where Shubael Williams, for whom the cove was named, and who was one of the first settlers on Islesboro, rose nobly to the occasion. He was not afraid of the British. He had once been kidnaped by a press gang and served an unwilling term in the British Navy; he has had more than one run-in with Colonel Campbell during the occupation, and even now was hobbling with a cane after forty lashes of the cat.

Cocking a snook at the British ships across the bay, he turned over his barn and part of his house to the scientists. They were not supposed to communicate with him, and he was not supposed to communicate with them, but foolish commands like that meant nothing to a man who had left his comfortable home in Tiverton, Rhode Island, twenty years before just to get away from British accents, and now had waked up one morning to find them anchored in his dooryard. He used to brag that he was glad he was too deaf to hear them.

The Harvard men set up their clock, fixed their telescopes, drew a meridian on the barn floor. The young Williamses were getting an education out of it all. Mrs. Williams and the girls cooked like mad; it must have been a delightful novelty for the girls to have six young undergraduates in the house. Shubael kept his eye out for any surprise visits from the British. Everyone found the whole affair novel and exhilarating—except the scientists, who were dismayed by the constant fog.

But on the morning of the 27th, the day of the eclipse, the fog cleared and the day was as beautiful as an October day on an island can be. The expedition made last-minute adjustments. At eleven the Williamses, the Pendletons, the Thomases, and the other Long Islanders joined together to watch the eclipse through bits of smoked glass. (The Williamses had the first glass windows in Islesboro.)

The eclipse was a wondrous experience, not only for the islanders but for the scientists themselves, who set down detailed observations. Because of the British restrictions, they had not been able to set up in the best possible place to see the eclipse; they were just outside the path of totality, so that about an eighth of the sun was visible to them. But something came out of that, the discovery of the phenomenon later known as "Bailey's Beads." "At the upper point [of the visible section of the sun] appeared two drops as bright as stars of the first magnitude," wrote James Winthrop.

Professor Williams wrote that after the last observation the bit of visible sun became like a very fine horn. "Both the ends lost their acuteness, and seemed to break off in the form of small drops or stars; some of which were round, and others of an oblong figure. They would separate to a small distance; some would appear to run together again, and others diminish until they wholly disappeared."

Now he moved to the larger telescope, to get the whole picture. "After viewing the sun's limb about a minute, I found almost the whole of it thus broken or separated into drops, a small part only in the middle remaining connected. This appearance remained about a minute, when one of my assistants, who was looking at the sun with his naked eye, observed that the light was increasing."

The scientists left the next day, giving the Williams family something to remember the rest of their lives, giving Shubael the particular satisfaction of a victory over the British, and having obtained observations that are a part of our scientific library today. A plain granite shaft shows the spot where they stood while the world grew dim about them in that year's miracle.

The town of Islesboro was incorporated in 1788, and included Long Island, Seven Hundred Acre, Lime, Marshal, and Lasell. It is about ten miles long, and quite narrow in places. It is not a tourist island, but there are some tourist homes, and cottages to let, and the island is now reached in about half an hour from Lincolnville by the splendid new car-ferry, *Governor Muskie*. One can ride on about fifty miles of good road from the ferry landing at the Sailor Memorial—once Grindle Point Lighthouse—up to Turtle Point on the northern end, and thence around and down to Dark Harbor on the easterly side. Between the few little villages on the island there are great summer estates, as there are at North Haven.

Islesboro is a lovely island, with some interesting old houses, beautiful shore line, and incomparable views of the bay and of the Camden mountains. It is lucky enough still to have some deep woods, in the midst of which the observant walker will find traces of the early settlement; cellar holes where lilacs still grow to remind one that human hands tenderly set out these shrubs two hundred years ago; and old cemeteries.

The comings and goings at the Tarratine Yacht Club at Dark Harbor, the arrival of the well-to-do for their island summers, the day trips by tourists—all these are a part of Islesboro today, but when one breathes the fragrance of that two-hundred-year-old lilac in the forest, or reads with difficulty the stones in the cemeteries, the activities going on outside the hush of the woods seem no more than the froth dancing and glittering atop the deep, dark, silently moving sea of history.

VERONA

Mention the name "Verona" and people think immediately of a medieval city in Italy, with all the citizens dressed in Elizabethan costumes and speaking Shakespeare's iambic pentameters—a setting which hardly ever pops into your mind when you drive across the high span of the Waldo-Hancock Bridge onto the island of Verona, and then shortly cross another bridge into Bucksport. Verona in this case is simply a place you pass over on your way to somewhere else. Once it was the place where you paid toll for crossing the big bridge. Now it is not even that. It comes as somewhat of a shock that Verona is an island surrounded by the Penobscot River, with Bucksport sprawling on the east bank and Fort Knox looking like an ancient fortification on the west bank; it is a high island, for as you cross it the Penobscot flows far, far below in what seems to be a deep gorge, with precipitous wooded banks descending to it.

Verona has a history quite as interesting as that of any other island, and an illustrious one too. It has been called by by many names. No one knows why it is called Verona, who of all its dwellers named it, and why of all its names that particular one appealed to everybody so that it remained. Once, when the island belonged to the Muscongus patent, it was called the Island of Lett. No one knows the why of this, either, but it is suggested that Lett may have been a contraction of the name Leverett, he being one of the holders of the Muscongus grant. It was also called Orphans' Island, another intriguing puzzle until we learn that the island became part of the Waldo patent after the Revolutionary War, and that after Samuel Waldo died the island was called Orphans' Island for his fatherless children.

Waldo's son later had a daughter who married Judge William Wetmore of Boston, who bought the island, and then it became Wetmore's Island. It passed through other hands but remained Wetmore or Whitmore until the town was incorporated in 1861. It became Verona at that time, which leads one to wonder if the ladies of the town had a Shakespeare club and chose the name. The Wetmores, or Whitmores, were and are prominent townspeople, even if the island is no longer called after them.

From the island, whoever was living on it during the Revolution probably looked downriver to watch the Lovell-Saltonstall-Revere naval fiasco before Fort George at Castine in 1779. General Wadsworth, Henry Wadsworth Longfellow's grandfather, wrote to the General Assembly in Massachusetts that a battery on the high bluff opposite the head of Orphans' Island would have saved the Continental fleet.

The Abbotts, the Blaisdells, the Carys and others came after the war. They found a good living on Verona's 5,600 acres, with neither bog nor swamp, but some rich farming land in spite of its rocky heights, and a river full of fish streaming by its feet. There was a brief frenzy of silver mining in 1870, when a company was formed and shares sold, but no silver found to speak of. In the '90's, spiritualism struck, and the Spiritualistic Society congregated in a sprinkling of cottages along the northwest shore.

All during this time the William Beasley Yard had steadily been building sailing ships that went almost everywhere in the world. Now that sailing vessels were seeing their last days, the yard was sold to McKay and Dix of New York. They began building ships for the Arctic. The largest was the five-masted schooner, *James W. Paul, Jr.*, built in 1901, at a cost of $100,000.

In 1904-5, the same company built the *Roosevelt*, Admiral Peary's ship. Charles Dix, who designed her, was not only a shipbuilder but a seaman himself, an Arctic traveler who knew what a vessel should have in order to survive in the ice. He gathered his materials from as far away as the Rio Grande. The keel was constructed of oak which had been soaked in ocean water for twenty-five years at the Portsmouth Navy Yard. She was covered with steel, braced, trussed, and bolted to the utmost. Her sides were about three feet thick. She had five watertight bulkheads, and a well so that a diver could go down to make repairs. The theory was that she would rise under pressure, and not cave in.

The *Roosevelt* was the last ship built at Verona. At least the industry did not peter out miserably but went out in a blaze of glory.

DEER ISLE

BIG DEER ISLE is nine miles long, and is in itself four or five islands; Little Deer Isle is three miles long. But Deer Isle proper is a township which includes all this territory and much more. It is, like Harpswell, a watery town of infinite allure, all the more so because it is not a highly developed tourist center. One can reach Deer Isle by island-hopping northeastward from North Haven, using Eagle, Butter, Bradbury, and Pickering Islands for stepping-stones; or in a tamer but just as beautiful way one can drive down the Blue Hill peninsula, and out over the bridge from Sargentville across Eggemoggin Reach, to find Deer Isle set like a big planet in the midst of a galaxy of small, smaller, and tiny islands, reaching all the way out to Isle au Haut. And each of these, even the least, has a bijou charm for the born island collector.

The islands of the present Deer Isle township passed out of Indian hands into white in the year 1696. Cotton Mather Olmstead, a fur trader, stands out in the history of the coast; indeed he stands out in all our early history, because he was one of the honest men whom the Indians respected. When the chief of the Penobscots was mauled by a bear, Olmstead tended his wounds and probably saved his life. By way of saying thanks, the chief gave him Deer Isle, the deed recorded on a piece of birchbark. The Government confirmed this deed a hundred years later, in 1795.

The very early settlers eagerly burned the forest growth to clear the land, and found themselves with not much left; they had to make a choice between farming and fishing, and with the thin poor soil they had left after the burning, soil clinging heaven knows how to the great sheets of ledge, they had to decide for fishing. Though there were plenty of fish, the life was hard; because of the wholesale burning of timber, firewood was always scarce. Salt was expensive—a dollar a bushel at a time when an average man rarely ever had a dollar in his hand—so it was difficult to cure the fish they caught. The erratic currents and tide rips around the islands were widow-makers. Ducks furnished meat, and feathers for featherbeds. Back in those hard days there were no grist mills, and the scanty corn had to be pounded into meal the way the Indians did it.

Deer Isle men began to build vessels to take them far from home to fish, out to the Grand Banks, and farther. And there were the quarries of pink granite; Stonington is aptly named. New York's Triborough Bridge (at least the stone for it) came from Deer Isle, and it took two hundred men two years to get out the granite and cut it into blocks.

Deer Isle's fortunes have risen, fallen, risen again. In the late 1800's perceptive visitors to the island were depressed by the sight of bankrupt quarries, great blocks of mortgaged granite, rusted machinery. The population was decreasing each year. Once the island had owned "as many as three hundred sail of vessel; now it was much if it had a score." The old men told how the profits of vessel fishing had gone down year by year, and how the Government had taken off the bounty of four dollars a ton. They were too old to go to sea and the young men were held at home by the lobstering, the quarries, and the "pogy" business—the catching of menhaden for their oil. For a time everybody had an oil press and everybody made a little something, until a Rhode Island company moved in with mass production, and the porgy was practically wiped out, very quickly. And lobstering then wasn't paying much more than a dollar a day.

But that was a long time ago, and the island today gives a far different impression. Deer Isle may not ever have returned to the glory of three hundred sail of vessel, but her ships are famous all over the United States, and so are her sailors. The Yard turns out big draggers that forge steadily through the heavy seas on the Banks, and yachts that skim like medricks through their winning races; of course it makes them even faster if they're handled by Deer Isle men, as the *Columbia* and the *Defender* were when they won their trophies.

Today lobstering is a going industry, with safeguards to keep it from being wiped out as the menhaden industry was. Many of the island women pack sardines in the season, which is through the summer up to December. Island men quarry stone from nearby Crotch Island.

Deer Isle's flower gardens blaze in the summer and autumn sun, and the houses are snug and warm in the winter. The boats are built to ride out storms with equanimity. And when the present-day islander drives his car along the causeway over Eggemoggin Reach, or takes his modern boat up by Wreck, Bare, or Devil Island into Deer Island Thoroughfare, or mentions with the familiarity of long usage the family names of other islands or coves, without knowing it he is preserving the talismans of his island's past. He is saying the words that conjure up the first hard-built log cabins, the small boats capsized in the tide-rip, the widows pounding corn in the Indian way, and the boys going far from home to fish, to see if they could do better and live longer than their fathers did.

ISLE AU HAUT

ISLE AU HAUT, named by Champlain and locally known as "Isle a Holt," lies south of Deer Isle, roughly between the Fox Islands and Swan's Island. It is six miles long and three miles wide, heavily wooded as it has always been since Champlain first saw it, and its highest point is 556 feet. The view from this height is incomparable, while seen from a distance the island itself appears as a mysterious blue cloud.

When the wind is southerly the ledges surrounding the island break heavily and are very dangerous. But this was never discouraging to early settlers. The first on Isle au Haut is thought to have been Peletiah Barter of Boothbay, who with his brothers Henry and William came in 1792. Close to the shore, in what later became Thoroughfare Village, Peletiah built a log cabin and dug his well. The old cellar hole can still be seen.

From this small beginning the population grew until there were around eight hundred people living on the island. Now there are only about fifty. The early settlers found a prosperous, though hard, way of life on the island, but their descendants, by the mid-1800's, were beginning to move away. In 1849 the gold fever struck a large number, and they built a small bark on the island in which men, women, and children sailed all the way from Isle au Haut to San Francisco by way of Cape Horn.

There seemed to be no reason why the remaining islanders shouldn't prosper. They were expert boatbuilders who could set up anything from a peapod to a pinky; the island was ideally placed for fishing; vegetation was plentiful, and there was space for farming. Still, more and more families were bothered by the isolation and kept moving away to the mainland.

At first the island was part of Deer Isle township, in Hancock County, but when it and the smaller islands surrounding it became Isle au Haut Township, in 1874, they were transferred to Knox County.

Then in 1880 Ernest Bowditch of Boston and a friend, Albert Otis of Belfast, discovered the island, liked its loneliness and wildness, and bought land on it; they gathered together some wealthy friends from Boston, New York, and Philadelphia to form a men's fishing club which they called the Point Lookout Club. A clubhouse was built, and cottages, and from these beginnings came a great change in the island's economy. It became a vacation island.

The members of the Club, who included such men as Charles Francis Adams, did much for the island, building roads and a strong wharf, improving the school, providing a library, and giving the men plenty of employment to supplement their income from lobstering. The Club still exists, though the original clubhouse has been sold to a private person who is tearing it down and will build a summer home on the spot.

One of the island's treasures is Crystal Lake, a mile and a quarter long, and stocked with landlocked salmon and trout. It also offers good smelt and eel fishing. Deer are a nuisance on the island, but are loved and protected nonetheless; there is a closed season on deer the year round. The island is not yet officially a game sanctuary, but Acadia National Park, to which the Bowditch heirs turned over a part of Isle au Haut, to be kept in its wild and natural state, is trying to make it so.

The island has one grocery store, a hundred-year-old church, and two post offices. The stone town building, which contains a library, a social hall, the selectmen's offices, and so on, was presented to the town by Mrs. Nathaniel Thayer of Boston in 1906 in honor of Mrs. Paul Revere III of Boston.

Isle au Haut is not an easy place to reach, and this protects it from the casual tourist. There is a daily mail boat from Stonington, and in the old days, when the winters were very cold, people were able to walk the six miles to Stonington over the ice. The last time this happened was in 1934. The Government has now dredged a channel between Kimball's Island and Isle au Haut so boats can pass over the intervening bar—a very dangerous business in the past—at any time. The town has also built a new dock so boats can moor there at all tides.

This island, so remote and inaccessible, is not easy to forget once one has made its acquaintance.

[V]

Eastward from Penobscot

BLUE HILL BAY TO
PASSAMAQUODDY BAY

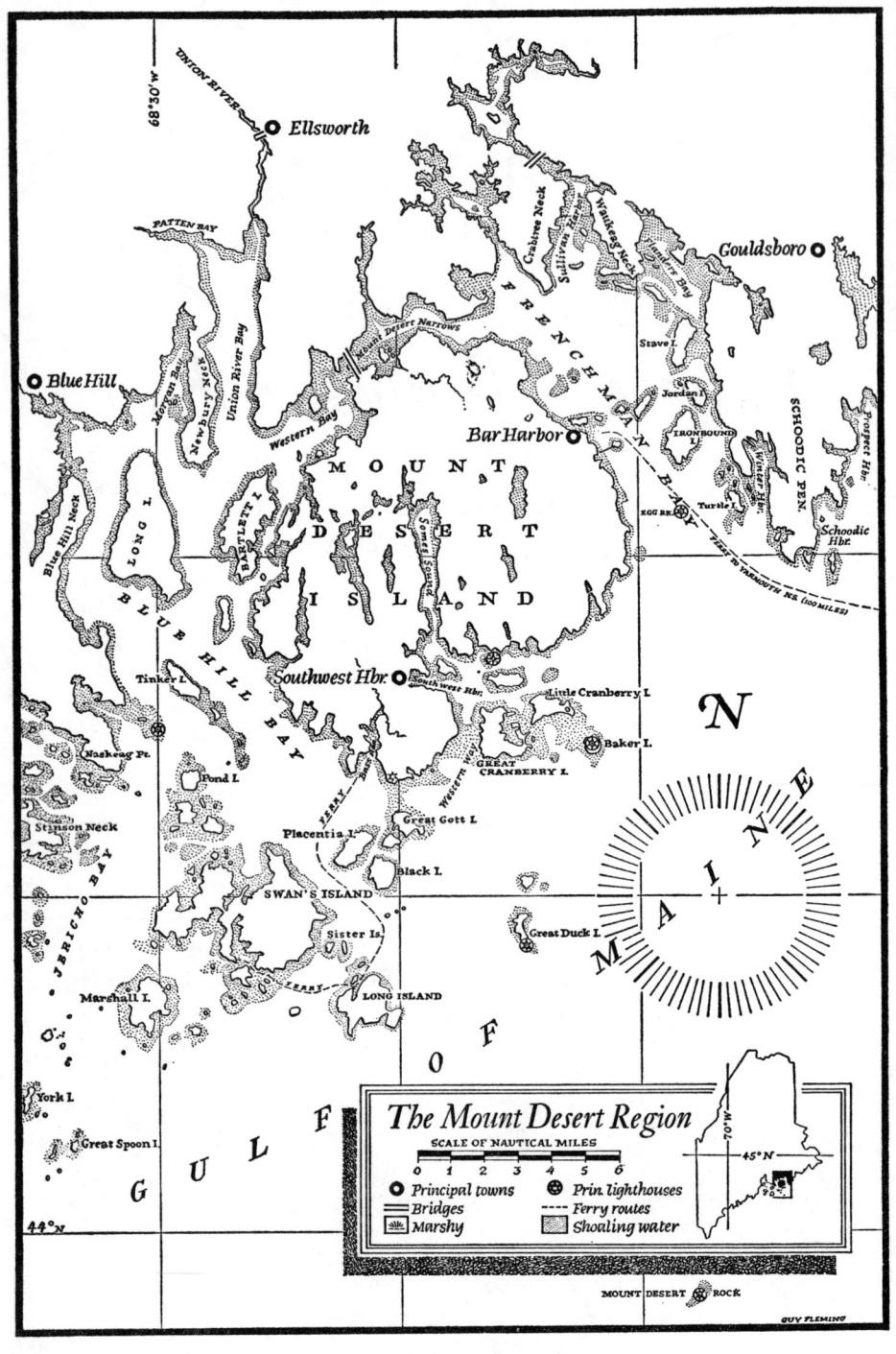

SWAN'S ISLAND

Swan's Island, a sizable spot with a very interesting shore line, and any number of attractive coves, lies between Isle au Haut and Mount Desert Island, both of which were so named by Champlain. (Placentia Island, to the northeast, he named *Petit Plaisant*, which confirms the suspicion that Champlain had a touch of the poet.) He did not miss Swan's, which he called *Brûle-Côte*, meaning "Burnt Hill." Therefore when he saw it in those enchanting days of discovery someone must have been living on it and have burned off one of its low hills. By means of a small careless change on each new chart and map, Brûle-Côte became Burnt Coat and sometimes Burnt Coal.

Someone besides the Indians, who used to camp there and who buried their dead near Hocomock Point, could very well have been living on Brûle-Côte in 1604. The picture of the coast and islands as empty country until the French expeditions came along is not exactly true. Hundreds of vessels crossed the ocean every year to fish along the Atlantic coast from Greenland down, and the shore line of Maine was speckled with the temporary camps of fishermen of a number of nationalities. Old Harbor on Swan's—which may have been the present long Burnt Coat Harbor, with Harbor Island at its mouth—was a very popular place.

After the French attempts at domination in this country ended and Massachusetts annexed the Province of Maine, great bites of it were promptly put up for sale. Wealthy men in the older Colonies bought much land in Maine. There was an apparently never-ending market for lumber, and the dense timberlands of Maine looked like a good investment. After the war, General Henry Knox, the Revolutionary hero and later Secretary of War, settled at Thomaston, where he built a mansion, "Montpelier," and began to live in the grand manner.

Colonel James Swan of Boston, who had known General Knox from the time they had both been clerks in the firm of Thaxter and Son, was not to be outdone by his old friend. He bought what was known as the Burnt Coat group. It consisted of the big island, once Brûle-Côte, and a number of smaller ones, some of them barely specks of land. In buying, he agreed to the conditions set up by Massachusetts, which were that a township of six square miles should have sixty Protestant families within six years; that each family was to have a house at least eighteen feet square, and to fit for tillage three hundred acres of land; and that the new town was to build a meeting house and hire a pastor.

Few of those who see Colonel Swan's name on the charts, or even those who live on his island, know much about him. He is worth a close look: an industrious character, a self-made man, who at the same time could be engagingly reckless and quixotic. When he bought the Burnt Coat group in 1784, he was around thirty years old, and had been merchant, politician, soldier, and author—most of these things before he was twenty-two. At eighteen he had written a book on the African slave trade. He joined the Sons of Liberty and helped dump 342 chests of tea into Boston harbor. He was wounded at the battle of Bunker Hill. At the end of the war he was a major in a cavalry corps, and because of his record he became secretary of the Massachusetts Board of War, and was elected a member of the Legislature and Adjutant-General of the State.

And with all this, Swan was lucky! He was left a fortune by a wealthy old Scots bachelor who perhaps admired the pluck and intellect of the boy who had come over from Fifeshire at the age of eleven and made his own way in the world. With his legacy Swan went into business on his own and shortly made himself a second fortune. He bought a great deal of land in Kentucky, West Virginia, and Virginia. He bought up confiscated Tory property through Boston and Dorchester. His winter home was at the corner of West and Tremont Streets in Boston; there he and Mrs. Swan raised their four children and lived in splendid style. He loved the French. Lafayette dined often at his house.

This was the charming self-made aristocrat who bought the Burnt

Coat group, set up sawmills at once, and had built for himself a large colonial mansion. (One wonders if he eagerly invited his friend Henry Knox to come to see it. Certainly he had dreams of living as Knox did, the beloved squire and military hero of his town.) The Colonel promised a hundred acres to any settler who would come to the island, bring his family, and build. At the end of seven years such a man would receive a deed for the land he had improved and developed; and he would surely deserve it, for the soil of the island had been nearly ruined by the cutting off of the original big hardwoods and subsequent burning.

People came from Deer Isle, Sedgwick, Mount Desert, and from even farther. The grist mills began to work with the first harvest. In the winter the men worked for Swan's lumber mills, cutting timber, and coasters stopped to take the lumber to Boston and points south, bringing back supplies on the return trip. Though the lumber business was the important one on Burnt Coat Island, the fishing industry was beginning in a small way. The new town was growing fast.

Then Swan's dreams of benevolently feudal grandeur came to a violent end. He failed in business, having taken one too many reckless plunges, and had to leave the country. He went to his beloved France, and promptly made money again through government contracts for supplying the French Army.

The French Revolution broke out while he was there and he remained in Paris, trying desperately to save his friends from the guillotine. He convinced a number of them that they should sail to America, there to settle down in freedom, and his ships were already loaded with their belongings when they were arrested and beheaded. The ships sailed anyway. One of the captains was Stephen Clough, of Wiscasset, Maine, who had written to his wife to prepare a house for Marie Antoinette. He was not to be allowed to carry her to America; instead he saw her execution, and was profoundly affected.

Prosperous, Swan traveled back and forth across the Atlantic with his handsome wife. On one trip he brought Prince Talleyrand to America and sent him along to Colonel Knox at Montpelier in Thomaston for a long visit. Meanwhile Joseph Prince, Swan's agent, lived on Harbor Island and looked after the affairs of the settlers on the Burnt Coat group. Swan himself was hardly ever at what was now known officially as Swan's Island, and the Big House stood in solitary magnificence. He was really too young—only forty at the time of Talleyrand's visit—for a settled existence, and his whole life had been full of excitement and conquest of one sort or another.

But on one trip to France he was arrested for a debt of two million francs, which he swore he did not owe. He was sent to the debtors' prison, St. Pélagie. He could have paid the money easily, but he refused. He did not owe it, he said, and to pay it would be a false confession of guilt. His wife gave up and went home to the children. Lafayette and his other French friends argued with him. It was no use. He stayed in St. Pélagie from 1808 to 1830, loved by his fellow prisoners, respected by his jailers. He paid the debts of many poor wretches and set them free. But always he refused to speak at all with the man who claimed the two million francs.

Forever a romantic, Swan used money his wife sent him, not to free himself, but to fit up an elegant apartment across the street from the prison, where he entertained his friends *in absentia*. His major-domo arranged great dinners, his stable and carriages and theatre boxes were maintained for the use of his friends, and always there was an empty place conspicuously left for him.

So he lived until the revolution of 1830 and the accession of Louis Philippe, who freed the debtors. But where was Swan to go? He was now an old man, he who had gone into prison in his vigorous prime. His wife was dead. He had one desire, and that was to embrace his old friend Lafayette. This he did, and then returned to the prison, wishing to become a prisoner again. Instead he died, suddenly, on the street.

On Swan's Island, Prince the agent had long given up and gone back to Massachusetts. The group of islands had been mortgaged by Swan, given up, bought back; now no one seemed to know who owned anything. Settlers came and chose their own lots, often setting up housekeeping in the Big House until they got their cabins built. The first permanent settler was David Smith, a veteran of the Revolution.

The timber on the island was almost all gone, so that Swan's stipulations that timber must be sawn out at his mills and carried in his ships meant nothing. There was some kiln-wood cutting in the winter, but no great lumbering operations as such. The biggest excitement was hunting bears.

More and more fishing was done, even though it was somewhat hampered by the War of 1812 and the British press gangs. Cod and haddock were *the* fish. Halibut were plentiful, but not salable, and a man considered it a nuisance to have to change his fishing berth because there were so many halibut around. Mackerel were ignored until suddenly, as if by a lightning stroke of genius, someone decided they were *good*. Then Abraham Lurvey invented the mackerel jig, and mackerel became, at least for the time being, the wealth of the sea.

At first the men went out in companies of little wherries. The larger boats of the time were the Chebacco boats, two-masted, weighing about fifteen tons. But the men needed still larger boats, as they had to go farther and farther to the fishing grounds, and the jigger or pinky was the answer, an extremely seaworthy boat which safely made fantastically long voyages in the worst kind of weather, riding out gales when there was no harbor near.

The Swan's Islanders of that time and of the present were and are mostly descendants of the earliest settlers: Smith, Kent, Sprague, Gott, Grindle, Davis, Staple, Joyce, and Torrey are a sprinkling of typical names. Hard-working, intelligent, and thrifty, these people deserved the good fortune that began to attend them around 1850, when they were able to build boats up to sixty tons and get their fish by seining instead of hand-lining. Net fishing made the island prosperous. From 1874 to 1889 the Swan's Island boats held either first or second place each year among the Atlantic fishing fleet; men came from other towns and islands to work on Swan's Island boats, their reputation was so high.

On the island there were many tangible signs of the new prosperity. Until that time there had been no regular roads, only paths and trails. If an islander wanted to visit someone on another part of the island, it was usually more convenient to go by boat. Now roads were laid out, horses were brought on to the island, and people went Sunday-calling in buggies. Some of the new houses were downright elegant. There was a regular schedule for steamboat landings and departures.

But as the granite boom was beginning to die out on Vinalhaven, Hurricane, and Deer Isle, the mackerel rush on Swan's began to decline. The big boats were sold, one after another. There was a brief flutter of excitement at one time about porgies, but it was short-lived.

Still, there was something else coming along—the lobster business. As early as 1857 a smack had run between Swan's Island and Boston, but in those days the lobstering was done by men too old to go fishing and by boys too young. Now as the fishing grew less the lobstering grew more. As methods of transporting live lobsters were improved, men began to stay home from fishing to go lobstering; here was a steadily growing market. They went first in small boats. Then, as it had happened in the fishing business, the need for larger boats came, so that a man could go winter-lobstering far from his island and feel safe. At first, too, the lobsters had been plentiful, and so close to the land that they could even be picked up under the rockweed at low tide. Later, with so many men lobstering, a man had to go farther and farther to get a decent catch.

The Legislature put laws into effect to preserve the supply, so that today lobstering still goes on, a bigger and better industry than ever, and the Swan's Islanders are getting their share. They are still great net fishermen too, and there are some big boats again in the Swan's Island fleet, draggers and seiners that range the coast like gulls looking for the great schools of fish.

Thus Champlain from France, Swan born in Scotland, and David Smith, the Revolutionary veteran and first permanent settler, are only the first three links in a chain that has come unbroken down to the present.

BARTLETT'S ISLAND

AT FIRST GLANCE, Bartlett's Island, lying snug against Mount Desert's western flank in Blue Hill Bay, with Long Island rising between her and Blue Hill Neck, and Newbury Neck thrusting down from above, is indistinguishable from any other island of the same size along the coast; that is, indistinguishable for anyone who does not have a personal connection with the island. Oh, one may see different views from its high spots, like sunrise over Mount Desert and sunset over Blue Hill Mountain, and there is the vista down the Bay across Hardwood Island to Tinker, and out to sea past Placentia and the Gotts; and then there is the northward aspect up toward Morgan and Union River Bays. Like other islands Bartlett's has its beaches, its birds and seals, its rocks, its first settler; its hardships and harassments, its share of all human tragedies, errors, and delights; all confined to a speck of soil about three and a half miles long and one and a half miles wide.

But since it is about to become—if indeed the process has not already started—a summer resort for the hundreds rather than the dozens, it is worth a second look if only to imprint indelibly on the mind a faint sense of what Bartlett's Island once was, before all memories are obliterated; before the old houses disappear from the landscape and the sounds of birds and wind and surf, and the striking silence of night and early morning (which are the continuity that joins us to the early islanders), are wiped out.

Christopher Bartlett, lieutenant in the Continental Army, may have traced his ancestry back to the Bartellots who crossed the English Channel with William the Conqueror, but very likely he did not bother. Probably the lands granted to his ancestors in 1066 for their work in the invasion mattered far less to him than did the grant of land his more immediate ancestors received in Weymouth, Massachusetts. And most important of all would have been his own possession of the small Maine island lying off the big one where he went looking for land after the Revolution.

The Bartletts multiplied and flourished greatly, but other families came to the island too: Ober, Dix, Salisbury, Butler, Robbins, Manley, Somes, Kane, Nutter, Herrick, Raymond, and Alley. These eighteenth-century pioneers opened up the seaward frontier as their descendants were to open up the Western one in the next century. The men were both fishermen and farmers, clearing the land of rocks and roots as settlers have done everywhere since time immemorial, while the women tended the stock and the gardens, spun the wool sheared from their own sheep and dyed it indigo blue or catechu red in the big brass dye pots that hung from the fireplace cranes. The exotic-sounding dye, catechu, came by vessel from South American ports. It had a preservative quality, so porgy nets were often dipped in it. A heap of scarlet net piled into a yawl or wherry on a gray day must have been as startling as a cry. The women wove their "coverlids" and clothing on their own looms, and made their medicines from their own herb gardens.

> For an emetic, steep thoroughwort down;
> For a laxative, steep thoroughwort up.

The pattern of island life stayed much the same for a long time, thrifty, ingenious, self-sufficient. There were changes, such as "boughten" cloth and an end to spinning and dyeing one's own cloth; sperm oil lamps succeeded homemade candles, and kerosene lamps followed sperm. But kerosene lamps are still used in places today, and older people still go out looking for skullcap to make a medicinal tea, and even much younger ones go down to the shore to clip the first goosetongue from among the rocks; probably not many of them think of the women a hundred and fifty years ago who cut goosetongue in the same places, starved for that first taste of green after a long winter on salt fish and meat and turnips.

Of course some things that were common on menus then are now delicacies to many people—lobsters, for instance. (Once it was a sign of poverty to eat too many lobsters, and they were sneaked home under cover of dark sometimes so the neighbors wouldn't know.) There were bushels of clams for the digging, cunners to be caught anywhere off the rocks; pea soup, baked beans, and always homemade bread, sour-milk biscuits or yeast loaves baked in the brick ovens beside the fireplace. "Marm stirred up a barrel of flour every three weeks," Otis Ober of Bartlett's recollected, "and I went to bed many a night when there were twenty people in the house."

The old men recollect other things, such as a cobbler's visit to the island every winter to make shoes for everyone from the leather that came by coaster from Boston: cowhide boots for men and boys —remember those little knee-high leather boots for small boys, with their copper toes and the tiny wooden pegs in the soles?—and shoes of laced kip hides for the women and girls.

Ellsworth, twenty miles away, was where the men went, either by sloop or oar power, to trade. In the very early days, when a man hardly ever saw a thousand dollars in cash all at once in his lifetime but had plenty to eat, wear, and burn and could leave his family well provided for, "trade" was the correct word. The Bartlett's men swapped dried fish, clams, and anything else their island produced for staples to take home. Eventually they built ships on Bartlett's Island, and could take their products direct to Boston from the island and come back with a load of goods. They went farther than that, to the West Indies and to Europe.

Polly Bartlett, who started the porgy-oil business on the island by selling the oil she saved from the porgies she caught to feed her hens, married old Uncle Aramiah Ballou, one of the first teachers on the island. Probably he wasn't "old Uncle" then, in the days when he boarded around from one family to another, taught his pupils well, and kept his voice lubricated with rum.

An even earlier teacher than Aramiah, John Carter, wrote a poem about Independence:

> When Independence was declared,
> To me it was good news,
> That we might pray
> And celebrate the day
> Like Esther and the Jews.

The long winter evenings held a fun and excitement that television today couldn't match, because nothing can come up to the joys of participation; there were games like "63" and Authors, singing classes, lyceums (debating clubs), and dances where "two hours' hard fiddlin' " earned two dollars.

When the men began going to the Grand Banks and to Greenland to fish, money in the actual sense—gold—came into their hands. Captain David Bartlett, returning from a voyage, drove a yoke of oxen to the shore to carry two kegs of gold up to the house.

"What you got in those nail kegs, Cap'n?" someone hailed him.

"Nails!" Captain David roared.

James Bartlett had a vessel crewed by his sons; he also had a good herd of cattle, about a hundred sheep, hogs, and two teams of oxen. He and his sons started southward in April, 1846, with a load of cobblestones from Duck Island, and were all lost off Cape Ann.

Merritt Ober began work at ten, stringing herring on Tinker's Island for twenty cents a hundred. He earned between eighty cents and a dollar a day. Another summer he worked as chore boy for nine dollars a month "and found." He was so small he had to stand on a box to yoke a pair of oxen. Otis Ober was captain of a lobster boat when he was thirteen, in the days when lobsters were sold to Underwood's cannery at Southwest Harbor.

The saga of Bartlett's Island tells of big men: of "Mr. David" Bartlett (not the Captain), who carried home four hundred-pound bags of meal in one trip, uphill, a quarter of a mile; who got beneath a mired cart his oxen couldn't budge, and lifted it; who could shuck clams so fast that a second shell would fly free before the first had touched ground. He was drowned in a squall that hit when he was on his way home from Blue Hill, and his body came ashore at Brig Landing Cove.

His son walked in his father's footsteps. Though it may be a legend, it is said that he carried on one shoulder an anchor weighing between 1,700 and 2,100 pounds from the wharf in Gloucester up to the center of the town, for a pair of horses to haul back.

Yet after such an energetic, crowded life, by 1900 the island had only a few people left on it. The new generations wanted much more than the island could provide, or it may have been that they wanted to make their own way, fight their own battles in the world as their grandfathers had done on Bartlett's Island. Anyway, the old houses with their massive fireplaces, their lilacs, their herb gardens gone wild, their alder-choked pastures, were deserted until the summer people discovered them.

They found here something which satisfied them and fed their souls, and they restored the old houses and lived in them as they were meant to be lived in. Various members of the Loring family of Boston soon owned all but a hundred acres of the island.

By 1933 there were only seven houses left standing on the island, but these, presumably, were loved and cared for. Eventually the Loring properties passed into the hands of the writer Phillips Lord, who vacationed and worked on the island until 1956, when he sold it to Mr. Herbert Meyer of New York, who would like to turn Bartlett's into a resort.

So it may be that the island will live again, in a fashion which Christopher Bartlett would find incredible. But at least it *will* live, and a whole new set of people will come to love it, and perhaps Christopher Bartlett would be glad of that.

MOUNT DESERT ISLAND

THE JESUIT PRIESTS WHO LANDED on Mount Desert in 1613 had really been bound for somewhere else along the coast. But at the end of a long fog mull they went ashore on the nearest land to stretch their legs and give thanks, and decided to stay. Thus a phenomenon of nature started something that resulted in a hundred and fifty years of trouble between French and English.

The journal of Father Pierre Biard tells about the way it began. But perhaps the accident of the weather had little to do with subsequent history after all, as the French had already discovered this large and goodly island with its mountains, lakes, its lovely fjord running in from the sea to the island's heart, and its clustering attendant islands. The Sieur de Monts and Samuel de Champlain found it on September 5, 1604, and Champlain was so impressed by the bleak grandeur of the mountains rising from the sea that he named the island *L'Isle des Monts Déserts*.

Pierre de Gast, the Sieur de Monts, was a wealthy French Huguenot who stood so high with Henry of Navarre, who was also Henry IV of France, that he had been given viceregal authority over the Atlantic coast of the New World, from what would be New Jersey now to New Brunswick. He was named Lord of Acadia, and sent to establish New France. Champlain came along to write the narrative of the voyage; if he had not been such a prolific writer we would not know much today about the French in Maine.

Henry Hudson anchored the *Half Moon* in what was later Somes Sound in 1609, the story goes, and went ashore to cut a tall pine to replace a mast lost in a storm. Then in 1613 de Monts, out of favor at home, sold his rights in Acadia to a Madame de Guercheville, who immediately fitted out an expedition to found a new colony at Kadesquit on the Penobscot River. This was the one that got lost in the fog and ended up on the island.

The Abenakis, who had good memories of Champlain and de Monts, welcomed the priests; again and again we find good relations between the French and Indians, more consistent and long-lasting than those between English and Indians. But this same year the governor of the Jamestown Colony, hearing that the French were in what he considered English territory, sent Captain Samuel Argall in the *Treasurer* to destroy the Mount Desert colony, St. Croix, where de Monts had planted his original settlement, and Port Royal in New Brunswick. Argall did so. The one memorial to that short-lived settlement on Mount Desert is the Jesuit Spring at Southwest Harbor, where the colony was.

Having taken it, the English did not know what to do with Mount Desert. Nobody really wanted to live there because it was so close to French territory. Toward the end of the century, in 1688, the King of France, who had never relinquished his claims, gave the island to the Sieur Antoine de la Mothe Cadillac. Cadillac, straight from the court of Louis XIV, is described as witty, shrewd, and able; he was also elegant, which term was never applied to an English patentholder. He had ideas of setting up a feudal estate on Mount Desert. He and his wife probably lived at what is now Hull's Cove. But his plans were not too successful; perhaps the underlings were already imbued with a sense of the freedom and equality of the New World. Or perhaps he really could not settle down. Cadillac went on to found Detroit, and later became governor of Louisiana. But he always signed himself *Seigneur des Monts Déserts*, doubtless with that nostalgia for the coast of Maine that has been afflicting people ever since.

In 1713 Louis ceded all Acadie except Cape Breton to England, but the fighting between the two powers, which started in Europe, kept up until the fall of Quebec in 1759 and the end of French influence on the eastern coast of North America.

There is a legend to the effect that Charles Maurice de Talleyrand-Périgord, Prince de Bénévent, was born at Southwest Harbor when it was a French fishing village; he is supposed to have been the child of a love affair between a village girl (of noble ancestry, of course) and a handsome young officer from a French frigate which took shelter in the harbor during a storm in 1753. Delphine, believing herself betrothed, kept expecting her beloved to come back to take her and their baby to France. Instead, there was no news until seven years later, when another French frigate arrived. This time an officer strange to her announced he had come to take the child to France to his father's family, who would give him everything he should have if his mother would relinquish all claim to him. Sad and bewildered, she did just that.

The legend finishes with a poetic touch; the visit paid by the great French statesman—perhaps the year he came over with Colonel Swan—to Southwest Harbor, now a Yankee town, to kneel at his mother's overgrown grave.

In 1759 the governor of the Massachusetts Bay Colony, Sir Francis Bernard, received title to Mount Desert Island as a gift from the Colony, and he gave one Abraham Somes of Gloucester a piece of land along the fjord, which became Somes Sound, and the new settlement became Somesville. By the time of the Revolution there was a small but self-sufficient community on Mount Desert, ruling itself by town meeting. For some reason the British left the island alone during this war, though they were to harass it severely during the War of 1812.

Two islanders fought in the Revolution, after a fashion. They took part in the ill-fated Lovell-Saltonstall-Revere attempt to clear the British out of Castine. The two men from Mount Desert who had gone patriotically to join the battle were properly shocked by the whole affair. When, after an incredible amount of argument and procrastination, the Colonials fled at the first sight of British force, the islanders came home and stayed home for the rest of the war.

With our Revolution ending, the ferment that was to cause the French Revolution was beginning to work like yeast overseas. Cadillac's granddaughter, Marie Thérèse de la Mothe Cadillac de Gregoire, and her husband fled from France, and she claimed a part of Mount Desert as her rightful inheritance. The de Gregoires had no papers to prove this, but Lafayette interceded for them, and Thomas Jefferson, who was President at the time, gave Madame de Gregoire the eastern half of the island. She and her husband had little to live on, but at least they were saved from the guillotine, and the other settlers were kind to them. They are buried in the old cemetery overlooking Hull's Cove.

Sir Francis Bernard's title to the island had been revoked when the Revolution began, for he had remained loyal to the King. He had already willed Mount Desert to his son John, however, and when the war was over Jefferson saw that the son received the western half of the island.

The islanders lived as quietly as if they were at the end of the world, and indeed they might have been, so little was known of Mount Desert until the first bridge was built to the mainland in 1836. Eight years later the painter Thomas Cole came upon the island by accident, as the Jesuits had done, and fell in love with the island and the whole Maine coast. Cole, of the Hudson River School of painting, glorified Mount Desert not only in his painting but by word of mouth. Soon other artists began to flock there, as they flocked to Rome when Cole turned that city into a romantic cult.

Wealthy people followed the artists, looking for the simple life even though they built great estates on which to live such a life. The Morgans and the Rockefellers were among the first of this rarefied genus of "summer people" to strike Mount Desert. Bar Harbor, that quiet little township of hard-working people, became a synonym for wealth. Now there are about 8,000 permanent residents on the island, and about 20,000 summer residents.

It was the summer people who were responsible for turning so much of the island into what is now Acadia National Park. They bought up land and gave it to the Government for the use and pleasure of anyone who cares to visit it, and as a memorial to Champlain, de Monts, and Cadillac.

Because of the Park, the deer live on the forested mountains as they did in the French days; the bald eagles circle aloof, far above the antlike comings and goings below. From the top of Mount Cadillac in the Park one can see the same spatter of islands that de Monts saw. And here are the memories of John James Audubon and Louis Agassiz, who found the island irresistibly attractive not because it was a good place in which to settle or to play, but because it is on the boundary line between two ornithological and botanical zones. It is the Promised Land for naturalists, who find plants and birds in incredible variety. In 1955, 655,000 people visited the Park.

In 1947 Mount Desert Island was almost destroyed by a fire whose flames were seen for forty miles up and down the coast. It is easy to sum it up by saying the island lost $2,000,000 in taxable property; this does not even begin to convey the nightmare that took place. Every town was evacuated and every road blocked. Besides all the homes that were burned, the mountainsides still bear the scars showing where thousands of acres of woodland and its wild life were destroyed.

One loss which could have been a tremendous tragedy to a great many people who had never seen or heard of Mount Desert, and probably never will, was that of the Roscoe B. Jackson Memorial Laboratory, one of the world's great centers for cancer research. Not only its records were destroyed, but a hundred thousand mice, each one of whom had an individual case history as part of the study of heredity in relation to cancer. Workers told of the tragic business of sorting over the small bodies and the happiness whenever a pair of bright little eyes showed up alive in a mouse face. The laboratory was rebuilt with the contributions of a great many organizations and people—even the natives of New Guinea have helped.

The green growth of Mount Desert is creeping slowly back; though many of the great houses could not be rebuilt, there are more hotels and motels for short-term tourists, and in summer the *Bluenose* sails every day between Bar Harbor and Yarmouth, Nova Scotia.

All things change, nothing stays the same; but whoever first wrote that didn't know about the granite spines of Maine islands, and islanders. Mount Desert with its lovely estates, its harbors full of yachts in the season, and its devoted attention to the summer visitor, is still an island where men must work hard for their daily bread; bemused by the glamour of summer, one is inclined to forget the shipyards, the sardine factories, and the lobstermen. It is true that a whole economic structure has formed around the summer trade like layers of pearl around the speck in the oyster, but the backbone of the island is the same as that of the other islands, formed of the men who live on it because they are islanders bred and born and could not imagine living anywhere else.

Mount Desert Rock Light, which lies twenty-seven miles in a southerly direction from the island, must have been even worse than Matinicus Rock for women in the days before it was a "stag" light. Mount Desert Rock is only a half-acre in size, and seventeen feet above water at the highest point. It is bare rock without grass, without anything, washed over by big seas all winter long, and the number of disasters caused by this rock in the days before the light was erected, in 1830, equals the record of Hatteras and Key West.

THE CRANBERRY ISLES

BIG ISLANDS ARE ALWAYS attended by little islands, like sharks with their pilot fish. Starting at its southwest tip, off Bass Harbor Head, Mount Desert is convoyed by Great and Little Gott Islands, Placentia, and Black; then, in a clockwise direction, Tinker, Moose, Hardwood, Bartlett's, Thomas, the Porcupines. Around to the southerly part again, on the east, outside Greening Island off Southwest Harbor lie the Cranberries.

The name "Cranberry Isles" is poetry with a Yankee accent. We think of the cranberry as a purely New England fruit, a paradox, like all New Englanders, with its bite and its warm rich bloom of ripeness. So the Cranberry Isles are New World cousins to all the isles of history and mythology: the Spice Islands, the Fortunate Isles, the isles of Greece, and Vachel Lindsay's "wizard islands, of august surprise."

Naturally they were named for the 200-acre cranberry bog on the largest island of the group, which is called Great Cranberry, and has 490 acres. The others are Little Cranberry, 73 acres; Baker's, 123 acres; and Sutton's, 174 acres. They lie in a strategic position to guard the entrance to Somes Sound, which was once *the* harbor of Mount Desert; ships coming in had to pass by the Isles either through the Western Way or the Eastern Way.

Much of the very early traffic along the coast probably touched at these islands; their rocks have doubtless heard many strange tongues, from those of the people who pre-dated the Abenaki to Norse, Basque, and others. But the first recorded visit is that of Champlain in 1604. It is likely that Father Biard explored the group in the few months he had on Mount Desert in 1613 before Captain Argall came up from Jamestown to destroy the settlement and take him prisoner.

The Cranberry Isles along with the great island were left to the Indians, then, until after Wolfe's victory at Quebec in September, 1759. Once the English possessed the whole coast, the islands, along with Mount Desert, were given to Massachusetts' governor, Sir Francis Bernard, who held them until the Revolution.

When that tragic lady, Marie Therèse de la Mothe Cadillac de Gregoire, granddaughter of the man who until his death signed himself *Seigneur des Monts Déserts*, claimed Mount Desert and was granted by Jefferson the eastern half of it, the Cranberry Isles fell into her portion. But she kept them for only a little while. She and her husband needed money, and they sold all their unsettled property to Henry Jackson, and lived as best they could at Hull's Cove until they died.

The Bunkers, Spurlings, and Stanleys were the first permanent settlers on the Cranberries, and there are still Bunkers on the Bunker land. John Stanley's descendants are found all over Hancock County and the islands, and the big Spurling clan has kept strong for five generations on Great Cranberry. Benjamin Spurling came from Portsmouth, New Hampshire, in 1768, and was one of the leaders of the community; he worked to have Mount Desert and the Cranberries made into a plantation with the right of self-government by town meeting. He made sure that everyone who wanted to vote had renounced any lingering partiality for the King of England, for he did not intend that anyone who had maintained Tory sympathies during the war, when the shaving mills harassed the coast making life miserable for the patriots, should have any say in town government afterward.

In the War of 1812 the outer communities were harassed again, this time by British privateers who forced them to pay tribute or else see their property destroyed. One shimmering August day, when we can imagine the magnificent prospect Frenchman's Bay presented, two fishermen were hailed outside Duck Island (south of the Cranberries, east of Swan's Island) by a British sloop of war, the *Tenedos*. The commander wanted the fishermen to pilot him to Somes Sound, but they refused, and must have been able to scud away out of the privateer's reach, because nothing happened to them. They seem to have got safely home and given the alarm, because it was no great surprise to anyone when the *Tenedos* sailed in through the Eastern Way and anchored off Sutton's Island.

Benjamin Spurling had two of his vessels hauled up in Norwood's Cove, in Somes Sound. He had taken the topmasts down and camouflaged the rigging with green trees so that the whole blended into the forest behind them. But the British had found out somehow that Captain Spurling of Great Cranberry had ships, and they sent word to him, demanding $350 or else the boats would be burned. Captain Spurling and a man rowed out to the *Tenedos*, and asked civilly for a little time in which to raise the ransom. The time was granted. What the commander of the *Tenedos* did not know was that there were five Spurling sons, and that these had been sent not to raise money but to raise the militia.

All through the night the word was passed from one man to another, and they began gathering in the woods at Norwood's Cove. Having not much ammunition, they had sent a messenger off to Ellsworth on horseback for more militia and more ammunition. When Captain Spurling went out to tell the *Tenedos*'s officers that he could not raise the money, they sent two armed barges toward the shore, with the Captain in one as a prisoner. The thirty-odd militiamen were waiting in the thickets. There were sixty men and a swivel gun in the bigger of the *Tenedos*'s two barges as they blindly approached what looked like dense but harmless woodland.

Captain Spurling slyly warned the commander not to go into the narrow passage under the bluffs that led into the cove. "I've got five sons over there," he bragged, "that could shoot a duck on the wing." He was told to hold his tongue, and the barges proceeded into the narrow way. Robert Spurling shouted unseen from the woods, warning them off, and was insulted in return. Then he asked them to let his father go, but the old man was knocked down into the bottom of the boat. Fighting mad by this time, he struggled up and yelled, "Never mind me, Rob, I'm an old man, but give these damned Britishers hell!"

They did. As the Minute Men picked off the British soldiers in 1775, so the island men picked off the sailors in the barges, who didn't know where to aim their swivel gun as the hail of bullets came from the green wall of the woods. The barges were ordered rapidly out of there, after seven men were killed; Captain Spurling was released, and the *Tenedos* departed. The Americans had one man wounded, Captain Samuel Hadlock of Little Cranberry. His hand was grazed by a bullet.

Captain Samuel was one of three Samuel Hadlocks on Little Cranberry, a line which began with the first permanent settler on this island. They were all fishermen. The one who was wounded in the attack on the *Tenedos* had already made quite a name for himself. In 1807, when the Napoleonic wars were making Spain very hungry, Samuel got a good load of fish off Labrador. Instead of coming home, he cured them on the Labrador shores and cleared for Spain. He got there safely, somehow just escaping the campaign of piracy carried on against American vessels by the French and English.

He made a good profit on his fish and came home with a load of salt and lemons. In spite of having to pay over $500 in duty at Marblehead, he still made a good thing out of it. He built a store on Little Cranberry, and today the Hadlocks are still the business people in the village of Islesford.

Captain Samuel built ships also, and he had five sons to command his vessels. All except Edward died at sea. The third son, Samuel, in command of the *Minerva*, was lost with all on board "at the ice" in 1829. What a world of bleak and freezing tragedy in that short phrase, "at the ice."

On Baker's Island the Gilleys come to mind; big handsome William and his equally strapping wife, Hannah Lurvey from Newburyport. During the War of 1812 (with more courage than sense, the critical might say) they decided to take possession of Baker's Island. They moved out there with three children, built their house and barn, started their farm going, and William also went fishing. They were supremely healthy and eventually had twelve children. There were enough girls to be a great help to their mother.

They grew practically everything they needed to eat and to wear, and lived off the sea as well as the land. Hannah had had an education and she taught all her children to read, write, and cipher. She approved of books as long as they were educational and informative. In the summer Hannah and the oldest children rowed the seven miles each way to Southwest Harbor to go to church every fine Sunday.

The Gilleys were therefore highly self-sufficient, and well-off to boot. Their fortunes improved even more when the Government built a lighthouse on Baker's Island in 1828 and appointed William the keeper. He received $350 a year, with house rent free and all the sperm oil his household needed. So he was able to put money away. The children all worked at home, contributing to the common good, until they were twenty-one or, in the case of the girls, until they were married.

It sounds idyllic and probably was in many ways, for these people were strong and also had good minds, which they were able to use for their own enjoyment and enrichment. But the Gilley story ends on an ironic and provocative note. William, at sixty-five, retired from the light, bought Duck Island, and went there to live. He stayed there, practically alone, until he was eighty, and then finished out his life with a married son on Baker's. Hannah stayed on Little Cranberry with a son until she died.

Why William's retreat to a hermitage? Was he tired of living in a crowd all these years? Did he hunger for solitude? No one will ever know but William.

Sutton Island was named by one Eben Sutton; he bought it from the chief of the Indians at what is now Southwest Harbor, for two quarts of rum. A larger island would have cost a gallon. Eben apparently bought the island on a quixotic impulse, as if it were a souvenir to take home and he wanted something easy to pack. There is no record that he ever lived on it. Abraham Somes, who was his companion on this search for a good place in which to start a fishing industry, came back to found Somesville on Mount Desert, and give his name to the deep cut running six miles into that island among the mountains.

However, someone must have lived on Sutton Island at one time —though how he escaped notice in town reports we can't guess— because when one of the numerous Gilleys, John, bought fifty acres on it in 1854, he got a house and barn with the land. They were in bad shape but he made them suitable to live in, and brought his bride there that fall. She was Harriet Wilkinson of Sullivan, with whom he had fallen in love when she was teaching school on Little Cranberry.

She was pretty but delicate, so John stopped going on the long fishing trips that had made his living. Their baby was born, and died. In three years Harriet herself was gone, and John had nothing left, neither wife nor baby son, nor money; only his island farm.

Harriet's cousin, Mary Jane Wilkinson, had come from Sullivan to look after her when she was ill, and about a year after Harriet's death she and John were married. She was husky, economical, and industrious. They did well, selling their farm produce, butter, and eggs, around on the other islands. And they raised three daughters.

During the Civil War, when the state of emergency made it hard to get linseed oil, John set up a porgy press, set out nets in the proper season, and was able to sell porgy oil for a dollar a gallon, for a period of about ten years. He used the leftovers for fertilizing his fields. With his porgy oil, smoked herring, butter, eggs, fowl, milk, and vegetables, John Gilley became indispensable. When summer people began moving on to Mount Desert in a sort of tidal wave, he could ask high prices and get them, because the buyer received good value for his money.

One of his daughters went through Castine Normal School and became a teacher; Hannah Gilley would have been proud of this, but not surprised, after the way she raised her children. Then in 1886 John began selling land to summer people and did well. Perhaps he could have retired, but he was faithful to his customers, and rowed every day two miles to Northeast Harbor to deliver his fresh vegetables, milk, and eggs. In the fall of 1896, after all the summer people had gone, he still made his trips because of one child who drank his milk. But his dory capsized one morning in an October blow, and his body was never found. President Eliot of Harvard wrote a book about him: *John Gilley, Maine Farmer and Fisherman*.

Benjamin Spurling and his five boys, the three Samuel Hadlocks, William Gilley, John Gilley—island men all, chosen as representative of the rest. They knew they were coming to no easy life when they chose islands for themselves; they rode out wars as their boats rode out storms, never turning stern to the gale; and they earned everything they came to possess by hard and honest means, and knew it, and were proud.

In 1830 the Maine Legislature incorporated the Cranberry Isles and Bear Island into a town called Cranberry Isles. The new town sent twenty-seven men to fight for the Union in the Civil War, and has kept up its record ever since. After incorporation, the old school system under which the number of children in a school determined the number of weeks of lessons they would have was thrown out, so that the Cranberry Isles children got a full school year. They have had good elementary schools ever since.

Cranberry Isles led in another way too, by having one of the first health officers in the country. In 1846 Michael Green was elected, to visit any house in which smallpox should be found, and he received twenty-five cents a day. Of course, the islanders did not find it necessary to elect another health officer the next year, or again until 1892, but now they have one full-time.

There is no longer any need to spend most of Sunday rowing to and from church, because the islands have their own churches now, with Sunday school during the winter and regular church services during the summer, both Protestant and Catholic.

And there is a social life such as Hannah Gilley's twelve children never imagined in the long winters when they entertained themselves by playing games, singing, and reading aloud. This of course was delightful for them, and we feel sorry for the children who have never known the pleasures of such home-grown amusements, but how the island women would have loved having a Ladies' Aid like the one that flourishes now, and how the men would have enjoyed meeting at the Firemen's Club and the Grange.

Of course they could not have dreamed of such a thing as a tourist business making jobs for them, and it would have been pure fantasy—"rum talk"—to them, to hear that some of their descendants would find it necessary to leave the islands in the winter to work on the mainland, or—strangest of all—to go to Florida to work on boats for the winter tourists who were summer tourists a few months before in the Cranberry Isles.

At home they drive cars on black roads, they watch television, they live a life far removed from that of their forefathers. Yet still the boats must observe the way of the tide around certain ledges, and the storms sweep down as they always did, and the whole vast stage of the bay, the mountains, and the islands stays the same. At the Sawtelle Museum in Islesford the evidence of the life the early settlers lived is there for anyone to see. Rachel Field, who lived summers on Sutton Island, has mirrored other sections of the past of the Cranberry Isles in her books, *Time Out of Mind* and *God's Pocket.*

Another thing which has probably remained the same since the days when the Stanleys, the Spurlings, the Hadlocks, and the others first came, is the bird life. The rare Leach's petrel nests on the cliffs. Gulls and terns breed here by the hundreds. It is a marvelous, apocalyptic sight to see them flying in crowds across a sunset sky; and then from that one should turn and look up at Mount Cadillac against the pale north.

THE MAINE SEA COAST MISSIONARY SOCIETY

VERY MUCH A PART of the Mount Desert region—and of the Maine islands—is the Maine Sea Coast Missionary Society.

Back in 1888 a young man with a resounding Scottish name came to Outer Long Island—Frenchboro—to teach school so that he could earn enough money to finish his education. It was an appropriate place for a MacDonald: in Scotland the MacDonalds were once hereditary Lords of the Isles, after they won the western islands from the last of the Vikings.

Alexander MacDonald found no religious life on the island where he taught, so he held meetings in the schoolhouse, and met a response which must have gratified his ardent young heart. When he finished at Bowdoin and at the Andover Theological Seminary, he came back to Maine to serve as a minister on the Cranberry Isles and Mount Desert.

It is true that the actual mission work was not started until 1905, but the beginning was in that island schoolhouse where a boy found people hungry for guidance back to the spiritual strength their forefathers had carried within them when they settled these islands.

While MacDonald was beginning his work on the Cranberry Isles, Captain George Lane was spending his summers sailing his own boat among the more isolated islands, giving out books and starting Sunday schools; it was he who took the first practical steps in clearing up the wretched situation at Malaga. By 1905 Captain Lane's health was failing, and he could not continue. The Congregational Church, which had sponsored him, wanted to keep up its missionary work, but as usual it was a question of money.

Alexander MacDonald had a brother Angus who was also a minister, at the Bar Harbor Congregational Church. The two loved the islands and the island people and, what is perhaps even more important, they understood them. They felt the best thing would be an interdenominational missionary organization rather than a strictly Congregationalist one. Having implicit faith that their plans would work out, they bought the sloop *Hope*, and sent her out with Captain Henry White, a lay preacher and good sailor to boot, as the first skipper and pastor. The Maine Sea Coast Missionary Society was incorporated on October 13, 1905.

"Either a fool or a saint," someone remarked, watching Captain White take the *Hope* out into a stormy sea on a mission errand. The first annual report of the Society, issued in the summer of 1906, began thus: "To sail a sloop in a parish extending from Kittery Point to Quoddy Head, along the broken coast of Maine in all kinds of weather, is no small undertaking."

The *Hope* was frail; she was feeling the strain. The second year a summer resident of Bar Harbor, Bishop Alexander Mackay-Smith, gave his thirty-eight-foot power yacht *Virginia* to the Society. She was rechristened *Morning Star*. Now the Society could go even farther afield and in worse weather. It engaged Alexander MacDonald as the missionary-minister, a work he carried on until he died aboard the mission boat *Sunbeam* in 1922. If he could have chosen the place of his death he might have chosen just that one.

The *Sunbeam I*, with her two gasoline engines, was a gift from Mrs. John S. Kennedy, another summer resident of Mount Desert. The little daughter of a lighthouse keeper, whose favorite hymn was "Jesus Wants Me for a Sunbeam," suggested the name. Until then the mission boats had not been able to go out in the winter, when often they were needed the most. But the *Sunbeam I* could sail in all weather, helping out in times of birth and death, raising morale by church services and good rousing hymn-sings afterward, the best sort of tonic in midwinter on an island far off the coast. The boat carried reading material to the isolated lighthouses and gave the keepers' wives a chance to visit with someone and do some company cooking. And when *Sunbeam* left, she almost always had passengers aboard, getting an unexpected and sometimes very necessary chance to go to the mainland.

Sunbeam I was retired after thirteen years of work. *Sunbeam II* was eighty feet long, and Henry Van Dyke wrote a poem about her. She was known along the coast and among the islands as "God's Tugboat," and the sound of her whistle as she entered the harbor brought everybody running. She might be coming to hold a dental clinic, or bringing a minister who would stay for a month or for the whole summer and organize church and Sunday school, recreation for the youngsters, lively discussion groups among the adults. Or perhaps she would be showing movies, or have someone aboard who had traveled far and made slides of his trip, and was kind enough to share his experiences.

Sunbeam III was launched in 1939, whereupon *Sunbeam II* began a new existence as a pilot boat at the mouth of the Mississippi. The new *Sunbeam* is Diesel-powered, with a three-man crew, and seventy-two feet long. She is ready for everything.

Now there are thirteen full-time Mission workers and many part-time helpers. The Reverend Neal D. Bousfield heads the work. In Bar Harbor are the offices and other buildings which the Mission owns, while the *Sunbeam*'s home port is at Seal Harbor, a few miles away. The Mission visits at about 170 places: islands, lights, and mainland ports. Naturally it concentrates on those with the greatest need, or those that are most isolated. It helps out, when necessary, with the schooling and housing of island children going to school on the mainland, just as once it used to supply teachers for the lighthouses when children lived there.

Of course at Christmas the Society makes a great effort; the work begins on January 1, for more than 2,500 persons are to be remembered. Those who are really impoverished are considered first, but the Mission does try to do something for all the children. In early December delivery starts. All the work of the Society is made possible by gifts from individuals, clubs, churches; from Catholic, Protestant, and Hebrew. The Sigma Kappa sorority has made the Mission its national philanthropy for more than forty years, and along with what the chapters, both college and alumnae, send in money, they ship enormous quantities of gifts to be given out at Christmas.

There have been many women ministers in the service of the Sea Coast Mission, and they are selfless, hard-working, and inspired in their service to the community where they are sent, whether it is a comfortable, fairly prosperous settlement or one on one of the more remote, bleak, and poverty-stricken islands.

Hannah Powell of Loud's Island was one such woman; another is the Reverend Gertrude Anderson, the present pastor on Monhegan Island. Miss Anderson is a lively person with the sort of career behind her that makes the average woman, and perhaps the average man too, take a sharp breath. She was born in Rochester, New York, around the turn of the century, and educated at Newton High School in Massachusetts, and Wellesley College. From there she went to teach for three years at Spelman Seminary, a school for Negro girls in Atlanta, Georgia. From 1921 until 1941 she served as a missionary in Burma, under the American Baptist Foreign Missionary Society. On leaves of absence from this work she attended Andover-Newton Theological Seminary, and took an agricultural course at Cornell University. From 1945 to 1949 she worked in the Belgian Congo.

Back in this country again, she joined the Maine Sea Coast Missionary Society in 1950, and began a new phase of existence. Her first parish was at Loud's Island, and after two years there she went to Monhegan. Here she continues her vigorous and devoted ministry in the same pattern which she set for herself at the very first, and she leaves the rest of us feeling rather out of breath and, in some cases, a little dissatisfied with our own lives.

Thomas Searls is the only living member of the original Sea Coast Mission group. He has been treasurer since the founding of the Society.

The Reverend Orville J. Guptill, who succeeded Reverend MacDonald on the *Sunbeam*, is lovingly remembered, and there are many others. Each person who has had experience with the Mission remembers a certain minister. The Reverend Anson Williams, for example, recollected when he saw art magazines in a house far up the coast that on an island far out to sea someone was trying to paint; and so on his next trip out there he brought the painter an armload of these magazines, which she cherished for years. This is just one example of the Mission's work, which covers all possible phases of human existence from the spiritual to the most physical facts of illness or accident.

Thus the ardor of a boy with an ancient Scottish name, whose ancestors sailed as feudal lords among their own islands, sent men sailing as missionaries among Maine's islands. And in the long saga of discovery and conquest along the coast, of battles, burning, and murder, the Society's story is a remarkable and satisfying chapter.

BEALS ISLAND AND GREAT WASS ISLAND

SOME SIX HUNDRED people live in the town of Beals, which is made up of two islands, Beals and Great Wass, the latter about four times the size of Beals. The town lies south of Jonesport, across a half-mile-wide stretch of clear deep water known as Moosabec Reach. The Reach is a short-cut from east to west, a sort of throughway for boats. The heavy traffic these days is made up of yachts, sardine carriers, and lobster smacks, where once the coasting schooners went by under sail. On calm seas the only sound would come from the bow dipping into the swells, and the musical swash along the sides, or the occasional slap of a sail. Nowadays only cruise schooners and yachts carry sail, and the rhythm of Diesel engines through the night is as common as the clamor of the gulls in herring time.

The two islands—though it is debatable whether Beals can still be called an island, now that it has a bridge (purists say it should *really* be called Beals Point)—are surrounded by a wondrous collection of islets and ledges with such names as Shabbit, Drisko and Little Drisko, Drown Boys Ledge (a little too evocative), Crumple, and Mistake. There are also on old charts The Virgin's Breasts and The Lecherous Priest. The names are all that comes down to us today, but there was a good reason for each of those names, and some we can guess at, and some simply delight us, we know not why. Speaking of delight, down to the west of Beals, by Bois Bubert, there is an island called Jordan's Delight, with Jordan's Delight Ledge tailing off it.

Beals and Great Wass had the usual early history of Indian ownership, then the gradual crowding by white men and the inevitable resentment, with the ending that everyone knows; each community had two flowerings, the second coming about a hundred years after the first brief one. So Manwarren Beal came to settle on his island about 1764, landing his wife Lydia and his children on Barney's Point.

Like many of the men in the island legends, Manwarren was a huge man, so big that he sent away to have a chair made for him. He was also a wise man, with a quick and clever trick of writing rhymes. With all these advantages of physique and brain, he was also a good provider; but so he would have to be, to live successfully on an island both winter and summer in that period.

There is a rather gruesome but vivid story about Manwarren Beal and an Indian. Beal and some other settlers were on a fishing trip and fog had driven them to the nearest island, where they were attacked by Indians. So they went out to their boat to sleep. When Manwarren discovered an Indian tampering with the boat's rudder, he hooked him in the jaw with his gaff, and tried to haul him aboard like a giant codfish. The Indian braced his feet against the side of the boat, pulled out the hook and swam away. But there was no more trouble that night.

There are also legends about "Long Barney" Beal, who sounds very like Manwarren, so that one wonders if they were the same man, or brothers, or father and son. Long Barney was even stronger than Manwarren, it seems, and once beat up fifteen men in a Falmouth pub. He did all kinds of other things too, but probably his greatest feat took place when he and his brothers, while seining, were overhauled by a British press gang. Long Barney threw the just-hauled seine, fish and all, over the British sailors and officer, and took them home as prisoners.

Around this time John Alley had settled on Great Wass Island. He moved his family from Bar Harbor, built a log cabin, and started lumbering. He bought the island, but no one knows just how, since the family was so hard up the boys had neither boots nor shoes. But the sons took turns chopping, and while one worked the other was in the cabin warming a plank on which he would stand while *he* chopped.

During this first winter the family built a huge log barn which has been torn down only recently, as time is measured; the sills can still be seen, and should be viewed with respect and some awe, as symbols of a time when men took great hardship for granted and called it not hardship if the land they worked was their own.

In the spring the Alleys shipped their wood to Camden and Rockland; it was the first shipment of wood from what is now the town of Beals. Then they turned to and built their permanent home, on the northeastern end of Great Wass Island near the log cabin. The house still stands today, more than a hundred and fifty years old and still lived in by those of Alley blood. John Alley's nine boys kept up the lumber business. They and their three sisters all settled on Great Wass Island when they grew up.

Meanwhile the Beals family was multiplying. The first post office on the island was run by J. A. Beal, and then by F. W. Beal, whose daughters clerked in the post office and ran a dry-goods store along with it, while Beal took care of his grocery store and bought fish and lobsters on Perio's Point.

In the very early days people hardly ever wrote letters because letter postage was so expensive, and the nearest post office was at

Columbia Falls, well up Pleasant River, which runs in between Ripley Neck and Cape Split. Mail was taken from there to Jonesport, twelve miles away, and then carried to Beals by boat. It would be given out from some certain house, where everyone gathered and made a pleasant social occasion out of the arrival of the mail. When the first official post office was set up, the mailtime ritual was already established as an enjoyable and stimulating break in the week. News of great events in the country was handed on by word of mouth before newspapers were common, so one never knew what to expect when he "met the boat."

Mrs. Susie Carver is postmistress now, and has been since 1912. She's a veteran of the long fight for better schools that goes on everywhere, and she and Mr. Carver can also feel a great personal pride in the new bridge, for which they worked so hard.

Beals was incorporated as a town in 1925, after being a part of Jonesport. The islanders had fought long and hard for their independence, and proved they deserved it by immediately breaking ground for their own high school so that the students needn't make the trip across the Reach twice a day; in winter it was sometimes downright dangerous. The men of the island worked all day to give the construction a good start, and the women served them dinner and supper.

Today Beals still maintains a Grade-A high school, and since its first graduation exercises, for three seniors in 1926, it has won many trophies in all fields, an average of two a year.

Beals people today are either lobstermen or seiners, sometimes both. The sea is their living, not summer people, though ironically enough they may have had the first one of the genus to hit the coast: one Thomas Hicks, who settled at Hicks Cove. He had a homestead on the mainland and a summer camp in the island woods. Of course, his wife was supposed to be a witch, so perhaps through some sort of inherited memory Beals people have distrusted summer residents ever since.

There are two clam-shucking plants in town, where the clams are shelled, cleaned, and shipped in big cans to western markets. Some Beals people work in the sardine factories at Jonesport. The town itself has five boat shops which are kept busy turning out the beautiful yet strictly functional boats which lobstermen demand.

The men have all the equipment they need to make a good living, and homes on Beals are pleasant and modern.

There is one other facet of Beals life which surely deserves mention, because it is one of the town's claims to uniqueness, and yet it goes along with its high school's record of well-doing. That is the continuous and creative energy of the five churches. What the children of the Advent Christian church did a few years ago is typical of the collective attitude of Beals people toward their churches. These youngsters, under the guidance of a committee of adults, worked so hard to enlarge their Sunday school, and got so many older people to come and increase the adult membership, that they won a contest in which there were 418 other competitors, in churches all over the world.

This really didn't surprise anybody who knew anything about Beals.

ST. CROIX

It has been called Neutral, Schoodic, DeMonts, St. Croix, and today it is called Dochet as well as St. Croix. It has probably had other names as well. Maybe the Vikings had a name for it. It is a small island that looks like two tiny ones lying together, not very significant in its appearance except for its lighthouse. But if one lands one sees a bronze tablet fixed to a boulder, reading: "To commemorate the discovery and occupation of this island by De Monts and Champlain, who, naming it *'L'Isle Saint Croix,'* founded here June 26, 1604, the French Colony of Acadia, then the only settlement of Europeans north of Florida. This memorial was erected by the residents of Saint Croix Valley. 1904."

Eastward from Penobscot · 215

Instantly the past of the island springs blazingly alive. Magic names are in the air, such as Norumbega, the Arabian nights city described by that classic liar David Ingram, who sent many an otherwise hard-headed adventurer haring off after phantoms; Champlain was one of them, but he had become disillusioned in his search the very fall of the year when the St. Croix colony was founded.

In the company that came over with DeMonts were nobles—hard, sinewy, spirited men; artisans of every sort needed to keep a settlement going—carpenters, mechanics, farmers, blacksmiths; soldiers to organize the necessary defenses, servants to look after those who were used to service. But perhaps the most remarkable thing about the group was that there were both Huguenots and Catholics, and clergymen of both faiths attended them. (It is said that the two clerics argued mightily whenever they got together.)

This group reconnoitered along the coast westward from Port Royal and when they entered Passamaquoddy Bay they chose the small island in mid-river as the safest possible spot; Indians would have to cross water on all sides of them, and there was a good height of land for the lookouts. They had brought sawn lumber with them, and at once set to work on their settlement.

This was June; the sun was warm, the seas blue, the views enchanting, the woods thick and green. It was easy to work hard in such surroundings, and life ahead must have looked anything but grim; men must have talked among themselves of sending for their wives and children, of beginning a new life far more abundant than anything they had known in crowded France, with its violent extremes of poverty and wealth. Champlain had the plan of the settlement all worked out, and his picture-plan exists today. It was efficient and comfortable; there were partially paved streets, a bakery, a blacksmith shop, a meeting hall; a church, and houses where the men were quartered in groups. It was protected by a fort and a high palisade. In the early summer sun the gardens seemed to spring to life as soon as they were planted.

Everything was on the side of the settlers. This was truly Arcadia. Even when Indians came looking for a fight they were won over, and the chief was baptized. It must have taken, because the Passamaquoddies have been peaceful and churchgoing ever since.

Champlain took time out to look for Norumbega and did not find it, but who cared? As the red and gold autumn came there was still no suspicion of what winter on an island between Maine and Canada could be. De Monts sent ships back to France for more men, leaving seventy-nine behind. He believed they were sufficiently provided for, with plenty of warm clothing and food supplies. But the winey weather of October gave way with lightning suddenness to the first snowfall, and now the Frenchmen knew that the houses built so lightheartedly in June were not fit for winter. There was no well on the island, and when the water supply ran out, the salt ice around the island was not hard enough to walk across to the mainland, though it was too hard to row through.

Still, things were not too bad by Christmas—this first Christmas in the northern part of the New World. The Protestants and Catholics each held their services in the little church, and then there was feasting on venison and wine.

Some progressive and practical brain in the group started the little newspaper, "Master William," named for the King's court jester. Everyone who could think of anything to contribute did so, and it must have been a perfect type of occupational therapy to take the settlers' minds—temporarily—off the fact that winter seemed to be lasting forever; that the vegetables were almost gone and scurvy was setting in; that the wines froze and they had to use bad water or drink melted snow.

One of the men, M. Lescarbot, wrote the story of that winter in *Nova Francia*. "Work on the handmill," he said, "was very fatiguing, since the most of us, having slept poorly, and suffering from insufficiency of fuel, which we could not obtain on account of the ice, had scarcely any strength, and also because we ate only salt meat and vegetables during the winter."

More than thirty of the seventy-nine settlers died before spring, and two of these were the priest and minister. Those who lived and were able to carry on the necessary work were those who drove themselves to exercise; it may have been that they had greater vitality to begin with, and reserves of strength to fall back on. But they were all glad to see the first signs of spring in 1605. As soon as the ships came back, they left the settlement and sailed down toward Massachusetts, but eventually came back to Port Royal.

In 1613, when the governor of the new colony in Virginia sent ships to clean out the St. Croix settlement, as they cleaned out the Jesuit settlement at Mount Desert, the English found nothing on the small island but the buildings of the deserted colony. These they burned with what seems a rather vicious thoroughness. But perhaps they wanted to report that they had accomplished something. At least, the chapel and the cemetery where the unfortunate thirty were buried were left alone—they were destroyed by later tides, and not by human hands.

Nobody paid much attention to St. Croix after that; only an occasional Indian or a fur trader camped there for the night. By the 1763 Treaty of Paris, which ended the French and Indian Wars, France ceded St. Croix, along with all her other holdings, to England. By another treaty, in 1783 after the American Revolution, the St. Croix River was chosen as the boundary line between Canada and the newborn United States. But which of three rivers was the St. Croix? And which island was *the* island?

A Canadian-American commission went to work on the problem, and in the course of their investigations they came to one island which gave up to their spades cannon balls, crockery, bricks, tools—enough to prove to them that these were the pathetic ruins of the first settlement of the Sieur de Monts, Lord of Acadie, Viceroy of New France.

Then the state of Massachusetts, which claimed all of Maine, deeded the island to John Brewer of Robbinston, and his heirs still owned it in 1856 when the Government bought the northern half of the island for a lighthouse.

On a June day in 1904, when the people of the St. Croix Valley set the bronze tablet in the boulder, vessels of four nations met at the island in remembrance of a June day three hundred years before; citizens and ships of Canada, France, Great Britain, and the United States took part in the commemoration exercises, and the woods echoed back the salute of the ships' guns.

The people who now live closest to the island, people like John Trimble, who used to take visitors out to St. Croix by boat, feel a passionate pride in its history. They want it to become a park, and they have worked to that end for a long time. Senator Owen Brewster set things in motion in 1946, and at last the Board of National

Parks, Historic Sites, Buildings and Monuments declared it to be a historic site. The dream is to turn it into a museum which will show what the archaeologists have found out about how the colonists lived, and with what tools they worked; there will be a collection of now widely scattered documents in the handwriting of Champlain and de Monts. And the island itself will be preserved as much as possible from the destructive tides that have eaten away the southern end of the island and long ago destroyed the cemetery; there will be a retaining wall built there.

At the moment it is all quiet; on the surface there is no great rush of action, which must be painfully frustrating to those to whom the fight for the restoration of St. Croix is a personal battle. Let us hope they win it soon.

DEPARTURE

At St. Croix we leave the islands, only to wish we could begin the odyssey again, this time sailing westward down the coast, touching at all the islands we missed on the eastward voyage; landing on each long enough to savor its individualism, and to find who named it and why, who lived on it once and who lives on it now, and why he is an island man for all or part of the year. What has this islander found there, we would ask, that he could not find somewhere else? And if he has his roots there, we would ask why he has never wanted to leave. Perhaps he could tell, perhaps not, but his very being there would be answer enough.

So we would go from island to island, always carried, in Swinburne's phrase, "far out with the foam of the present that sweeps to the surf of the past."

We are not in love with yesterday; we may be anxious about the future, but we do not really want to turn back the clock three hundred years, to a time when there was also considerable anxiety about the future, when a man went to bed at night knowing that the very next day might hold death from an Indian attack or the start of a lethal epidemic. The perils of today are different and in some ways more terrible—if there can be degrees of terror where death is concerned—but we are conditioned and prepared for them as the early settler was prepared for his. To take the islands simply in their present sense affords a great deal of pleasure, because the charm that islands hold for people is eternal and universal. There is a fascination in being surrounded by water, cut off, separate, unique. The air is different; the wind sounds different; and there is so much sky, a world of space and light wherever we look, and to mount a high rock is to feel like the King of the Castle. The past and the future of the island, and ourselves, do not matter beside the delight and satisfaction of *now*.

And yet what has prepared us for anticipating and experiencing this peculiar pleasure is the past, whether or not we give it conscious thought; the procession of people whose memories we have inherited since the birth of man, those who went to islands for one reason or another—to live a holy life, or a private one, or an independent one, or a safe one. Like it or not, we are the fruits of them.

Narrowing this collective experience down to the almost immediate past, we cannot escape history, and the islands of Maine are the beginnings of Maine. They are granite monuments to the Founders which cannot be expunged from sight and memory by intensive building, parking lots, and freeways. They will always be there, and as long as man lives to remember this, they will have a significance as deep and as ancient as time.

ACKNOWLEDGMENTS, BIBLIOGRAPHY, AND APPENDIX

ACKNOWLEDGMENTS

Material on the islands dealt with in this book (listed in the order of the contents) was gathered and organized by the following members of the Maine Writers Research Club:

The Islands of Saco Bay; Richmond Island	Bhima M. Sturtevant
Cushing Island	Mabel Rogers Holt
Peaks Island	Rosemary Clifford Trott
Long Island	Dorothy Shaw Libby
Chebeague	Eric Kelly
Jewell Island	Miriam S. Thomas
Mackworth Island	Dorothy Shaw Libby
Cousins Island	Bhima M. Sturtevant
Harpswell's Islands; The Dead Ship of Harpswell	Margaret Burr Todd
Malaga Island	Miriam S. Thomas
Swan Island	Abbie Giggey
Squirrel Island; Mouse Island; Ram Island; Fisherman's Island; Damariscove	Bernice Bassett Wyman
Loud's Island	Susie McKechnie

Hog Island	Doris Ricker Marston
Monhegan	Elsie Holway Burleigh
Matinicus; Matinicus Rock	Florence Agnes Nelson
Criehaven	Frances Wright Turner
Monroe's Island; Sheep Island	Daphne Winslow Merrill
North Haven	Argie Buzzell
Hurricane	Ina Ladd Brown
Islesboro	Marion M. Springer
Seven Hundred Acre Island	Helen Batchelder Shute
Verona	Mabel Demers Hinckley
Little Deer Isle	Susan Shaw
Bartlett's Island	Stella L. Hill
Mount Desert Island	Hill–Hamlin
The Cranberry Isles	Susie McKechnie
Beals Island	Martha Meserve Gould
St. Croix	Doris Ricker Marston
Index of Tidewater Islands of Maine	Lillian W. Lewis

The Maine Writers Research Club and the author are grateful to the many individuals who have contributed valuable and generous assistance in compiling the material for this book. Since this work has covered many years, the following can be only a partial listing of those to whom thanks are due:

Mrs. Sylvina Alley; the Rev. Gertrude Anderson; Richard Bailey; Professor Thomas Barbour, Harvard University; Robert Barter, Town Clerk, Boothbay Harbor; Hon. Percival P. Baxter; the Rev. and Mrs. Neal Bousfield; Hon. Owen Brewster; W. F. Brock, Coast Guard commander, Rockland; Charles E. Campbell; Annie Clark; Dr. Bernard Cohen; Mrs. Ruie L. Curtis; Mrs. C. W. Demereaux; Mrs. Mary D. Devereux; Mrs. Norma Millay Ellis; Mrs. Elizabeth Bowditch Eustin; Hon. Raymond Fellows; Dr. Harry Emerson Fosdick; Mrs. Ruth Lepper

Acknowledgments · 225

Gardner; Charles Dana Gibson; Mae Gorham; Bruce Jordan, BMC, Damariscove Lifeboat Station; Georgie Leeman, Postmaster, Round Pond; A. E. Libby, Town Clerk, Vinalhaven; Mrs. Isabel B. MacDonald, Town Clerk, Isle au Haut; the Rev. Malcolm A. MacDuffie; H. Eola Mayo, Bangor Public Library; Mrs. Emma Murray; Mrs. Kathleen Newcomb; Mrs. Thelma Newcomb; Merritt T. Ober; Otis M. Ober; Velton Peabody; Peter Pepicello; the Rev. Hannah Powell; Charles Rawlings; Marion Rowe; Abram Sansom; Olive M. Smythe, Bangor Public Library; Roland Stimpson; Mrs. Marion Stubbs; John E. Sylvester, Sr.; William E. Sylvester, Sr.; Velma Teel; Mrs. Esther Terrill; Dorothy Vaughan, Librarian, Portsmouth; Harold Vinal; Edgar N. Walls; Lucy Whitmore; Dr. John Henry Wilson; Mrs. Thelma Woodward; Mrs. Bradbury Young.

Thanks are also due to the Central Maine Power Company, the Director of Inland Fisheries, the Harvard University Press, the Maine Development Commission, the Maine Historical Society, the Maine Publicity Bureau, the U.S. Navy, First District, Boston, and the Navy Department, Washington, D.C., the Waterville Public Library, and to the following publications: the Boothbay Harbor *Register*, the Boston *Herald*, *Down East*, the Lewiston *Journal*, *Outing*, and the Portland *Telegram*.

A SELECTIVE BIBLIOGRAPHY

The following list does not include the numerous pamphlets and guidebooks, town registers and other local documents consulted, nor many of the privately printed works on local history and general reference works on American history used in compiling material for this book.

Abbott, John S. C., *History of Maine* (1892)
Attwood, Stanley Bearce, *The Length and Breadth of Maine* (Lewiston, Me., 1946)
Baxter, James Phinney, *The Trelawny Papers* (1884)
Beck, Horace, *The Folklore of Maine* (1957)
Beston, Henry, ed., *White Pine and Blue Water: A State of Maine Reader* (1950)
Bisbee, Ernest E., *State o' Maine Scrap Book of Stories and Legends of Way Down East* (Lancaster, N. H., 1940)
Chadbourne, Ava H., *Maine Place Names and the Peopling of Its Towns* (1955)
Coffin, Robert P. Tristram, *Yankee Coast* (1947)
Dean, Jasper, *Narrative of the Sufferings, Preservation, and Deliverance of Captain John Dean* (1711)
Dole, Nathan H., and Gordon, I. L., *Maine of the Sea and Pines* (1928)
Eaton, Cyrus, *History of Thomaston, Rockland and South Thomaston* (Hallowell, Me., 1865)
Eliot, Charles W., *John Gilley, Maine Farmer and Fisherman* (1904)
Elkins, Leon Whitney, *The Story of Maine; Coastal Maine* (Bangor, Me., 1924)
Federal Writers Project, *Maine: A Guide "Down East"* (Boston, 1937)
Folsom, George, *History of Saco* (1830)
Grant, W. L., *Voyages of Samuel de Champlain* (1906)

Greene, Francis B., *Boothbay, Southport and Boothbay Harbor* (1906)
Holt, Harrison Jewell, *The Calendared Isles: A Romance of Casco Bay* (1910)
Ingersoll, Ernest, *Down East Latch Strings* (1887)
Jenney, Charles Francis, *The Fortunate Island of Monhegan* (1922)
Jones, Herbert G., *The Isles of Casco Bay in Fact and Fancy* (Portland, Me., 1946)
Maine Federation of Women's Clubs, *The Trail of the Maine Pioneer* (Bangor, Me., 1916)
Maine Historical Society Collections
Mitchell, Dorothy, *Along the Maine Coast* (1947)
Munson, Gorham, *Penobscot* (1959)
Parker, Arlita D., *A History of Pemaquid with Sketches of Monhegan, Popham and Castine* (Boston, 1925)
Pearson, Edmund, *Murder at Smutty Nose, and Other Murders* (1926)
Rich, Louise Dickinson, *The Coast of Maine* (1956)
Rowe, William Hutchinson, *The Maritime History of Maine* (1948)
Small, H. W., *History of Swan's Island, Maine* (Ellsworth, Me., 1898)
Smith, George Otis, *The Geology of the Fox Islands* (1896)
Smith, John, *Generall Historie of Virginia, New England & the Summer Isles* (2 vol., 1907)
Snow, Edward Rowe, *Pirates and Buccaneers of the Atlantic Coast* (1944)
——————, *True Tales of Pirates and Their Gold* (1953)
Spencer, W. D., *Pioneers on Maine Rivers* (Bangor, Me., 1930)
Starkey, Glen W., *Maine, Its History, Resources and Government* (1920)
Sterling, Robert T., *Lighthouses of the Maine Coast and the Men Who Keep Them* (1935)
Stetson, W. W., *History and Civil Government of Maine* (n.d.)
Street, George Edward, *Mount Desert: History*; ed. by S. A. Eliot (Boston, 1905)
Synge, Martha B., *A Book of Discovery* (1925)
Varney, George J., *History of Maine* (1888)
Vinal, Albra Josephine, *History of Vinal Haven* (1900)
Wasson, George S., *Sailing Days on the Penobscot* (Salem, Mass., 1932)
Wheeler, George A. and Henry W., *History of Brunswick, Topsham and Harpswell* (1878)
Williamson, W. D., *History of the State of Maine* (Hallowell, Me., 1832)
Winslow, Sidney L., *Fish Scales and Stone Chips* (1952)
Young, Hazel, *Islands of New England* (Boston, 1954)

Appendix:
THE TIDEWATER ISLANDS OF MAINE

The list that follows includes only *islands*—i.e., bodies of land which are surrounded by water, either all the time or at high tide, and which support some soil and vegetation. It does not include *ledges*, which do not ordinarily support vegetation, except for those that have lighthouses manned by keepers.

Opposite the name of each island is that of the town or township in which it is located, or, if the island is itself a town, the county to which it belongs. Where there are two or more islands of the same name in the same town or county, the latitudes and longitudes of each are given. Islands more easily identified by the group to which they belong—as those comprising the Muscle Ridge, or Ridges, south of Rockland in the approaches to Penobscot Bay—are so designated.

An asterisk (*) indicates that a lighthouse is located on the island.

This list has been compiled from the maps of the U.S. Geological Survey and the charts of the U.S. Coast and Geodetic Survey. Stanley Bearce Attwood's *The Length and Breadth of Maine* was also helpful; and I have drawn on local knowledge for some names of islands shown but not named on any available map or chart.

Note that with the exception of Swan's Island, the apostrophe is not countenanced by the U.S. Board on Geographical Names. In most cases the Maine native has paid no heed to the policy of this board!

LILLIAN W. LEWIS
Belfast, Maine

Island	Town or location	Island	Town or location
Allen	St. George	Bar	Trescott
Alley	Beals	Bar Is. (2)	Deer Isle
Alley	Trenton	Barnes	Harpswell
Andrew	Muscle Ridge	Barney's Little	Beals
Andrews	Stonington	Barred	Deer Isle—44-10-
Anguilla	Roque Bluffs		00; 68-43-14
Appledore	Isles of Shoals, Kittery	Barred	Stonington
		Barred Is. (2)	Deer Isle—44-16-
The Ark	Southport		00; 68-50-01
Arrowsic	Sagadahoc County	Barred Is. (8)	Deer Isle—44-13-55; 68-48-30
Ash	Muscle Ridge	Barter	Boothbay
Ash	Sorrento	Barter	St. George
Ash	Sullivan	Bartlett	Mount Desert
Aunt Mollie	Penobscot	Bartol	Freeport
*Avery Rock	Machiasport	Barton	Vinalhaven
		Basket	Cumberland
Babbidge	North Haven	Basket	Saco
Babson	Brooklin	Bass	Kennebunkport
Baileys	Harpswell	Bates	Cumberland
Baker	Cranberry Isles	Battery	Isle au Haut
Bakers Is. (2)	Swan's Island	Battle	Penobscot
Bald	North Haven	Beach	Deer Isle
Bald Porcupine	Bar Harbor	Beal	Georgetown
Ballast	Jonesport	Beals	Washington County
Bare	Machiasport		
Bare	Stonington	Bean	Sorrento
Bareneck	Georgetown	Bear	Deer Isle
Bar	Addison	*Bear	Mount Desert
Bar	Bar Harbor	Bear	Phippsburg (New Meadows River)
Bar	Bristol (Muscongus)		
Bar	Gouldsboro	Beaver	Bristol
Bar	Harpswell	Ben	Harpswell (Quahog Bay)
Bar	Jonesport		
Bar	Machiasport	Benner	St. George
Bar	Milbridge	Berry	Georgetown
Bar	Mount Desert	Berry	Wiscasset (Back River)
Bar	Muscle Ridge		
Bar	Roque Bluffs	Bickford	Kennebunkport
Bar	St. George	Biggers	Winter Harbor
Bar	Tremont	Big Hen	Harpswell

Island	Town or location	Island	Town or location
Big Nash	Addison	Browney	Beals
Bills	Isle au Haut	Browns	Vinalhaven
Birch Is.	Addison	Buckle	Stonington
Birch	Deer Isle	Buckle	Swan's Island
Birch Is.	Edmunds	Buck	Cape Rosier (Brooksville)
Birch	Georgetown		
Birch	Harpswell	Bucks, see Harbor	
Birch	Mount Desert	Bum Key	Bar Harbor
Birch	Muscle Ridge	Bumpkin	Kennebunkport
Birch	South Bristol	Burial	Lubec
Birch	Vinalhaven	Burnt Coat, see Swan's	
Black	Bar Harbor	Burnt Coat	Phippsburg
Black	Friendship	Burnt	Isle au Haut
Black	Long Island	Burnt	North Haven
Black	Mount Desert	Burnt	Pembroke
Black	Swan's Island	Burnt	St. George
Black Horse	Isle au Haut	*Burnt	Southport
Blubber	St. George	Burnt	South Thomaston
Bluff Head	Vinalhaven	Burnt Is. (2)	Vinalhaven
Bluff	Scarboro	Burnt Porcupine	Bar Harbor
Bois Bubert	Milbridge		
Bold	Stonington	Bush	Harpswell
Bombazeen	Harpswell (New Meadows River)	Bushy	Phippsburg
		Bustins	Freeport
		Butter	Deer Isle
*Boon Island	York		
Boston	Boothbay (Sheepscot River)	Cabbage, see Independence	
		Calderwood	North Haven
		Caldwell	St. George
Bowman	Freeport	Calf	Beals
Bradbury	Deer Isle	Calf	Bremen
Bragdons	West Bath	Calf	Gouldsboro
Bragdons	York	Calf	Roque Bluffs
Bremen Long	Bremen	Calf	Sorrento
Brick	Bowdoinham	Calf	St. George
Brimstone	Swan's Island	Campbell	Deer Isle
Brimstone	Vinalhaven	Campbell	Phippsburg
The Brothers	Cape Elizabeth	Camp	Muscle Ridge
The Brothers	Falmouth	Camp	Stonington
The Brothers	Roque Bluffs	Cape	Southport
The Brothers	St. George	Cape Porpoise	Cape Porpoise

Island	Town or location	Island	Town or location
Cape Wash	Cutler	Cone	Addison
Capitol	Southport	Coombs	Brunswick
Carleton	Blue Hill	Coombs	Stonington
Carlisle	Boothbay (Damariscotta River)	Cooper	Lubec
		Coot, see Combs	
		Cousins	Yarmouth
Carlow	Eastport	Cow	Bremen
Carrying Place	Addison	Cow	Brunswick-Topsham (Androscoggin River)
Carrying Place Head	Phippsburg		
Carver	Vinalhaven	Cow	Harrington
Castle	Arrowsic	Cow	Portland
Castle	Georgetown	Cow	Saco River
The Castle	Steuben	Crab	Freeport
Cedarbush	Southport	Cranberry	Friendship
Cedar	Friendship	Cranberry	Harrington
Cedar	Isles of Shoals, Kittery	Cranberry Isles, see Great and Little Cranberry	
Cedar	Vinalhaven	Crane	Friendship
Center	Harpswell (Quahog Bay)	Crane	Vinalhaven
		Crawford	Bath
Chamberly	Milbridge	Crescent	Muscle Ridge
Chance	Cutler	Criehaven	Approach to Penobscot Bay
Chandlers	Addison		
Chatto	Brooklin	Cross	Cutler
Chebeague (Great)	Yarmouth (Casco Bay)	Cross	North Haven
		Crotch	Cushing
Clam	Bremen	Crotch	Friendship
Clam	Stonington	Crotch	Stonington
Clapboard	Falmouth	Crotch	Vinalhaven
Clark	Kittery	Crow	Brunswick
Clark	St. George	Crow	Cumberland
Cliff	Portland (Casco Bay)	Crow	Deer Isle
		Crow	Five Islands, Georgtown
Closson	Blue Hill		
College	Portland (Long Island)	Crow	Georgetown (Kennebec River)
Colt Head	Deer Isle		
Combs	South Thomaston	Crow	Harpswell
Compass	Deer Isle	Crow	Long Island
Conary	Deer Isle	Crow	Milbridge

Island	Town or location	Island	Town or location
Crow	Muscle Ridge	Doliver	Isle au Haut
Crow	Portland (Long Island)	Double Shot Is.	Cutler
		Double Shot Is.	Roque Bluffs
Crow	South Bristol	Douglass Is.	Milbridge
Crow	Swan's Island	Doyle	Jonesport
Crow	Winter Harbor	Drake	Wells
Crumple	Beals	Dram	Pembroke
*The Cuckolds	Southport	Dram	Sorrento
Cundell	Vinalhaven	Drisco	Addison
Currant	Milbridge	Drum	Long Island
Curtis	Camden	Duck	Isles of Shoals, Kittery
Cushing	Portland		
Cushing	South Thomaston	Duck Is. (3)	Vinalhaven
Cutters, see Fog		Dudley	Lubec
Cutts	Kittery	Dumpling	Stonington
		Dumpling Is. (5)	Cutler (Cross Island)
Dagger	North Haven		
Damariscove	Off Ocean Point, Boothbay	Dunn	Jonesport
		Dyer	Harrington
Darling	Blue Hill	Dyer	Vinalhaven
Daniel	Addison		
Davids	Southport	Eagle	Addison
Davis	Edgecomb	*Eagle	Deer Isle
Davis	St. George	Eagle	Harpswell
Davis	South Bristol	Eagle	Saco
Deer Isle	Cutler	Eagle	St. George—43-57-00; 69-18-00
Deer Isle	Deer Isle		
Deer Isle	Harrington	Eagle	St. George—43-59-03; 69-09-36
Denbow	Lubec		
Despair	Roque Bluffs	Eagle	Swan's Island
Devil	Stonington	East Brown Cow (The Cow)	Phippsburg (eastern Casco Bay)
Dingley	Harpswell (New Meadows River)		
		Eastern	Steuben
		Eastern Ear	Isle au Haut
Dix	Muscle Ridge	Eastern Mark	Stonington
Dix	Phippsburg	Eastern Sheep	Beals
Dobbins	Beals	Eaton	Deer Isle
Dochet, see Saint Croix		Eben	South Thomaston
Dog	Eastport	*Egg Rock	Frenchmans Bay
Dogfish	Vinalhaven	Elm Is. (2)	Harpswell

Island	Town or location	Island	Town or location
Elwell	St. George	Fox	Georgetown
Emery	Owls Head		(MacMahan
Ensign Is. (2)	Islesboro		Island)
Ewe	Isle au Haut	Fox Is. (5)	Phippsburg
Ewe Is. (2)	Woolwich	Fox Islands, see North Haven and Vinalhaven	
Falls	Trescott	Foxbird	Wiscasset
Fan	Machiasport	*Franklin	Friendship
Farrel	Stonington	Freds	Trescott
Fellow	Roque Bluffs	Freese	Deer Isle
Fiddle Head	Deer Isle	French	Freeport
Fish Hawk	Boothbay	French House	Beals
Fisherman	Beals	Freyer	Brunswick
Fisherman	Boothbay		(Androscoggin
Fisherman	Muscle Ridge		River)
Five Islands, see Georgetown, Malden, Hen, Crow, Mink		Friendship	Friendship
		Frost	Perry
Five Is. (5)	Harrington		
Flag	Harpswell	Gander	Brooklin
Flag	Muscle Ridge	Garden	South Thomaston
Flake Is. (2)	Isle au Haut	Garden (2)	Swan's Island
Flash	Harpswell	Garrison	Friendship
Flat	Addison	Gay	Cushing
Flat	Islesboro	Gem	South Bristol
Flat	Winter Harbor	George	Harpswell
Flea	Stonington	Georges Islands, St. George, see Allen, Benner, Burnt, Little Burnt, Davis and Thompson	
Fling	Deer Isle		
Flint	Harrington		
Flye	Brooklin	Georges Head	Stonington
Fog	Georgetown	Georgetown	Sagadahoc
Fog	Isle au Haut		County
Folly	Kennebunkport	Gerrish	Kittery
Folly	Mount Desert	Gibbs	Addison
Fort	Damariscotta River (Boothbay)	*Goat	Kennebunkport
		Goat	Phippsburg
		Gooseberry	Kittery
Fort	Harrington	Gooseberry	Phippsburg
Foster	Harrington	Gooseberry	Stonington
Foster	Machiasport	Gooseberry	Swan's Island
Foster	South Bristol	Gooseberry	Trescott
Fox	Lubec	Goose	Addison

233

Island	Town or location	Island	Town or location
Goose	Brooklin	Green Is. (2)	Long Island
Goose	Islesboro	Green Is. (5)	Southport
Goose Is. (5)	Beals and Jonesport	Greening	Southwest Harbor
Goose Nest	Cumberland	Greer	Vinalhaven
*Goose Rocks	Fox Island Thorofare	Griffin	St. George
		Griffith Head	Georgetown
The Goslins (2)	Harpswell	Grog	Stonington
Graffam	Muscle Ridge	Guard	Harrington
Gravel	Penobscot		
Great Chebeague, see Chebeague		Haddock	Bristol
Great Cranberry	Cranberry Isles	Haddock	Harpswell
Great Diamond	Portland	*Halfway Rock	Casco Bay
*Great Duck	Long Island	Halifax	Englishmans Bay
Great Mark	Harpswell	Hall	Friendship
Great Moshier	Yarmouth	Hall	Jonesport
Great Spoon	Isle au Haut	Hallowell	Edmunds
Great Spruce	Jonesport	Halls	Vinalhaven
Great Spruce Head	Deer Isle	Harbor	Boothbay
		Harbor	Brooklin
Great Wass	Beals	Harbor	Brooksville
Green	Addison	Harbor	Friendship
Green	Bar Harbor	Harbor	Isle au Haut
Green	Beals	Harbor	Long Island
Green	Biddeford	Harbor	Phippsburg
Green	Boothbay	Harbor	Swan's Island
*Green	Brooklin	Hardhead	Deer Isle
Green	Jonesport	Hardwood	Beals
Green	Kennebunkport	Hardwood	Isle au Haut
Green	Milbridge	Hardwood	Jonesport
Green	Mount Desert	Hardwood	Tremont
Green	Roque Bluffs	Hardy	Waldoboro
Green	Stonington	Harper	Westport
Green	Swan's Island	Harris	York
Green	Vinalhaven—44-04-25; 68-54-55	Hart	St. George
		Haskell	Harpswell
*Green	Vinalhaven—44-02-16; 68-27-20	Hat	Swan's Island
		Hay	South Bristol
		Hay	Vinalhaven
Green	Vinalhaven—44-04-12; 68-46-34	Hay Is. (5)	Vinalhaven

234

Island	Town or location	Island	Town or location
Head Harbor	Jonesport	Hopkins	Harpswell (New Meadows River)
Heart	Deer Isle		
Hemlock	Addison		
Hen	Deer Isle	The Hop	Gouldsboro
Hen	Five Islands, Georgtown	Horn	Kittery
		Horse Head	Deer Isle
Hen	Harpswell	Horse, see Harbor Island, Phippsburg	
Hen	Phippsburg		
Hen	St. George	Horse	Harpswell
Hen Is. (2)	Vinalhaven	Hospital	Brooksville
Heron	South Bristol	House	Portland
Heron	Swan's Island	Huckins	Lubec
Heron	Winter Harbor	Hungry	Bremen
Heron (3)	Phippsburg	Humpkins Islet	Stonington
Hewell or Hewett	Muscle Ridge	Hunting	Southport
		Hurricane	Muscle Ridge
Hickey	Machiasport	Hurricane	Vinalhaven
High	South Bristol	Hutchinsons	Islesboro
High	Muscle Ridge	The Hypocrites (4)	Boothbay (east entrance Boothbay Harbor)
High St. George	St. George		
High Sheriff	Swan's Island		
Hodgdon	Boothbay	Independence	Boothbay (Liniken Bay)
Hodgdons	Bristol		
Hog	Bremen	Indian	Bristol
Hog	Brooklin	Indian	Freeport
Hog	Damariscotta	Indian	Rockport
Hog	Deer Isle	Indiantown	Boothbay
Hog	Gouldsboro	Ingalls	Sorrento
Hog	Islesboro	Inner Green	Portland
Hog	Lubec	Inner Heron	South Bristol
Hog	Machiasport	Ironbound	Winter Harbor
Hog	Matinicus Isle	Irony	Harpswell
Hog	North Haven	*Isle au Haut	South of Stonington
Hog	Steuben		
Holbrook or Hooks	Brooksville	Isle of Springs (Sweet)	Boothbay
Holmes	Winter Harbor	Islesboro, see Long Island (Penobscot Bay)	
Hooper	St. George		
Hope	Cumberland	Isles of Shoals, see Appledore, Cedar, Duck and Smutty Nose	
Hope	Roque Bluffs		

235

Island	Town or location	Island	Town or location
Jacquish	Harpswell (Baileys)	*Libby Is. (2)	Machiasport
		Lime	Islesboro
Jamaica	Kittery	Lines	Bath
Jed (2)	Surry	Little Babson	Brooklin
Jenny	Harpswell	Little Bangs	Cumberland
Jewell	Portland	Little Birch	Harpswell
Jim	Eastport	Little Black	Long Island
Job	Islesboro	Little Bois Bubert	Milbridge
John	Long Island		
John	Mount Desert	Little Brimstone Is. (6)	Swan's Island— 44-00-28; 68-46-26
John	Stonington		
Johns	Bristol		
Johns	Swan's Island	Little Burnt	St. George
Johnson	Waldoboro	Little Bustins	Freeport
John White	Addison	Little Caldwell Is.	St. George
Jones Garden	Bristol		
Jordan	Winter Harbor	Little Calf	Gouldsboro
Jordans Delight	Milbridge	Little Camp	Stonington
Junk of Pork	Portland	Little Chebeague	Cumberland
Junk of Pork	Sorrento		
Kemps Folly	Milbridge	Little Cranberry	Cranberry Isles
Killick Stone	Bristol	Little Deer	Deer Island
Kimball	Isle au Haut	Little Diamond	Portland
Knight	Jonesport	Little Dochet	Robbinston
		Little Drisco	Addison
The Ladle	Addison	Little Duck	Long Island
Lairey	Vinalhaven	Little French	Freeport
Lamb	Georgetown	Little George Head	Stonington
Lamp	Swan's Island		
Lane	Freeport	Little Gott	Tremont
Lane	Vinalhaven	Little Green	Matinicus
Large Green	Matinicus	Little Green	Muscle Ridge
Lassell	Islesboro	Little Hardwood	Jonesport
Lazy Gut Is. (6)	Deer Isle	Little Hurricane	Vinalhaven
Leadbetter	Vinalhaven	Little Iron	Harpswell
Leavitt (also called Darlings)	Harpswell (Cundys Harbor)	Little Island	Boothbay Harbor —43-51-30; 69-36-10
Lee	Phippsburg	Little Island	Boothbay Harbor —43-51-10; 69-40-02
Lewis (also called Miles)	Boothbay		

236

Island	Town or location	Island	Town or location
Little Island	Bowdoinham	Long	Islesboro (Waldo County)
Little Island	Bristol		
Little Island	Friendship	Long	Lubec
Little Island	Harpswell (Cundys Harbor)	Long	Portland
		Long	Vinalhaven
		Long Porcupine	Bar Harbor
Little Island	Islesboro	Lord	Harrington
Little Island	Matinicus	Louds, see Muscongus	
Little Island	New Harbor (Bristol)	Lower Basket	Cumberland
Little Island	Owls Head	Lower Clapboard	Falmouth
Little Island	Vinalhaven		
Littlejohn	Yarmouth	Lower Goose	Harpswell
Little Knubble	Georgetown	Lower Mark	Southport
Little Mark	Harpswell		
Little Mark	Roque Bluffs	MacMahan	Georgetown
Little McGlathery	Stonington	Mackworth	Falmouth
		Mahoney	Brooklin
Little Moose	Winter Harbor	Major	Lubec
Little Moshier	Yarmouth	Malaga	Phippsburg
Little Pond	Muscle Ridge	Malden	Five Islands, Georgetown
Little Ram	Beals		
Little Ram	Roque Bluffs	Manana	Monhegan
Little River	Cutler	Man	Jonesport
Little Sheep	Jonesport	Marblehead	Owls Head
Little Sheep	Stonington	Mark	Harpswell
Little Spoon	Isle au Haut	Mark	Islesboro
Little Spruce Head	Deer Isle	Mark	Jonesport
		*Mark	Stonington
Little Spruce	Jonesport	Mark	Winter Harbor
Little Stage	Kennebunkport	Marr	Georgetown
Little Whaleboat	Harpswell	Marshall	Swan's Island
		Marsh	Bristol
		Marsh (part of Roques Island)	Jonesport
Little Wood	Phippsburg		
Lobster	Gouldsboro		
Lobster	North Haven	Mash Harbor	Addison
Locust	Waldoboro	Mathews	Eastport
Long	Blue Hill	Matinicus	Entrance to Penobscot Bay
Long	Georgetown		
Long	Frenchboro	*Matinicus Rock	Matinicus
Long	Harpswell		

237

Island	Town or location	Island	Town or location
McFarland	Boothbay Harbor	Mouse	Jonesport
McGee	St. George	Mouse	Southport
McGlathery	Stonington	Muscongus	Bristol
Merchant	Isle au Haut		
Merritt	West Bath	Narrows	Harrington
Merrow	Boothbay	Narrows	Vinalhaven
Merry	Edgecomb	Narvo	Vinalhaven
Metinic Green	Matinicus	*Nash	Addison
Metinic	Matinicus	Nathan	Isle au Haut
Middle	Islesboro	Nautilus	Brooksville
Middle Mark	Georgetown	Navy Yard	Kittery
Miles	Boothbay	Ned	Winter Harbor
Miller	Bristol	Negro	Boothbay
Miller	Waldoboro	Negro	Saco
Millett	Stonington	Negro Is. (2)	Castine
Ministerial	Cumberland	Negro (Camden)	see Curtis Island
Mink	Addison	Nigger	Arrowsic
Mink	Beals	Nigger	Kennebunkport
Mink	Cutler	Night Cap	Addison
Mink or Lower	Five Islands, Georgetown	Nipple	Jonesport
		Nipps	Perry
Mink	Lubec	No Mans	Stonington
Mink	Muscle Ridge	No Mans Land	Matinicus
Minot	Islesboro	Norris	Winter Harbor
*Mistake	Jonesport	Northern	St. George (Tenants Harbor)
*Monhegan	Off Muscongus Bay		
Monroe	Owls Head	North Haven	Penobscot Bay
Moore	Brooksville	North Sugar Loaf	Phippsburg
Moose	Addison		
Moose	Eastport	Norton	Addison
Moose	Stonington	Norton	Beals
Moose	Tremont	Norton	St. George
*Moose Peak, see Mistake Island		*Nubble	York
Morse	Friendship	The Nub	Blue Hill
Mosquito	St. George		
Mount Desert	Hancock County	Oak	Harpswell
*Mount Desert Rock	Hancock County	Oak	Muscle Ridge
		Oak	North Haven
Mouse	Isle au Haut	Oak	Woolwich
Mouse	Islesboro	Oar	Bremen

Island	Town or location	Island	Town or location
Old Man	Cutler	Pole	Harpswell (Quahog Bay)
Opechee	Swan's Island		
Orono	Swan's Island	Pomp	Beals
Orrs	Harpswell	Pond Cove	Roque Bluffs
Otter	Harrington	Pond	Deer Isle
Otter	Friendship	Pond	Harpswell
Otter	Muscle Ridge	Pond	Milbridge
Otter	Vinalhaven	*Pond	Phippsburg (mouth of the Kennebec)
Outer Bar	Gouldsboro		
Outer Green	Portland		
Outer Heron	Boothbay	Pond	Swan's Island
Outer Ram	Beals	Pond	Winter Harbor
Overset	Portland (Long)	Pond Is. (2)	Muscle Ridge
		Pop	Steuben
Parker	Lubec	Popes Folly	Lubec
Partridge	Harrington	Porcupine	Machiasport
Pea	Milbridge	The Porcupines, Long, Sheep	see Bald, Burnt,
Peabow	Bristol		
Peaks	Portland		
Peggy	Georgetown	The Porcupines (2)	Deer Isle
Pell	Isle au Haut		
Perch	Boothbay	Potato	Stonington—44-08-00; 68-39-10
*Perkins	Georgetown (Kennebec River)		
		Potato	Stonington—44-08-20; 68-35-35
*Petit Manan Island	Steuben	Potato	Vinalhaven
		Pound of Tea	Freeport
Pettingill	Freeport	Pound of Tea	West Bath (New Meadows River)
Phebe	Georgetown		
Phinney	Swan's Island		
Phoebe	Stonington	Powderhorn	Boothbay (Sheepscot Bay)
Pickering	Deer Isle		
Pig	Beals		
Pine	Woolwich	Pratt	Southport
Pinkham (formerly Ram)	Harpswell	Preble	Waukeag
		Pudding	Criehaven
Pinkham	Milbridge	Pumpkin	Boothbay
Placentia	Long Island	Pumpkin Is.	Deer Isle
Pleasant	Muscle Ridge	Pumpkin Knob	Freeport
Plummer	Addison	Pumpkin Nob	Portland (Peaks Island)
Plummer (2)	South Bristol		

Island	Town or location	Island	Town or location
Rabbits Ear	Isle au Haut	Resolution	Deer Isle
Rackliff	St. George	Richmond	Cape Elizabeth
Ragged, see Criehaven		Ringtown	Swan's Island
Ragged	Harpswell	Ripley (2)	Harrington
Ram	Addison	Roberts Is.	Vinalhaven
Ram	Arrowsic	Rock	Stonington
Ram	Bath	Rodger	Jonesport
Ram Is. (3)	Beals	Rodgers	Lubec
*Ram	Boothbay	Rogue	Harpswell
Ram	Bremen	Rogues	Cumberland
Ram	Brooksville	Roland	Winter Harbor (Schoodic)
Ram	Cape Elizabeth		
Ram	Friendship	Roque	Jonesport
Ram (now Pinkham)	Harpswell (Merryconeague Sound)	Rosebud	Isle au Haut
		Ross	Bristol
		Round	Machiasport
Ram	Harpswell (Orrs Island)	Round	Stonington—44-07-25; 68-37-40
Ram	Isle au Haut	Round	Stonington—44-09-00; 68-39-00
Ram	Long Island		
Ram	Machiasport	Round	Swan's Island
Ram	Portland	Rumell	Tremont
Ram	Rockport	Rum Key	Gouldsboro
Ram	Saco	Rutherford	South Bristol
Ram	St. George—43-59-42; 69-10-09		
		Saddle	Islesboro
Ram	St. George—43-55-25; 69-18-00	Saddleback	Stonington
		Saddleback	Swan's Island
Ram	Stonington	*Saint Croix	Calais
Ram	Woolwich	Saint Helena	Stonington
*Ram Island Ledge	Portland	Sally	Gouldsboro
Raspberry	Addison	Sally Islands (Steuben), see Western, Outer Bar, Bar, Sheep, Sally and Eastern	
Raspberry	St. George (Port Clyde)		
Razor	Lubec	Salt	Machiasport
Read	Woolwich	Salter	Georgetown
Red	Perry	Sand Is. (2)	Addison
Reddington	Perry	Sand	Cumberland
Redin	Kennebunkport	Sand	Stonington
Reed	Boothbay	Sand Is. (10)	Friendship

Island	Town or location	Island	Town or location
The Sands	Pittson (Kennebec River)	Sheep	Gouldsboro
		Sheep	Harpswell
Sargeants	Winter Harbor	Sheep	Jonesport
Sawyer	Beals	Sheep	Mount Desert
Sawyer	Boothbay	Sheep	Muscle Ridge
Scabby (2)	Machiasport	Sheep	Steuben
Scallop	North Haven	Sheep	Stonington
Schoodic	Winter Harbor	Sheep	Swan's Island
Scotch	Cutler	Sheep	Vinalhaven
Scott (2)	Deer Isle	Sheep Porcupine	Bar Harbor
Scrag	Deer Isle		
Scrag	Harpswell	Sheldrake	Addison
Scrag	Swan's Island	Sheldrake	Sullivan (or Sorrento)
Scraggy	Stonington		
Scrub	Lubec	Shelter	Harpswell
Seal (*also called* Folwells)	Islesboro	Shingle	Stonington
		Ship	Tremont
Seal	Matinicus	The Shivers (2)	Stonington
Seal	Phippsburg	Shoppee	Roque Bluffs
Seal	St. George	Simpson	Machiasport
Seal Is. (2)	Georgetown	Sister	Freeport
Sears	Searsport	Sister Is.	Long Island
Seavey	St. George	The Sisters (2)	Harpswell
Sebascodegan (*also called* Great)	Harpswell	The Sisters	Cape Elizabeth
		The Sisters	Saint George
		Slate	Beals
*Seguin	Georgetown	Sloop	Deer Isle
Seguin	Jonesport	Smith	Vinalhaven
Seven Hundred Acre	Islesboro	Smutty Nose	Brooklin
		Smutty Nose	Isles of Shoals, Kittery
Shabbitt	Addison		
Shabby	Deer Isle	Snow	Harpswell (Quahog Bay)
Shag	Harrington		
Shark	St. George	South Sugar Loaf	Phippsburg (mouth of Kennebec)
Sheep Head	Deer Isle		
Sheep	Addison—44-29-47; 67-42-15		
		Southern	St. George (Tenants Harbor)
Sheep	Addison—44-31-34; 67-45-30		
		Southern Mark	Isle au Haut
Sheep	Brooksville	Southport	Lincoln County
Sheep	Deer Isle		

241

Island	Town or location	Island	Town or location
Sow and Pigs (4)	Freeport	Sugar Loaves (2)	Vinalhaven
Soward	Sullivan	Sutton	Cranberry Isles
Spar	Georgetown	Swan	Kennebec River opposite Richmond
Spar	Jonesboro		
Sparks	Penobscot		
Sparrow	Isle au Haut	*Swan's Island	Hancock County
Spaulding	South Thomaston	Sweet (*also* called Isle of Springs)	Boothbay
Spectacle	Eastport		
Spectacle	Newcastle		
Spectacle	Vinalhaven		
Spectacle	Winter Harbor	Tabbetts (Tibbetts)	Addison
Spectacle	Muscle Ridge		
Spectacle Is. (2)	Boothbay	Teal *or* Tiel	St. George
Spectacle Is. (2)	Brooksville	Ten Pound	Matinicus
Spectacle Is. (3)	Jonesport	Thief	Bristol
Spectacles (2)	St. George	Thomas	Bar Harbor
Spruce	Islesboro	Thompson	Bar Harbor
Spruce	Stonington	Thompson	St. George
Sprucehead	South Thomaston	Thorne	Bath
Squid	Mount Desert	Thorpe	Boothbay
Squirrel	Southport	Three Bush	Swan's Island
Stage	Biddeford	Three Islands (3)	Harpswell and West Bath
Stage	Georgetown		
Stage	Kennebunkport	Thrumcap	Bar Harbor
Starboard	Machiasport	Thrumcap	Brooksville
Stave	Cumberland	Thrumcap	Gouldsboro
Stave	Deer Isle	Thrumcap	Islesboro
Stave	Gouldsboro	Thrumcap	South Bristol
Steel Harbor	Jonesport	Tibbet	Boothbay
Stepping Stones (3)	Portland (Long Island)	Timber	Kennebunkport
		Tinker	Tremont
Steve	Stonington	Tommy	Harrington
Stevens	Addison	Tommy	South Thomaston
Stimpsons	North Haven	Torry Is. (2)	Brooklin
Stockmans	Cumberland	Trafton	Harrington
Stoddard	Vinalhaven	Tread (3)	Trescott
Stone	Machiasport	Treasure	Sorrento
Stone	St. George	Treat	Lubec
Stratton	Saco	Trott	Kennebunkport
Strout	Harrington	Trumpet	Tremont
Sturdivant	Cumberland		

Island	Town or location	Island	Town or location
Tumbler	Boothbay Harbor	Whaleboat	Harpswell
Turnip	Georgetown	Wharton	Friendship
Turnip	Harpswell	Wheat	Isle au Haut
Turtle	Winter Harbor	Wheaton	Matinicus
The Twinnies (2)	Bar Harbor	White Bull (The Bull)	Harpswell
Two Bush	Deer Isle	* Whitehead	Muscle Ridge
Two Bush	Matinicus	Whitehorse	Isle au Haut
* Two Bush	Muscle Ridge	White	Deer Isle
Two Bush	St. George	White	Harpswell
Two Bush	Stonington	White Is. (2)	Boothbay
Tyler Is. (3)	Westport	White (5)	Kittery
		White (14)	Vinalhaven
Uncle Zekes	Harpswell	Whittum	Westport
Upper Coombs	Brunswick	Widow	Vinalhaven
Upper Goose	Harpswell	William	West Bath
Upper Green Is. (2) (The Green Nubs)	Cumberland	Williams	Freeport
		Winslow	Penobscot
		Witch	South Bristol
Upper Flag	Harpswell	Wolsgrover	Friendship
Upper Mark	Westport	Wooden Ball (The Ball)	Matinicus Isle
Vaill	Portland (Long Island)	Wood	Bath
		Wood	Kittery
Vaughn	Kennebunkport	Wood	Phippsburg—43-44-00; 69-52-10
Verona	Verona (Penobscot River)		
* Vinalhaven	Penobscot Bay	Wood	Phippsburg—43-44-20; 69-46-45
Virgin Is.	Jonesport	* Wood	Saco
		Wood	Georgetown
Warren	Islesboro	Woodward	Jonesport
Water	Jonesport	Wreck	Bristol
Webber	Boothbay	Wreck	Stonington
Webber Is. (2)	Georgetown	Wyer	Harpswell
West Barge	Tremont		
West Brown Cow	Cumberland	Yarmouth	Harpswell
Western	Deer Isle	Yellow	Winter Harbor
Western, see Sally Is.		Yellow Head	Machiasport
Western Ear	Isle au Haut	Yellow Ridge	St. George
Western Sheep	Beals	York	Isle au Haut
Westport	Lincoln County	Youngs (3)	Penobscot

INDEX

Abbott family, 148, 175
Abenaki Indians, 14, 194
Acadia, 15, 195, 214, 217
Acadia National Park, 180, 197
"Acaraza Man" ("the Professor"), 89
Ada Barker, 55-56
Adams, Abraham, 70
Adams, Charles Francis, 179
Adams, John, 122
Adams, John Quincy, 157
Agamenticus, Mount, 25
Agassiz, Louis, 197
Albany, 170, 171
Aldrich, Thomas Bailey, 23
Allen's Island, 129, 130
Alley family, 190
Alley, John, 212
Alexander family, 87
Alves, Joe, 154
America, 82
American Museum of Natural History, 136
Ames family, 148
Ames, Capt. Stuart, 145
Ames, Stuart, Jr., 146
Among the Isles of Shoals, 20, 23
Anderson, Mr. and Mrs. Carl, 154
Anderson family, 155
Anderson, Rev. Gertrude, 209
Andrews Island, 47
Andrews, James, 47, 48
Andrews, Jane, 68, 69
Andrews, Samuel, 68, 69
Androscoggin River, 53
Ann, Cape, 192
Appledore Island, 19-21, 23, 24, 147

Ararat, Mount, 148
Archangel, 130
Archer, 91, 117
Arey family, 163
Arey's Harbor, 163
Argall, Capt. Samuel, 194, 199
Arrowsic Island, 94, 115, 116, 127
Aspinquid, 25
Aucocisco Bay, 54
Audubon, John James, 197
Audubon Society, 135, 136
Augusta, 133, 134

Babb, Philip, 24
Back Cove, 64
Bagnall, Walter, 34, 35
Bailey Island, 86-87, 94, 102
Bailey, Timothy, 86-87
Baker Island, 199, 202, 203
Baker, John Hopkinson, 136
Ball, Col. Samuel, 119
Ballou, Aramiah, 191
Bangs Island, 48
Bangs, Capt. Joshua, 48
Bar Harbor, 197, 198, 207, 208, 212
Bare Island, 178
Barker family, 111
Barker, Jacob, 111
Barker, Robert, 111, 112
Barney's Point, 211
Barstow, Jacqueline Stewart, 140
Barter, Henry, 179
Barter Island, 129
Barter, Peletiah, 179
Barter, William, 179
Bartlett, Christopher, 189, 193

244

Index · 245

Bartlett, Capt. David, 192
Bartlett, David (not Capt.), 192
Bartlett, Polly, 191
Bartlett's Island, 189-193, 199
Bass Harbor Head, 199
Bath, 96
Baxter, Hon. James P., 71-72
Baxter, Gov. Percival, 72
Bayley, Rev. Jacob, 113
Beal, F. W., 212
Beal, J. A., 212
Beal, "Long Barney," 212
Beal, Lydia, 211
Beal, Manwarren, 211-212
Beals, 210, 212, 213
Beals Island, 210-214
Bear Island, 94, 204
Beck, Horace, 152
Bellows, George, 140
Bennett's Island, 152
Bernard, Sir Francis, 195, 196, 200
Bernard, John, 196
Berry, Maj.-Gen. Hiram G., 71
Biard, Father Pierre, 193-194, 199
Bibber, Albert, 91
Bibber, Charles, 92
Bickford family, 139
Biddeford Pool, 31, 32, 45
Big Hen Island, 101
Big House, 184, 186
Big White Island, 126
Bingham, Mrs. Millicent Todd, 135-136
Birch Island, 98, 99
Birch Point, 75, 77
Bisbee, 67
Bishop, Mr., 131
Black Head, 141
Black Island, 199
Black Point, 40
Black, Will, Jr., 86
Black, Will, Sr., 86, 87
Black William of Saugus, 35
Blackbeard, 22
Blaisdell family, 175
Blaney's Point, 74, 76
Block Island, 169
Blue Hill, 192
Blue Hill Bay, 189
Blue Hill Mountain, 189
Blue Hill Neck, 189

Blue Hill peninsula, 176
Bluenose, 198
Bluff Island, 28, 30, 31
Blythe, Capt., 127
Board of National Parks, Historic Sites, Buildings and Monuments, 217-218
Bodwell Granite Co., 163
Bois Bubert, 211
Bombazeen (Indian sagamore), 99
Bombazeen Island, 99
Bona-waggon, Cape, 116
Bonney, Judge Percival, 122
Boon Island, 25-27
Boon Island Light, 26
Boone, Samuel, 81
Boothbay, 84, 115, 179
Boothbay Harbor, 115, 118, 121-124
Boothbay islands, 115-129
Bousfield, Rev. Neal D., 208
Bowditch, Ernest, 179
Bowdoin, 117
Bowen, Michael, 165
Boxer, 127
Boyce, John, 85
Brackett, Thomas, 50, 51
Bradbury Island, 176
Bray, Richard, 75
Bremen, 130
Brewer, John, 217
Brewster, Senator Owen, 217
Brig Landing Cove, 192
Bristol, 132-134
Broad Cove, 34
Brookman, Henry, 153
Brothers of the Way, 125
Brown, Charles, 166
Brown, J. O., 166
Brown, John, 48, 131
Brûle-Côte Island. *See* Swan's Island
Brunswick, 41, 79, 85, 99
Brunswick, Union Bank, 71
Bucksport, 154, 174
Bull, Dixey, 35, 128
Bulwark, 32, 33, 116
Bunganac, 105
Bunker family, 200
Burgess, Abby, 151-152
Burgess, Capt., 151
Burgess family, 148
Burnett, Frances Hodgson, 23

Burroughs, Capt., 127
Bustin's Island, 74
Butler family, 190
Butter Island, 176
Byles, Mrs. Matthew, 83

Cabot family, 166
Cabot, John, 138, 160
Cadillac, Mount, 197, 206
Cadillac, Sieur Antoine de la Mothe, 194-195, 197, 200
Cady, William, 81
Cagawescoe, 46
Calderwood family, 163
Caldwell Island, 129, 130
Calf Island, 109
Calista D. Morrill, 145
Camden, 169-171, 212
Cammock, Thomas, 36, 38
Camp Berry, 71
Campbell, Colonel, 171, 172
Canada Indians, 50
Cape Breton Island, 21, 195
Cape Island, 116
Cape Newagen Island, 115
Carter family, 133, 134
Carter, John, 191
Carver, Mr., 213
Carver, John, 163
Carver, Reuben, 163
Carver, Mrs. Susie, 213
Carver, Thaddeus, 160-163
Carver's Harbor, 161, 162
Cary family, 175
Casco Bay, 14, 45-47, 49, 56, 59, 69, 79, 91, 97, 104
Casco islands, 75
Casco Neck, 64
Castine, 161, 170, 175, 196
Castine, Baron, 70
Cathedral Woods, 142
Catherine, 32
Cato, 55
Cedar Island, 19, 20
Cedar Ledges, 100
Central Maine Power Co., 77-78
Chamberlain (lawyer), 133
Champlain, Samuel de, 14, 15, 34, 138, 178, 179, 183, 188, 194, 197, 199, 214-216, 218
Chandler's Cove, 60

Chase, Capt., 66-67
Chase, Ethan Allen, 120
Chase House, 121
Chebeague Island, 53, 59-62, 75-77
Chebnood, 148
Christensen, Anetha, 23
Christensen, Karen, 23
Christensen, Maren, 23
Church, Benjamin, 50, 169
City of Portland, 157
Clam Cove, 34
Clapboard Island, 105
Clay, Henry, 119
Cleaves, Ebenezer, 76-77
Cleeves, Elizabeth, 47, 51
Cleeves (Cleeve), George, 38, 47, 74
Cliff Island, 64, 65
Clough, Capt. Stephen, 185
Coffin, Robert P. Tristram, 90-91, 102
Coggswell, Francis, 160, 161
Colby College, 119
Cole, Nicholas, 81
Cole, Thomas, 196
Columbia, 178
Columbia Falls, 213
Condon family, 148
Condy, William, 81
Cook, Elisha, 83
Corbin's Sound, 127
Corneille, Pierre, 30
Cornfield Point, 74-75
Cosemes, 148
Cousins Island, 72-78
Cousins, John, 73-75, 78
Cousins River, 74
Cranberry Island, 129, 130
Cranberry Isles, 199-207
Cranberry Isles (town), 204-205
Crie, Horatio, 156
Crie, Robert, 153, 156
Criehaven Island, 56, 148, 152-156
Crumple Ledge, 211
Crystal Lake, 180
Cuckolds, The, 115, 118, 124
Cumberland, 62
Cundy's Harbor, 81, 82, 93
Curtis, Hannah, 86-87
Cushing, Ezekiel, 48, 55
Cushing, Francis, 56
Cushing, Hannah, 55
Cushing House, 58

Index · 247

Cushing, Ignatius, 55
Cushing Island, 46-51, 70, 71
Cushing, Lemuel, 49, 71
Cushing, Phebe, 55
Cushing, Thomas, 55
Cutts, Colonel, 32, 33

Damarell, John, 65
Damarill, Humphrey, 126, 129
Damarill's Isles, 126
Damariscotta River, 126, 127, 146
Damariscove Island, 15, 123, 124, 126-129
Danforth, Thomas, 81
Dark Harbor, 169, 173
Darling, John, 90
Dash, 103
Davenport, Albert, 122
Davenport Cove, 119, 120
Davis family, 187
Davis Island, 129
Dean, Jasper, 26, 27
Dean, Capt. John, 26-27
Decker, Ebenezer, 117
Decker, William, 117
Decker's Cove, 117
Deer Isle, 176-178, 185, 188
Deering, James, 70
Defender, 178
Delphine (mother of Talleyrand), 195
DeMonts Island, 214
Descartes, René, 30
Devil Island, 178
Devil's Wall, 97
Devon, 127
Diamond Island, 46
Dingley family, 118, 120, 121
Dingley, Frank, 121
Dingley, Nelson, 122
Dirigo House, 58
Discoverer, 160
Dix, Charles, 175
Dix family, 190
Dochet Island. See St. Croix Island
Don Pedro del Montclova, 88
Don Pedro Salazar, 104, 105
Donnell, Capt. Joseph, 63, 64
Donnell, Nathaniel, 81
Douglas brothers, 92
Douglas, Oliver, 92
Down East (magazine), 92

Dresden, 109, 111-113
Drinkwater, Joseph, 76
Drinkwater Point, 76
Drisko Island, 211
Driver, Mrs. Robert M., 92
Drown Boys Ledge, 211
Drowne, Shem, 131, 139
Drowne, Thomas, 139
Duck Island, 19, 20, 192, 200, 203
Dumaresq family, 110
Dumaresq, James, 110, 111
Dumaresq, Jane F. R., 111
Dumaresq, Philip, 110, 111
Dunbar, Col. David, 118
Dunbar, Edward, 132
Dyer family, 163
Dyer, Capt. Howard, 165-166

Eagle Island, 28, 31, 91, 99, 176
Eastern End, 153
Eastern Mark Island, 100
Eastern Way, 199, 201
Eaton, 162
Ebenecook Harbor, 117
Eggemoggin Reach, 176, 178
Elerette, Louis, 54
Eliot, Charles W., 204
Eliot, John, 25
Elizabeth, Cape, 31, 34, 36, 53, 63, 104
Elizabethans and America, The, 30
Ellsworth, 191, 201
Elm Island, 98
Emily-from-California, 76-77
Emita, 56
Enterprise, 127
Epic of Hog, The, 135
Equator, 32
Erickson family, 154
Express, 56

Falmouth, 48, 50, 64, 68, 70-72, 100, 212
Felt, George, 47, 73
Fern Cliff, 153
Fernald family, 148
Field, Capt. Earl, 141
Field, Rachel, 72, 205
Fisherman's Island, 123-126
Fisherman's Passage, 157
Five Islands, 118

248 · INDEX

Flag Island, 100
Fletcher's Neck, 32
Fly, 162, 163
Folklore of Maine, The, 152
Folsom, George, 31
Fore River, 46
Fort George, 175
Fort Island, 47
Fort Knox, 174
Fort Loyal, 70
Fosdick, Dr. Harry Emerson, 122-123
Fox, George, 30
Fox Islands, 147, 159-168, 178
Franklin Island, 129
Freeport, 89, 103, 104
Frenchboro, 206
Friendship, 129, 130
Frenchman's Bay, 200
Fulton, Robert, 111

Galileo, 30
Gallatin, Albert, 111
Garden Island, 109
Gardiner, 110, 111
Gardner family, 87
Garrison Cove, 87
Garrison Island, 130
Gast, Pierre de, 194
Gaston, William, 168
Gay's Island, 129, 130
Georges Islands, 129-130
Georgetown Island, 94, 115, 118
Ghost Cliff, 97, 98
Gibbins Island, 32
Gibbins, James, 32
Gibson, Charles Dana, 169
Gibson, Richard, 37, 40-41
Gibson, Mrs. Robert, 34, 41
Gilbert, Sir Humphrey, 138
Gilley family, 202-205
Gilley, Hannah, 202, 203, 205
Gilley, John, 203, 204
Gilley, William, 202, 204
Gilpatrick, Harold, 122
Gimlet Eye, 60-61
Gloucester, 192, 195
God's Pocket, 206
Gomez, Estévan, 14, 138, 160
Goodyear, Moses, 36
Goose Islands, 101
Gordon, John True, 24

Gorges, Sir Ferdinando, 29, 30, 36, 45, 53, 68, 69, 74, 128, 131, 138
Gosling Islands, 101
Gosnold, Bartholomew, 138
Gosport, 21, 24
Gott family, 187
Gott Islands, 189, 199
Gould, Dr. Edwin, 156
Gould, Maj. John, 95-96
Governor Muskie, 173
Grand Manan, 14
Granite Spring Hotel, 58
Grant family, 151-152
Gray, Amos, 119
Great Chebeague Island. *See* Chebeague Island
Great Cranberry Island, 199
Great Diamond Island, 72
Great Gott Island, 199
Great Island. *See* Sebascodegan Island
Great Mark Island, 100
Great Wass Island, 210-212
Green Islands, 63
Green, Michael, 205
Green, Mrs., 147
Greening Island, 199
Greenleaf, William, 119
Green's Island, 148, 160, 168
Gregoire, Marie Therèse de la Mothe Cadillac de, 196, 200
Greystones Hall, 124-125
Grindle family, 187
Grindle Point Lighthouse, 173
Guercheville, Madame de, 194
Guptill, Rev. Orville J., 210

Haddock Island, 129
Hadlock family, 202, 204, 206
Hadlock, Edward, 202
Hadlock, Capt. Samuel, 202
Haley, Capt. Samuel, 22, 24
Hall, Capt. Albert, 155
Hall, Daniel, 147, 148
Hall, Ebenezer, Jr., Mr. & Mrs., 148, 153, 161
Hall, Ebenezer, Sr., 147, 149
Hall, Hannah, 161
Hall, Harriet, 153
Hall Island, 129
Hals, Franz, 31
Ham, J. B., 118-122

Index · 249

Hamilton, Jack, 77
Hancock County, 179, 200
Harbor Island, 130, 183
Harbridge, Harry, 155
Hardwood Island, 189, 199
Harpswell, 78, 79, 88, 98, 103, 176
Harpswell, dead ship of, 101-106
Harpswell Center, Lookout, 102
Harpswell, Hermit of, 90
Harpswell Islands, 78-106
Harpswell Neck, 63-65, 67, 78, 81, 91, 98, 104
Harpswell Township, 83
Harvard College, 81
Harvey, William, 30
Harward, George, 112, 113
Haskell Island, 91-92, 99
Haskell, Mr., 91
Hatch, Charles, 40
Havre de Grâce, 54
Hawkins, Capt. Marius, 37
Hawthorne, Nathaniel, 23
Haynes, William, 74
Hayward, Mary, 75
Helen Eliza, 52
Hendrick's Harbor, 116, 117
Hendrick's Head, 118
Henri, Robert, 140
Henrietta, 56
Hermione, 32
Heron Islands, 99, 115, 123, 126
Herrick family, 190
Hicks Cove, 213
Hicks, Thomas, 213
Higgins, Ed, 155
Hill, Mrs. John Fremont, 140
Hippocras. See Hypocrites Islands
Hiram Ricker & Sons, 96
History of Saco, 31
Hockamock Point, 135, 183
Hoffse family, 134
Hog Island, 135-137
Homestead in the Willows, The, 48
Hood, Robin, 81
Hooper Island, 129
Hope, 207
Horn family, 140
Horn, Francis, 139
Horse Island, 93, 95
House Island, 46, 50
Housewife's Sound, 53, 58

Howard, Judith, 81-82
Hudson, Henry, 194
Huggins, G. Ellsworth, 122-123
Hull's Cove, 195, 196, 200
Humphrey (of Haskell Island), 91-92
Hungry Island, 129
Hurricane Island, 160, 166-168, 188
Husseys Sound, 53
Hypocras. See Hypocrites Islands
Hypocrites Islands, 115, 123-125

Increase, 25
Ingram, David, 215
Inner Heron Island, 126
Ipswich, 160
Irony Island, 101
Island Shepherd, The, 141
Isle of Bacchus, 34
Isle au Haut, 176, 178-180, 183
Isle au Haut Township, 179
Isles of Shoals, 14, 19-24, 45
Isles of Shoals Unitarian Association, 24
Islesboro, 169-174
Islesford, 205

Jackson, Henry, 200
Jacques, Richard, 83
James W. Paul, Jr., 175
Jefferson, Thomas, 196, 200
Jemima Leonard, 167
Jesuit Spring, 194
Jewell, George, 63
Jewell Island, 63-67, 75, 91
Job's Island, 169
John Dawn, 102
John Gilley, Maine Farmer and Fisherman, 204
Johnson, David, 89
Johnson family, 87
Johnson's Cove, 60
Jones family, 51
Jones Garden Island, 129
Jones, Nathaniel, 48
Jonesport, 210, 213
Jonson, Ben, 30
Jordan, Clement, 42
Jordan, John, 41, 42
Jordan, Robert, 41, 69
Jordan's Delight, 211
Jordan's Delight Ledge, 211

Jose, Charles, 103-105
Josselyn, Henry, 146
Josselyn, John, 146
Joyce family, 187
Juniper Point, 122

Kadesquit, 194
Kane family, 190
Kellogg, Rev. Elijah, 98
Kennebec River, 53, 65, 99, 104, 109, 139
Kennebunk River, 45
Kennedy, Mrs. John, 207
Kent family, 187
Kent, Rockwell, 140
Kidd, Capt., 60, 66, 128
Kilgore, Dr., 97
Kimball's Island, 180
Kittery, 80, 139, 147
Kittery Point, 207
Knox, Colonel, 185
Knox County, 179
Knox, Gen. Henry, 183-185

Lafayette, Marquis de, 184, 186, 196
Laighton, Thomas, 23
Laighton's Hotel, 23
Lamont family, 166
Landers, John, 168
Lane, Cora, 95
Lane family, 134
Lane, Capt. & Mrs. George, 96, 207
Lange Eylande, 53
Lapthorn, Steven, 40
Lasell Island, 169, 173
Lattimore (pirate), 128
Laughing Mary, 131
Laura B., 141
LeBlanc, Simon, 154
Lecherous Priest, 211
Leighton, Jennie, 76
Lescarbot, M., 216
Lett, Island of, 174
Leverett, Capt. George, 103-106, 174-175
Levett, Christopher, 15, 35, 45-47, 49, 50, 115, 116
Levett's River, 46
Lewis, Mary, 41
Lime Island, 173
Lincoln Galley, 171

Lincolnville, 169
Linekin Neck, 118, 123
Little Cranberry Island, 199-203
Little Deer Isle, 176
Little Drisko Island, 211
Little Gott Island, 199
Little Harbor, 54
Little Irony Island, 101
Little Mark Island, 91, 100
Little Sebascodegan, 83
Little Squirrel, 118
Little Swan Island, 109
Little White Island, 126
Littlefield, Samuel, 81
Long Cove, 65
Long Island (Blue Hill Bay), 189
Long Island (Casco Bay), 48, 50, 53-58, 64
Long Island (Penobscot Bay). *See* Islesboro
Lord, Phillips, 193
Loring family, 193
Loring, Short & Harmon, 96
Loud family, 134
Loud, William, 131, 139
Loud, William Solomon, 131-132
Loud's Island, 97, 130-135, 209
Loudville, 134
Louisbourg fortress, 21, 60, 146, 147
Lovell, General, 170
Lowe, Edward, 22, 88, 128
Lowell, James Russell, 23
Luckse Sound, 53
Lurvey, Abraham, 187
Luxton, George, 53
Luxtons Sound, 53

MacAfee, Tom, 125-126
McCobb, Mr. & Mrs. Samuel, 130
MacClure, "Mike," 154
MacCullum, Bart, 52
MacDonald, Rev. Alexander, 134, 206-207, 210
MacDonald, Angus, 207
McGee Island, 129
McKay and Dix, 175
Mackay-Smith, Bishop Alexander, 207
McKeen family, 67
McKenny, James ("King Jim," "King of Malaga"), 56, 93-96
MacMillan, Commander Donald, 117

Index · 251

MacMullen, Archibald, 165
McVane, Charles, 57
Mackerel Cove, 86
Mackey's Island, 69, 71
Mackworth, Arthur, 68-69
Mackworth Island, 68-72
Mackworth, Jane, 69, 70
Mackworth's Point, 68
Maine Federation of Women's Clubs, 95
Maine Sea Coast Missionary Society, 97, 134, 156, 206-210
Malaga Island (Isles of Shoals), 19, 20
Malaga Island (Casco Bay), 93-97, 134, 207
Maliseet Indians, 160
Manana Island, 137, 138, 141, 142
Manasquesicook Island, 146
Manley family, 190
Maquoit Island, 80
Mark Island, 169
Marr's Harbor, 116
Marsh Island, 55
Marshal Island, 173
Marshall family, 148
Marston, Benjamin, 65
Mary A., 56, 145, 146
Mason, Capt. John, 53
Matinicus Island, 56, 145-156, 160, 161
Matinicus Plantation, 148
Matinicus Rock, 148, 150-152, 163, 198
Mayflower, 35
Maxwell Cove, 114
Maxwell, Louisa Hatch, 112
Menikoe, 68
Mere Point, 99, 101
Merriman, Walter, 98
Merryconeag Neck, 63-65, 67, 79, 83, 91
Merryconeag Sound, 102
Merryman family, 87
Merrymeeting Bay, 109, 112
Merrymount (Mass.), 15, 35
Methodist Home Missionary Society, 149
Meyer, Herbert, 193
Michael's Island, 51
Micmac Indians, 160
Middle Bay, 99, 101
Millay, Edna St. Vincent, 98
Millet (of Sebascodegan), 82

Mills brothers, 91, 92
Milne, Captain, 32, 33
Minerva, 202
Mistake Ledge, 211
Mitchel, Peter, 154
Mitton, Michael, 47, 50, 51
Mitton, Sarah, 47
Mitton's Island, 51
Modobt, 148
Monhegan Island, 15, 127, 129, 137-142, 209
Monroe, Hugh, 157
Monroe's Island, 156-159
Montpelier, 184, 185
Monts, Sieur de, 194, 197, 214-218
Moosabec Reach, 210
Moose Island, 199
Morgan Bay, 189
Morgan family, 196-197
Morning Star, 207
Morrell, Mary, 112
Morrow family, 166
Morse Island, 129
Morton, Thomas, 15, 35
Motions, The, 128
Moulton, Capt., 99
Mount Desert Island, 183, 185, 189, 193-199, 203, 204, 206, 207, 217
Mount Desert Rock, 198
Mouse Island, 118, 121-123
Mowatt, Capt. Henry, 100, 171
Mugdumbawit, 148
Mullin (of North Haven), 166
Munjoy, George, Mr. & Mrs., 50
Munjoy's Island, 51
Murder on Smutty Nose, 23
Murphy, Jerry, 96
Murphy, Dr. Robert Cushman, 136
Muscle Ridges, 156-157
Muscongus Bay, 97, 124, 135
Muscongus Island, 130, 132-133, 139
Mussel Cove, 34
Mussey, Theodore, 71
Mussey's Island, 69, 71

Neale, Captain, 35
Negro Island, 28, 31
Nekrangan, Cape, 115
Neutral Island, 214
New Brunswick, Canada, 194
New Casco, 70

INDEX

New Damariscove Island, 91
New England Council, 45
New England Rareties, 146
New Harbor, 131, 137
New Meadows River, 79, 80
Newagen, Cape, 115, 116
Newagen Inn, 118
Newagen Island, 127
Newaggon, Cape, 115
Newark, The, 85
Newbury Neck, 189
Newton Island, 69
Newwaggin, 86
Niclas, Yolla, 141
Noble, Fanny, 110
Noble, Lazarus, 110
Norridgewalk, 99
Norridgewock Indians, 50
Norsemen, 14, 160
North Haven, 160, 162, 163-166, 169, 173, 176
North Island. *See* North Haven
North Yarmouth Island, 79, 101
Northeast Harbor, 204
Norumbega, 215, 216
Norwood's Cove, 201
Nottingham Galley, 25, 27
Nova Francia, 216
Nowell, Sumner, 81
Nubble, The, 54
Nutter family, 190

Obed's Rock, 54
Ober family, 190
Ober, Merritt, 192
Ober, Otis, 191
Ogilvie, Elizabeth, 152
Old Harbor, 183
Old Lambo, 82
Old Whitehead, 46, 49
Oliver, Alfred, 56
Olmstead, Cotton Mather, 176-177
Oram, Mary, 132
Oram, Robert, 132, 133
Orphans' Island, 175
Orr, Clement, 83
Orr family, 87
Orr, Henry, 85
Orr, Joseph, 83
Orr's Island, 83-87, 89, 90, 100, 102
Osier family, 134

Otis, Albert, 179
Ottawa Hotel, 49
Otter Island, 129
Outer Heron Island, 126
Outer Long Island, 206
Overset Island, 55
Owl's Head Bay, 157, 159
Owl's Head Light, 157, 158, 162

Page, Miss, 57
Palmer, John, 50, 51
Palmer's Island, 51
Parker, John, 80
Parker Point, 73, 74
Parsons family, 51
Passamaquoddy Bay, 215
Passcattaway, 41
Pattishall, Capt. Richard, 129
Peaks Island, 46-48, 50-53
Pearl of Orr's Island, 83
Pearson, Edmund, 23
Peary, Admiral Robert E., 99, 175
Pejepscot Proprietors, 81
Pemaquid, 25, 35, 126-128
Pemaquid Neck, 129
Pemaquid Point, 124, 139
Pendleton family, 172
Pendleton Point, 169
Penobscot Bay, 37, 145, 146, 150, 154, 157, 159, 160, 170
Penobscot Indians, 50, 147, 148, 176
Penobscot River, 174, 194
Pepperell, William, 21-22, 146
Perio's Point, 212
Perry (of Malaga), 97
Peterson, George, 75
Petit Plaisant, 183
Pettengill, Stephen, Mr. & Mrs., 57
Peverly, John, 35
Philbrook family, 148, 163
Phillips, Ray, 141
Phippsburg, 93, 94, 97
Picaroon, 82
Pickering Island, 176
Pierce, Capt. Jonathan, 116
Pine Point, 30
Piscataqua River, 26, 45, 65
Placentia Island, 183, 189, 199
Plaisted, Gov., 96
Pleasant Cove, 98
Pleasant River, 213

Index · 253

Plummer, Rev. Abram, 149
Plymouth (Mass.), 25
Plymouth Company, 109
Plymouth Council, 34, 35, 80
Poland family, 134
Pond Island, 87-91
Popham's Colony, 109
Porcupine Islands, 199
Porpoise, Cape, 29
Port Clyde, 129, 137
Port Royal, 194, 215, 216
Porter, Samuel, 103
Porter, Seward, 103
Portland, 38, 41, 47, 50-52, 56, 58, 59, 74, 90, 91, 104, 147, 165
Portland Harbor islands, 45-52
Portsmouth (N. H.), 19, 23, 27, 132, 200
Portsmouth Navy Yard, 176
Potts Harbor, 91, 101, 106
Potts, Margaret, 64
Potts Point, 64, 65, 91, 106
Potts, Richard, 64, 91
Potts, Thomas, 64-65
Powell, Rev. Hannah, 134, 209
Preble, Jedediah, 42, 48, 49, 70
Preble, Jonathan, 75
Presumpscot River, 46, 68, 69
Priest, Mr. & Mrs. M. C., 113-114
Prince, Joseph, 185, 186
Prince Point, 73
Pring, Capt. Martin, 14, 15, 80, 160
Prior, Cecil, 134
Prior, Mrs. Lettie, 134
Pripet, 169
Prout's Neck, 30, 31
Pryor family, 134
Pulpit. *See* Haskell Island
Pulpit Harbor, 166, 169
Pumpkin Island, 115
Purchase, Thomas, 41, 80
Purrington, John, 81, 82

Quack, 46
Quoddy Head, 207

Ragged Arse, 152
Ragged Island (Casco Bay), 97-98
Ragged Island (Penobscot Bay). *See* Criehaven

Racketash, 152
Raleigh, Sir Walter, 80
Ram Island (Boothbay Harbor), 123-124
Ram Island (Casco Bay), 100
Ram Island (Isles of Shoals), 28, 31
Raymond family, 190
Red Paint people, 14
Redman, Capt., 56
Reed, Jane, 112
Reed, Samuel, 112
Reid State Park, 118
Rennie, James, 70-71
Reynolds (of Appledore), 21, 22
Revere, Paul, 170
Revere, Paul, III, Mrs., 180
Rhodes, Mr. & Mrs. Fred, 156
Richards, Sarah, 110-111
Richmond, 37
Richmond, Duke of, 34
Richmond, George, 34-35
Richmond Island, 31, 33-42, 47, 48, 65, 69, 70, 74, 109, 112
Ricker, Capt., 56
Ridley, Capt., 95
Rigby family, 74
Ring family, 148
Rio de Gomez, 160
Ripley Neck, 213
Robbins family, 190
Robbins, Granny, 165
Robbinston, 217
Roberts, Kenneth, 26
Robinson, John, 48
Rockefeller family, 196-197
Rockland, 56, 145, 212
Rockland Harbor, 157
Rockport, 169
Rocky Bar, 31
Roosevelt, Franklin D., 60, 175, 176
Roscoe B. Jackson Memorial Laboratory, 197
Rosier, James, 130
Ross Island, 129
Round Pond, 134
Rouse, John, 48
Rowse, A. L., 30
Royal Rivers, 73, 74, 77, 103
Royal Tar, 165
Royal, William, 73
Russell, James, 54, 55

Russell, Richard, 54
Rut (explorer), 138

Saco, 32-33, 40, 41
Saco Bay islands, 28-42
Saco River, 45
Sagahadoc River, 34, 46
Sagettawan, 81
Sagunto, 22
Sailor Memorial, 173
St. Croix Island, 35, 194, 214-219
St. Croix River, 217
St. Croix Valley, 214, 217
St. George River, 130
Salem (Mass.), 29
Salisbury family, 190
Saltonstall family, 166
Saltonstall, Capt. Gurdon, 170
Samoset, Chief, 45, 46, 124, 126, 130, 131
Samoset House, 122
Samoset's Island, 130
Sandy Point, 75
Sarah, 103-105
Sargent, Stephen, 37
Sargentville, 176
Sawtelle Museum, 205
Sawungun Island, 99
Scarboro, 30, 31, 146
Schoodic Island, 214
Schooner Head, 153
Scott family, 51
Sea Flower, 56
Seagirt Refuge, 34
Seal Cove, 156
Seal Harbor, 208
Searls, Thomas, 209
Seavey Island, 129
Sebago Lake, 69
Sebasco, 95
Sebascodegan Island, 79-83, 90, 99, 100, 160
Sedgwick Island, 185
Seguin, 124
Sequeson Island, 73
Seven Hundred Acre Island, 169, 173
Sewall, Stephen, 171
Seymour, James, 85-86
Shabbit Island, 211
Shapleigh, Maj. Nicholas, 80
Shearwater, 162

Sheep Island, 156-159
Sheepscot Bay, 115, 116
Sheepscot Island, 127
Sheepscot River, 53
Shelter Island, 101
Shepard (of the *Picaroon*), 82-83
Shepard's Point, 82
Shirley, Gov. William, 48, 131, 146
Shute, John, 110
Simonton (of Cape Elizabeth), 99
Simpson, Alfred, 154
Simpson family, 155
Singing Beach, The, 54
Simpson, Fred, 154
Simpson, Herman, 154
Sinnett family, 87
Sinnett, Michael, 84-85, 98-99
Sinnot, Micah. *See* Sinnett, Michael
Skillings, Simon, 48, 49, 51
Skitterygusset, 46, 48
Slatterlay, Roger, 40
Small, Elizabeth, 80
Small, Francis, 80
Small Point, 80
Smith, David, 186, 188
Smith family, 187
Smith, Captain John, 15, 19, 109, 118, 124, 126, 127, 131, 137
Smith, John (not Capt.), 55, 161
Smith, Payson, 95
Smith's Isles, 19
Smutty Nose Island, 19, 20, 22-24
Snakey, Robert, 68
Somes, Abraham, 195, 203
Somes family, 190
Somes Sound, 194, 195, 199, 200, 201
Somesville, 195, 204
Soule, Sarah, 103
South Freeport, 103
South Harpswell, 92, 100
South Island (Fox Islands). *See* Vinalhaven
South Island (Penobscot Bay). *See* Criehaven
South Matinicus Island. *See* Criehaven
Southampton, Earl of, 130, 131, 138
South Portland, 50
Southport Island, 115-118, 121, 127
Southwest Harbor, 192, 194, 199, 202, 203

Index · 255

Southwest Point, 153, 155
Spaulding, Ann, 109-110
Spaulding, Cora A., 166
Spaulding Island, 109
Speedwell, 160
Spiritualistic Society, 175
Split, Cape, 213
Sprague family, 187
Sprague, Phineas, 31, 42
Spray, 120
Spring Point, 49
Spurling, Benjamin, 200-202, 204
Spurling family, 200, 204, 206
Spurling, Robert, 201
Squid, The, 122
Squirrel Island, 118-122
Squirrel Island Association, 120, 122
Stafford, Mrs. Marie Peary, 99
Stage Island, 28, 31, 33
Stage Island Monument, 32
Standish, Myles, 71, 124
Stanley family, 200, 206
Stanley, John, 200
Staple family, 187
Star Island, 19, 20, 21, 24
Starks, 119
Starling family, 140
Starling, Josiah, Jr., 140
Starling, Josiah, Sr., 139
Starling, Mary, 140
Starling, Phebe, 140
State o' Maine Scrap Book, 67
State School for the Deaf, Mackworth Island, 72
Stepping Stones, The, 54
Sterling family, 50
Stevens, Benjamin, 40
Stirling, Earl of, 138
Stonington, 180
Stowe, Harriet Beecher, 83, 85
Stratton Island, 28-31
Stratton, John, 29-31
Strong family, 166
Styleman, Elizabeth, 42
Sullivan, 203, 204
Sunbeam I, 207, 208, 210
Sunbeam II, 208
Sunbeam III, 208
Sutton, Eben, 203
Sutton Island, 199, 201, 203, 205
Swan Island (Kennebec River), 109-114

Swan Island Game Management Area, 114
Swan, Col. James, 184-186, 188, 195
Swan's Island (off Mount Desert), 178, 183-188, 200
Sylvester, Charles, 90

Tailer, William, 83
Talleyrand-Périgord, Charles Maurice de, 185, 186, 195
Tarbox, Jesse, 32
Tarratine Indians, 46, 47, 147
Teach (pirate), 22, 60
Teel, Adam, 130
Teel, Henry, 130
Teel Island, 129, 130
Tenant's Harbor, 155
Tenedos, 200-202
Thaxter, Celia (Laighton), 20, 23, 24
Thaxter, Levi, 23
Thayer, Mrs. Nathaniel, 180
Thevet, André, 138
Thief Island, 129
Thomas family, 172
Thomas Island, 199
Thomaston, 24, 183
Thompson, David, 45
Thompson Island, 129
Thoroughfare, The, 160
Thoroughfare Village, 179
Thrumcap Island, 115
Tide, 152
Tillson, Gen. Davis, 167
Tilton brothers, 160
Time Out of Mind, 206
Tinker Island, 189, 192, 199
Titcomb, Eldridge, 91
Todd, Mr. & Mrs. David, 135
Todd, Dr. James M., 136
Todd Wildlife Sanctuary, 135, 136
Tolman family, 148
Torrey family, 187
Townsend, 117
Townsend Gut, 117
Treasurer, 194
Trefethren family, 50, 140
Trefethren, Henry, Jr., 139, 142
Trefethren, Henry, Sr., 139
Trelawny, Robert, 34-36, 38-42
Trimble, John, 217
Trott, Benjamin, 50, 51
Tubbs, Major, 114

Tuck, John, 21, 24, 163
Tucker, Richard, 38
Turnip Island, 101
Turtle Point, 173
Twins, The, 86

Uncle Zeke Island, 101
Union River Bay, 189

Van Dyke, Henry, 208
Vaughan, William, 146-147
Vaughn, Edward Winslow, 140
Vernon, Fortescue, 170, 171
Verona Island, 174-176
Verrazano, Giovanni da, 14, 138, 160
Vikings, 146, 214
Vinal family, 163
Vinal, Harold, 164, 168
Vinal, John, 162
Vinal, William, 162, 167, 168
Vinalhaven, 148, 160-164, 167, 188
Vines, Richard, 36, 40, 68, 69, 74
Virginia, 207
Virgin's Breasts, 211

Wadsworth, Gen. Peleg, 171, 175
Wagner, Louis, 23, 24
Waite, Capt. John, 51
Wakeley family, 70
Waldboro, 129
Waldo, Samuel, 175
Waldo-Hancock Bridge, 174
Wallace, David, Mr. & Mrs., 57
Wallace family, 148
Ward, Mary, 84-85
Watch Point, 34
Waterville College, 119
Wawenock Indians, 116, 131
Way, Eleazer, 81
Way, George, 80
Wentworth Ricker, 62
Western Head, 34
Western Way, 199
Wetmore, Judge William, 175
Wetmore's Island, 175
Weymouth, Capt. George, 130, 138
Whale Rock, 91
Wharton, Richard, 80, 81
Whidden, Abigail, 110
Whidden, Capt., James, 110, 113
White Head, 141, 152, 157

White Island, 123, 126, 162
White Island Light, 23, 24
White, Capt. Henry, 207
White, Sam, 154
Whittier, John Greenleaf, 23, 102-103
Whitworth, Miles, 27
Wicasset, 110, 185
Wild Rose, 155
Wilkinson, Harriet, 203, 204
Wilkinson, Mary Jane, 204
William F. Wyman Station, 78-79
Williams, Rev. Anson, 210
Williams' Cove, 171
Williams family, 171-173
Williams, Rev. Prof., 170-173
Williams, Shubael, 171, 172
Will's Island, 86, 87
Will's Strait (Cut, Gut), 86
Wilson, Dan, 101
Wilson, Capt. John, 100
Wilson, Dr. John Henry, 125
Wingards Eylant, 34
Wingut Island, 34
Winnegance, 94
Winslow, Edward, 126, 139
Winte Island, 34
Winter, Andrew, 140
Winter, John, 34, 36-41, 47, 74
Winter, Mrs. John, 34, 37, 38, 40, 41, 74
Winter, Sara, 37, 38, 40, 41
Winthrop, Adam, 109
Winthrop, James, 171, 172
Wood Island, 28, 31, 94
Woodbury family, 51
Woody Mark Island, 100
Woolwich, 112, 127
"Wreck of the Hesperus, The," 52
Wreck Island, 129, 178
Wright, Mr., 47
Wyeth, Andrew, 130

Yankee Coast, 91
Yard, William Beasley, 175
Yarmouth, 73, 76, 77, 104
York, 75, 81
York River, 45
Young family, 148
Young, Granny, 99-100
Young, Joseph, 149
Young, Judson, 155
Young, Mrs. Scott, 149